The Soviet Empire: Its Nations Speak Out

Soviet Studies

A new series on current informed opinion and discussion of events in the Soviet Union. Each book will have a thematic focus and will consist of translations of Russian articles from Moscow-based and regional periodicals.

Editors: Oleg Glebov and John Crowfoot, Moscow

Volume 1
THE SOVIET EMPIRE: ITS NATIONS SPEAK OUT
Edited by Oleg Glebov and John Crowfoot

This book is part of a series. The publisher will accept continuation orders which may be cancelled at any time and which provide for the automatic billing and shipping of each title in the series upon publication. Please write for details.

The Soviet Empire: Its Nations Speak Out

The First Congress of People's Deputies,
Moscow, 25 May to 10 June 1989

Edited and Translated by

Oleg Glebov and John Crowfoot
Moscow

with an Introduction by

Ernest Gellner
William Wyse Professor of Social Anthropology,
Cambridge University, UK

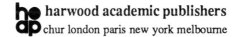 harwood academic publishers
chur london paris new york melbourne

Harwood Academic Publishers

Post Office Box 197
London WC2E 9PX
United Kingdom

58, rue Lhomond
75005 Paris
France

Post Office Box 786
Cooper Station
New York, New York 10276
United States of America

Private Bag 8
Camberwell, Victoria 3124
Australia

Library of Congress Catalog Card Number

89–24613

ISBN: 3-7186-5000-2 (hardcover)
ISBN: 3-7186-5017-7 (softcover)
ISSN: 1046-1809

CONTENTS

PREFACE

Opinion surveys held during the Congress found that half the people claimed to be following its proceedings all the time, with countrywide variations from 44% in Alma Ata, Kazakhstan to 85% in Tbilisi, capital of Georgia. People's opinions of what was happening there varied greatly. For some, including impatient deputies, it was a "great television entertainment" of frequently doubtful value; unproductive when it was not positively harmful. Others watched and listened compulsively to this quite unpredictable "thriller". One participant of the Congress, who sat immediately below the tribune, thought it was at times almost like a "Shakespearean drama". As we describe in the last chapter, however, only some felt a cathartic cleansing after the performance was over. Others, thinking this was the whole play, or that the performers would not be allowed a second chance, felt cheated by its inconclusive ending. Yet it was, after all, only the first act.

The compilers and translators of this selection are neither academics nor journalists, and make no pretensions to doing the jobs of those professions. Both are Moscow-based editors and translators who, with millions of others, daily listened to and watched the Congress, and then, after a week's interval, closely followed the first 6 weeks of the Supreme's Soviet's activities.

Our task as we conceived it was to make available, as rapidly as possible, some of the most important statements made at the Congress. Since the problems of 'democratising' such a vast state are inextricably and uniquely entangled with its multi-national character, we decided to give this selection such a regional and ethnic slant. With an additional, indispensable minimum of explanatory notes and statistical information, our aim was to provide Western readers with direct access to the historic First Congress of People's Deputies by October 1989, when the Second Congress was due to meet.

The complete transcripts, translated and annotated, will doubtless appear sometime in the future. By then the full figures for the January 1989 population census will also be available. Our task was instead dictated by the urgency of unfolding events.

Our principle of selection was to pick the most striking, typical or clear statements and arrange them chronologically for each major geographical and cultural region of this vast country. Some have already attracted the attention of the Western media, others have not. We excluded Gorbachev and Ryzhkov's speeches (they have already been translated by *Novosti*), and the many routine and repetitive statements. Some dozen speeches have been reproduced almost in full; others are quoted in several different chapters (for instance Janis Peters' shrewd comments on a wide range of issues are split between several different entries). An index of speakers' names enables the reader to follow up references and reconstruct the overall complex picture. Of course, we regretfully excluded a number of excellent contributions that could not be fitted into our plan, for reasons of subject and space: after all, the entire Congress and first Supreme Soviet transcripts would make a hefty book in themselves.

We have tried to be representative in all respects, though since conservatives (as opposed to certain reactionary spokesmen) made traditional statements of limited interest, they are under-represented: however, the votes on various issues show how numerous they were. That so many writers are quoted here is no accident. They certainly expressed themselves more coherently than almost all party officials, on the national issue, and on many others. Yet there is more to it than that: the traditional Russian writer's vocation of being not an entertainer but a teacher and mentor has been exaggerated, under Soviet political conditions, into their becoming a kind of substitute politician whose personality and position *is* well-known, unlike those of the formal 'leaders' of the country. The emergence of real politicians like Mikhail Gorbachev and Boris Yeltsin, and the overt political involvement of academics, legal specialists, party officials and others may herald a change in this and many other traditions — if this experiment continues, or the transplant operation proves successful.

Yet perhaps most striking of all has been the discovery of the number of people, from the farthest reaches of the country who, once given the chance, have the ability and courage to speak their minds. In a vast assembly of over 2000, many did not have an opportunity to speak and only in the Supreme Soviet did some first display the qualities that got them elected. One such revelation was when Valentina Kiseleva, an industrial worker from Belorussia, firmly took the Defence Minister Dmitry Yazov to task.

The extraordinarily rapid acquisition of political skills by deputies and the continuing educational effect of these broadcasts on their electors is impressive. Despite conservative and (private) liberal misgivings that the people are not ready for democracy, it seems that a great many of them most certainly are. Whether this experiment will take root and continue, or be disrupted by the snowballing course of subsequent events only time can tell: the concluding chapter gives some contradictory indications.

In the introductory note to each regional chapter we attempt, very briefly, to indicate salient points about each republic. More hard data is provided in the appendix. Klara Hallik's speech provides a good introduction to ethnic issues and policy in the Soviet Union. Faith and confession are included as an important component of culture and ethnic identity, especially in its pre-national stages. It is difficult to give figures for the numbers of practising Christians, (and Muslims, Buddhists, Jews, etc.,) but baptismal registers, according to the claims of the Orthodox church in the 1970s, indicated a total of 50 million, while revered figures such as Vasgen, Catholicos of Armenia, and also certain Russian Orthodox hierarchs were elected or nominated to such an assembly for the first time. The greatest omission is information on the economy — but there are books on the subject so we restricted ourselves to the revealing indicator of urbanisation.

We are thankful to Professor Ernest Gellner, another witness of this exceptional event, for his impressions and reflections. We should add that his *Nations and Nationalism* (1983) has been translated into Russian and will, finally, be published here, despite some initial official problems, in a few months time.

John Crowfoot and Oleg Glebov
Moscow, September 1989

Note on sources

Throughout the Congress and the first sittings of the new Supreme Soviet there was very full Russian-language coverage on TV and radio and in the press.

Direct live transmission of the proceedings were shown throughout the day and evening on the Soviet second TV channel (reaching 70% of the country's land area). Full transmission of the renewed Supreme Soviet proceedings after 20 June was resumed following public pressure. However, the daily newspaper *Izvestiya* (officially published by the Presidium of the Supreme Soviet) ceased to provide more or less complete transcripts after 14 June.

The following translations of speeches and excerpts are based on the reports in *Izvestiya*, supplemented where necessary by the live TV transmissions. Occasional explanatory notes are provided in square brackets.

Chapters 1, 2 and 5 were prepared by John Crowfoot, Chapters 3 and 6 by Oleg Glebov and the rest were prepared jointly. Of course, the editors bear joint responsibility for the entire book.

For those who read Russian the cryptic numbers that follow each name refer to the (Moscow) issue of *Izvestiya* in which the speech was published.

Explanatory notes written by the editors have been set in italics, except when they appear at the beginning of a chapter. The speeches are always in roman script.

INTRODUCTION

> ... the other day I was browsing through an old encyclopaedia and came across the following text: "In 1682-90 the Kremlin witnessed stormy disputes about 'faith'. The soldiers (streltsy) gathered there and the traders from outside the city walls, demanding greater rights, and that all the rulers should be replaced." (Commotion in hall) You see: from time to time, perhaps every fifty or hundred years, it is the practice in Russia to gather together like this. It would be all very fine but for one thing: that each time, we begin again from the beginning. As though this vast country, with the most varied national nuances and customs, had no historical experience.
> *Sergei Zalygin, Writers Union*

Modern methods of mass communication have an interesting consequence: from time to time, they allow an entire nation, however large or anonymous its population, to communicate with itself. They allow it to follow, at one and the same time, the same thoughts, and be moved by the same feelings. In England, I recall only one occasion on which this actually occurred: it was the Football World Cup Final in 1966 which England in the end won, beating Germany 4:2. The game remained agonisingly undecided for a very long time, and the entire country was glued to its television and radio sets. In the much populated waters off Chichester Harbour, for instance, between the mainland and the Isle of Wight, pleasure crafts without radio anxiously shouted to those better endowed, *How is it going?*

In the Soviet Union in late May and early June 1989, for two whole weeks, the country was in a similar condition, though, in the main, nothing weighty was actually being decided at once. Walking around Moscow, one could see people carrying transistors and listening to them; if one arrived at an office, most rooms were empty, and one could finally locate their intended denizens in a special room, which sounded as if a public meeting were going on in it. But the voice which held their attention then turned out to be not that of anyone actually present, but the transmitted voice of someone addressing the great *Syezd* or Congress, *How is it going?*.

There were interminable discussions of the finer points of performance and affirmations of the various speakers. I can think of no political event in the recent past which has so gripped the imaginations and the mind of a nation. In Britain, both the Suez Crisis and the Falklands War

xi

certainly captured the attention of the nation: but in each case, people had in the main adopted their positions and, though anxious to know the development of events, they were not passionately attentive to the finer nuances of the points scored by participants in a complex, many-sided and many-stranded debate. They already knew where they stood.

The attention conferred on the debates of the Congress was not due to some similar single and passionately absorbing issue, which would have been either argued out or fought out. The attention was bestowed on what can only be described as an open debate, a discussion which raised a whole set of tangled issues, on many of which the listeners had not altogether — or even at all — made up their minds. An enormous nation, a group of nations, was publicly and freely re-examining its own ideas. The fact that it had not done so for the past 70 years, endowed the exercise with its unquestionable fascination. It was probably a unique event in world history.

To appreciate the nature of the impact of the Congress, one must remember the nature of the Soviet political and, also, conceptual and moral system as it had developed and crystallised in the course of the previous 70 years. That system is made up of three main elements, which one can conveniently visualise as three pillars. The first is the formal political system as prescribed by the Constitution — admirably democratic, and, as far as it goes, ensuring that elected authorities are responsible to the electorate. But this formal machinery was systematically complemented by another, by the concentration of real power and decision-making in the Party, a self-selecting and well organised sub-set of the community, which constitutes the second pillar. This has been formally recognised in the Constitution itself since 1977; it is not merely one of those cases where a group or social stratum simply captures the real levers of power. The Constitution is democratic in some of its passages, and it indicates just where power should be, in others.

Was there, then, a contradiction between one aspect of the system, abstractly democratic, and another, endorsing the real concentration of power in one part of society? Outsiders generally believe this to be so. Was this contradiction not noted and queried? Did it not bother anyone?

The answer lies not *only* in the fact that, for most of Soviet history, no one who felt such doubts dared to make them publicly known. Of course this was a major factor, but it was not the only one. On its own, this consideration would probably not have been quite sufficient to explain how the system was brought into being (though we shall never know for sure): the important thing is that the system worked not only by fear, but also by faith. It probably could never have been established by fear alone, though it is by now quite impossible to perform the experiment which would tell us whether this could indeed have been done. In any case, both fear and faith were present, and I for my part strongly suspect that both were indispensable. Fear may well have actually confirmed faith: there is the story about a Renaissance visitor to Rome, who came back from the holy city convinced of the truth of Catholicism. He argued thus: nothing but divine favour could explain the survival of an institution quite as rotten as this. Similarly, I suspect that the faith of many was sustained under Stalinism by an analogous reflection: nothing other than the truth of Marxism could account for a terror of such unique scale, pervasiveness and horror.

Within the terms of the pervasive System, as supplied by itself, there was indeed an answer to the problem as to how the formal democracy of the nominal Constitution could co-exist with the real concentration of power in the Party. The Soviet Union was, as Raymond Aron used to put it, an *ideocracy*. The ultimate authority lay, in a sense, not with a man or an institution or a procedure, but with a Theory. The truth about human nature, human society, the pattern of history, was available to man, or at any rate to some men. That theory was not merely, so to speak, a dispassionate though important piece of sociological information: it also defined the very nature of what is Right and Wrong in human and social life. It set up the moral framework of the scheme of things. The theory assures us that the social and political world is not static, but is irresistibly moving in a certain direction, and its terminus is deeply significant morally. This alone confers meaning on all history or human life. The process of history will bring about a condition in which all that is good in human nature will at long last find unhampered fulfilment, free of exploitation, oppression, and of scarcity. This doctrine is the third and indispensable pillar of the edifice.

Now the emergence of this Truth in history is itself a historical fact, and its manner of operation is allowed for within the theory itself. The theory was held to be unquestionably true, and the theory saw itself as the touchstone of Truth and Error, including, ominously, moral and political error. The carriers of the truth are blessed by it: they and they alone are the legitimate agents of historic fulfilment. They may not be lukewarm or soft in the performance of their task; that would be treason and dereliction of duty. Those who reject the truth thereby show themselves to be the enemies of the people. Truth, Spinoza said, is the touchstone both of itself and of error. The Bolsheviks certainly held such a view of Marxism, and indeed themselves.

This background of theory both explained and justified the political domination of the Party. The Party could be defined as the disciplined association of those committed to the implementation of the truth, an implementation which is of course in the true interest of *all* men. So it is in effect truly democratic. Khomeini has pointed out that Iranian democracy as instituted by himself implemented the divine rather than the popular will — but of course in the absence of corruption on earth, the two actually went together. Similarly, the Party's implementation of the will of history was the *truest* implementation of the popular will.

So, if Truth of this trustworthy, salvation-bringing kind is indeed available, and in possession of the Party, then it naturally follows that domination of society by the Party is democratic in a far deeper and more important sense, than would be a mere mechanical, formal implementation of democratic procedure, as envisaged by the more abstract articles of the Constitution on such matters, when seen in isolation. Such formal democracy on its own is a sham, typical and characteristic of the deception practised in bourgeois democracies. In any case (given the premises), the question concerning the conflict between formal democracy and party decisions is abstract and unreal. The people understand their true interest, the party understands the realities of the situation, and the two will inevitably converge, unless some alien and hostile force interferes — and if it does, then it is only right and proper that this force be thwarted and ruthlessly destroyed. To do any less would be an inexcusable dereliction of duty.

The circle of ideas is complete. Given the various premises, there is indeed no escape from it. Government by Truth, so to speak, constitutes the Third Pillar in the system. It essentially completes the other two, the formal constitutional democracy and the political monopoly of the Party. It rounds off the edifice and confers harmony on the other elements.

The System contains two important and complementary illusions. One is the absence of factions or fractions in the Party. Lenin proscribed this. In reality, of course, no large body of this kind could possibly function, were it genuinely composed of nothing but atomised, individualised units, bound only by their joint devotion to the Corporate Body and to the Truth which it serves. Such genuine atomisation, even or especially when the faction-less body is made up of sincere believers, would lead to a total volatility, unpredictability and waywardness of all movements of the total association. Any crackpot with a plausible idea and tongue would sway the entire body. This is not tolerable or possible and it does not happen. Covertly, the Party was of course always composed of factions struggling for control. But these alignments, aggregated ideas and interests gave the inner life of the party a certain coherence and stability.

The other illusion, or piece of False Consciousness, to use the Marxist expression, is the idea that the Corpus of Truth contains or engenders uniquely correct solutions for all the practical political and other problems which may arise, and that the party is there to implement these uniquely valid solutions. The truth of the matter, of course, is nothing of the kind. The world is enormously complicated, ambiguous and fluid. The body of propositions and ideas which constitutes the Truth is fragmentary, incomplete, ambiguous and often contradictory, and like all other belief systems it cannot really spew out a unique, clear and convincing 'line' with respect to each situation and each problem which arises. The idea that the "correct Marxist solution" is uniquely determined, and will be recognised by every competent and *bona fide* Marxist is a complete illusion, but one inherent in this thought style. On the contrary, any competent theologian of the System, as of any other, can extract almost anything from it, as and when required.

The two illusions complement each other, and enable each other to persist with at least a tiny measure of plausibility. Unacknowledged informal but often tight factions do of course exist, and at most times one of them will prevail. Its victory will, however, be presented as the historical self-revelation of the unique Correct Solution. The victorious faction will now have the power to impose its own interpretation of the Truth, which will in turn obligingly confirm the legitimacy of the faction — though no one will dare call it such — and the iniquity of those who dared oppose it. The rivals were in error, and error is not innocent.

How is the unique truth in fact recognised and accepted by the Body whose historic role is to be the Recogniser, Carrier and Enforcer of the said Truth? There is an old quip of Berthold Brecht's to the effect that in a democracy, if things go badly one changes the government, but in a dictatorship one changes the people. Reality is a little subtler. Under the dictatorship of the proletariat, you cannot exactly change the people (though you can diminish their numbers, on occasion quite significantly). But the Party is much more adjustable than the people: you can, not merely eliminate, by exclusion or liquidation, past members who have become unsatisfactory; you can also actually make new ones, from the available raw material, ready for co-optation.

During crucial changes of direction, this is precisely what is done: the old membership is purged, and a new membership, whose endorsement then proves the Correctness of the Line, has been coopted into the charismatic community. The Prophet has said that the community will not agree on an error: so communal consensus is the touchstone of truth. In Marxism it is the Party, and not the total society, which constitutes the charismatic community and which works on this principle, thus defining or creating truth by its own consensus. The convergence of Party consensus and Truth is made tautological and ever-applicable and manipulable by controlling the membership of the Party. He who rules the Party, controls truth.

In the course of Soviet history, this system has gone through various stages. Up to some point in the 1920s, a genuine debate about correct policy existed between the informal fractions. Thereafter, under Stalin, control over the identity of the sacralising Party and the truth was in the hands of him who controlled the secret coercive services, accountable only to Him. It is interesting that these services in turn did in fact obey him, for it is not possible to explain this in terms of their own self-interest. They were far more at risk than anyone else, they connived in their own annihilation, and obedience was in no way a sufficient condition of survival.

But obey they did, perhaps because they did not fully understand their own predicament, and partly, I think, because their loyalty was sustained by Faith as well as by fear.

Under Khrushchev and thereafter and thanks to him, the system was transformed, and during the long period of Stagnation, it obeyed new rules. Repression lost the enormously massive and largely random quality which it had had under Stalin, and the incomparably smaller number of those repressed (give and take a few errors and specific injustices) were people who genuinely, even if mildly, opposed the system. Retirement replaced execution as the method of disposal of those vacating key positions. This meant that now, at any rate, those who believed, and those who outwardly conformed, were relatively safe, and their conformity could be described as rational, from the viewpoint of their own interest. Random terror ceased, and fear greatly diminished.

But another curious thing happened, though it was not immediately visible at the time: not only fear, but faith also vanished — faith more so than fear. Russia entered this new era still endowed with faith — Khrushchev was still very much a believer (hence his vast campaign against the Church) — and left it, three decades later, without any. It was a kind of sleep, and when awakening came, faith had evaporated. However, during the Age of *Zastoi* (stagnation or immobility) from 1965 to 1985, public decencies were observed: though faith was ebbing, this was not discussed in public. This regime was as prudish about lack of faith as it was about sex. Appearances were maintained, and society functioned on the surface *as if* it still were a charismatic community, bound by a messianic faith. Individuals may have noted that their own faith had vanished, but they did not probe into the fidelity of others. So the assumption that the Founding Faith was upheld continued, in a vague general kind of way, to pervade the atmosphere. People knew and understood the rules, and there are some merits in such a situation. You knew at least just which fibs to honour, which makes life a damn sight easier than trying to seek out the tangled truth.

It was in this atmosphere that Perestroika made its dramatic appearance, under the impulsion of ruinously heavy military spending, economic slowdown and failure. The important thing about Perestroika is that it is an attempt at social transformation, which defines itself in opposition not to one, but *two* quite distinct antitheses: the Stalinism which is still a matter of living memory for the older generation, and the Stagnation which is remembered by all. These two "perversions" of socialism do not resemble each other much. This is important. The first, Khrushchevian liberalisation was accompanied by the conviction that all will be well in the none-too-distant end, economically and otherwise, if only the perversion of the Cult of Personality is overcome. Foolishly, a precise date - 1980 - was actually specified as the time of this imminent Secular Second Coming. But what characterised the Age of Stagnation was not some dramatic, exaggerated cult of the leader's personality, but, quite on the contrary, something which the Soviet historian Batkin described as serocracy, the *rule of the grey*, of a faceless, dreary, and un-dynamic bureaucracy. A sleazy, edgy, corrupt, and far from affluent world was emerging.

It was Oscar Wilde who observed that losing one parent was something that could happen to anyone, but losing two looked like carelessness. Likewise, any ideal can be smitten by one tragic perversion; but to suffer two, and of such a divergent character, is one too many. This, above all, is the underlying reason for the current lack of faith and of cynicism. The formal position, implied (but without too much conviction) in official pronouncements, is that the initial idea of the October Revolution was perfectly sound, and continues to be binding, but something had alas then gone wrong. This attitude is publicly externalised by the ubiquitous representations of Lenin: Lenin good, and what followed, bad. But if you work out what this means, it is clearly rather odd. Of the 70 odd years of Soviet power, only a little over half a decade is seen as good, though this was a period when policy was in any case dictated first by the requirements of the Civil War, and then exemplified, para-doxically, by what at the time was seen as the temporary expedient of the New Economic Policy. The overwhelmingly larger remaining period is disavowed. The peculiar balance, in historic time, of various forms of Perversion, compared with the rather strange and admittedly untypical period when the ideal could manifest itself in its "undeformed" and true character, and when in reality it had compromised with non-socialist enterprise, can hardly inspire much conviction. Now, the market is invoked as a matter of principle, then it was a temporary expedient. One important Soviet social thinker, actually employed by the Central Com-mittee of the party, has openly reached the conclusion that the time has now come to *re-examine October itself* (his own words). The fault, it would seem, lies not in the perversions but in the idea itself.

It was against this kind of half-unspoken background reasoning that the great May/June Congress was held; it externalised and made public and explicit such a mood. One highly significant moment of the Con-gress occurred with the speech, or should one say outburst, of the retired Major Chervonopisky, a severely disabled veteran of the Afghan war. He began with a bitter and unquestionably deeply-felt, and no doubt justified, account of the manner in which veterans were treated by the bureaucracy on their return. The artificial limbs he received came from a factory so antiquated that it dated back to a present from Lady Churchill at the end of World War II! But then he changed gear: apart from an attack on Academician Sakharov for his criticism of certain moral aspects of the way the Afghan War was conducted, he noted that in all the deep soul-searching that was going on at the Congress, the word Communism had not even been mentioned! Was it not time to return to our ideal? And he went on to propose that they should heed the trinity of Empire, Fatherland and Communism ...

It was indeed the *absence* of allusion to what had once been the legitimating ideal of this society which was truly striking. The Congress was a public, free, not to say uninhibited collective self-examination, but one carried out without any invocation of that set of once sacred ideals, to the implementation of which the Soviet Union had been dedicated.

What then did the Congress do to the three pillars of the political system? It visibly and dramatically marked its restructuring, and the drastic shift in the load each of the three pillars in the edifice were now expected to bear.

Take the first pillar, the formal elective democratic system which had always been there both on paper and as a kind of empty ritualised activity, a theatre of endorsement. What the Congress and the elections which preceded it had done was to take this mechanism out of the cupboard, shake off the dust, and make it operational. It wasn't altogether easy. It had lain in the cupboard so long, it had been an empty formality for so many years, that literally no one knew the rules which were to govern its real employment. In the past it did not matter: there were only *ad hoc* instructions, no real rules. The Administrative-Command system had applied in the polity as well as in the economy.

I repeatedly asked people about the rules of the Congress, and no one knew the answer. The rules were complicated, ambiguous, indeterminate, or simply non-existent. No one seemed to know, for instance, by just what procedures the two chambers of the Supreme Soviet were to be selected from within the totality of the Congress. No one knew how long the Congress would sit and who had the power to dissolve it. Everything had to be decided on the spot. The deputies had arrived and were not supplied with any agenda or the necessary papers. Rumours circulated that the Party members had been instructed to make it short and sweet and to ensure dissolution after three days, before too much damage had been done. (These rumours proved to be false.) Subsequently, rumours circulated that the Congress would terminate itself after two weeks, because Gorbachev did not wish to miss his state visit to West Germany. (This proved to be correct.)

In the event, the Congress had to, and did, make up its own rules as it went along. It turned out to be a unique example of a Presidential Parliament, in which the effective head of state was also the Speaker or vice versa, and treated his fellow members with a curious combination of comradely familiarity and effective leadership. His attitude to the Congress combined, attractively if not altogether consistently, the two ideals emphatically proclaimed in Moscow — the rule of law, and democracy. For instance, at one point, when a proposal was made, he fussed and worried with unfeigned anxiety about whether the proposal was *legal*: we don't, he said with a troubled mien, want to do something stupid (commit a *glupost'*). Was there a lawyer in the house? There was indeed. His advice was sought (and subsequently, after further speeches in support of the measure, ignored). At another point, on the other hand, Mikhail Gorbachev stressed that we — the Congress — are the supreme sovereign body, and hence free to decide what we shall do. We make the law. At the Congress and elsewhere, Gorbachev's leadership has an appealing Harun al Rashid quality; he by-passes intermediate officials and addresses himself with great directness to people and issues, in a manner which is all at once egalitarian, and yet that of a man who knows well who is boss.

It is a marked feature of the present situation that no one pretends for a moment that the system was, even in the recent past, not to mention, of course, the nightmare of Stalinism, an example of either democracy or of the rule of law. The absence of each of these is freely and unquestioningly admitted. These things are to be striven for, but they are not yet with us. In the old days of faith and constant official boasting, the rule of Truth-and-Party was of course claimed to be far more truly democratic than the spurious constitutional facades of bourgeois democracy, which merely camouflaged the protection of the interests of the dominant class minority. With the working class in power, insistence on those formal niceties was redundant: substantive justice overruled formal justice. The question asked now, however, is not whether those formal safeguards, the rule of law, are indeed necessary (everyone now recognises that they are), but rather, given the present political framework, whether they are *possible...*

Consider what the *Syezd*, as the most dramatic expression of Perestroika, has done to the previously formal and cosmetic constitutional pillar. It has endowed it with a measure — no one knows for how long and just how much — of real power. Effective sovereignty is no longer the Party-and-Truth, but is, in some measure at least, shared by an assembly, which acts as a public platform for airing ideas and unpalatable truths. Admittedly the Supreme Soviet was elected by a complex, imperfect and only half-intelligible procedure, and further sifted by an additional and manipulable internal selection procedure, with many lacunae in the system of genuine, contested election. Yet, for all that, it is a body which clearly contains an independent, vocal, and assertive element, not susceptible to intimidation, and which turns it into something quite other than a rubber stamp: thus its debates can fascinate and succeed in holding the attention of an entire nation for two weeks on end. This independent and critical minority in the *Syezd* could always be outvoted, if necessary, by the delegations from the Russian backwoods, and the patron-bound deputies from the Muslim Mezzogiorno, so to speak. But it would not be silenced, cowed, or deprived of influence. Gorbachev's strategy evidently consists of using it as the stimulus of Perestroika, whilst at the same time using the Conservative elements to restrain it, in turn, within certain limits.

What has the Congress done to the third pillar, the unique Truth to be implemented in society and history by its guardians and carriers? It has dramatically destroyed, at any rate for the time being, its monopoly of intellectual legitimacy and truth. Official doctrine is no longer the standard of truth or error. Orthodoxy was brazenly defied not only with impunity but with manifest legitimacy. Heresy is affirmed and the heavens do not fall. Heretics are treated with respect and courtesy, as valued participants in the political process. The freedom of speech within the Congress was dramatic and extreme. Baltic and Georgian deputies openly and unambiguously challenged the very legitimacy of the inclusion of their republics in the USSR ...

Admittedly freedom of speech in the media had already for some time been remarkable — I could never quite believe that I was really hearing the things which I did hear on TV — but the affirmation of heresay on a formal political platform gave these expressions of erstwhile un-tolerated heterodoxy a quite special weight. Government by Revealed Truth is over, at any rate for the time being. Truth is no longer so easy to come by. (History examinations in the educational system have had to be suspended: old textbooks are clearly no longer usable, new ones are not yet available, and the teachers felt unable to teach, and even more so, to examine, without textbooks to guide them.) It has now been publicly shown that the Truth is no one's exclusive property, that dissent and disagreement are legitimate, that honest doubt and debate are in order, that losing factions — if and when they lose — are therefore not necessarily sinning against nation and history, and thereby eligible for legitimate exclusion from the political arena.

That leaves the middle pillar of the old edifice, the Party. One of the paradoxes of the Congress was that the proportion of party members amongst the delegates was actually higher, not lower than used to be the case in the old days for formalistic rubber-stamping sessions of the Supreme Soviet. In the past, the number of such members was kept down to a certain ratio, as a kind of deliberate demonstration of the alleged national unity of the party and of the party-less. (This was actually an official slogan.) This ratio could now no longer be controlled, given that a significant proportion of seats was being genuinely contested, and so the proportion of party members actually went up. This illustrates, not a strengthening of the party, but the fact that party membership cuts across the crucial political dividing line, and membership itself is not always very significant. The increase in the proportion of party members reflects the fact that the deputies now were, much more often, people genuinely eager to take part in political decision-making; such people frequently chose, for a variety of reasons which do not always include total conviction, to be party members.

This paradox has a certain similarity to another — namely, that some of the legal measures adopted in the last year or so, e.g. the July 1988 edict on the holding of public meetings, are more, not less, severe and restrictive than earlier legislation. Liberals are naturally and quite properly incensed by this. But there is a certain logic in it. In the days of the dominance of substantive, "class" justice, the authorities had little need of legislation to keep a check on unwanted associations and meetings. They could and did do so easily without the benefit of any legal blessing. (*Meetingovat'* is now a Russian verb, with a somewhat negative emotive charge.) Hence formal legislation, like the constitution, could be admirably liberal. But now that the authorities intend to, or are constrained to, act within the law, they are, not without some measure of justification, eager to possess themselves of legal means for controlling assemblies which certainly can lead to a disturbance of the peace, sometimes with lethal consequences.

But to return to our middle pillar: the fact that there is now a rival centre of authority and legitimacy, namely the erstwhile formal structure, and that men can act independently in that rival structure even if they are party members, means that the old monopoly is lost — and so is the fiction of a seamless, undivided party. Unity, monopoly of political and indeed any association, and the underwriting by a supposedly unique Truth, have all gone.

The question as to whether the new democracy can work without a multi-party system has inevitably and openly been raised. Gorbachev has not endorsed this suggestion, but the manner in which it is held in abeyance is interesting. (Party members can state publicly, on T.V., that they favour such a system). There is no suggestion that it constitutes an unspeakable heresy. Commenting on the present single-party system on television some time prior to the Congress, Gorbachev observed with seeming carelessness, *"tak istoricheski sluchilos'"*, it just so turned out, historically, that we are landed with a single-party system. This is the contingent historical situation which we have inherited: we may or may not like it, but we have to work within this framework, at any rate for the time being. This rather offhand reasoning is a very far cry from any convinced reaffirmation of the Leninist view, that the party was and should be the authoritative Advance Guard of the Proletariat.

So this is what the Congress has visibly, conspicuously done. It has severely undermined the ideocratic pillar. It has endowed the formal, erstwhile cosmetic institutional pillar with a real role in the system — certainly not yet an exclusive or dominant one, but nevertheless, a genuine one. It has given it a real load to bear. And it has left what remains the main concentration of power, the middle pillar, with an acknowledged question mark hanging over it; it is faced with the need to deal with the newly enfranchised formal structure, and to do so without the support of, or the ability to invoke and manipulate at will, the third, ideological element. The Party is now legitimated not by a Sacred Doctrine, but rather by the weighty, but pragmatic rather than ideological consideration that it is the only body standing between society and chaos. Only the State-and-Party- bureaucracy possess the organisations and habits of discipline which hold society together.

The Soviet Union under Perestroika is now a pragmatic and *not* an ideocratic society, and one trying to overcome the disastrous unintended institutional consequences of the Faith which it no longer really upholds, but which it cannot formally disavow. It is trying to cope with the crisis by using the best institutional tool to hand: that very state-and-party bureacracy which was in fact engendered, but not intended or foreseen, by the Faith. The endeavour is of course hampered by the fact that its success is not in the interests or to the taste of all members of that very bureaucracy. The Faith cannot be clearly disavowed, because this would completely disorient that power hierarchy which is the only effective executive agency of Perestroika, and furthermore, it would provide those numerous members of it who stand to lose by the changes, with a platform. So the balancing act, with its tacitly anti-Party End of Ideology element, goes on. It is complemented by the contrary and contradicting theme, to the effect that all this is the protection and revival of the Socialist and Communist heritage. How this new compromise system will develop further remains to be seen: but one can only stress the remarkable changes which have already occurred in it.

What next? Two, not one, menacing swords hang over the Perestroika enterprise. One is the conjunction of economic failure; the other, ethnic explosions. If one thing is obvious, it is that neither of these problems can be taken lightly. Four possible fates await the present trend in the USSR. The most hopeful one, from the viewpoint of the leadership, is that there will be economic improvement and that ethnic conflict will be contained. The most disastrous scenario is *the conjunction of* economic collapse and ethnic explosion. In between lie two middle possibilities: imposition of restraint on the ethnic irredentists, but one accompanied by continuing economic stagnation; or the achievement of economic growth, but one paid for by the continuation of national troubles. Only a rash man would predict which of these four possibilities will actually take place.

The ethnic situation obviously is a very severe threat to the system. Stalinism and stagnation had stifled and hidden, but in no way eliminated, sources of ethnic conflict. The Soviet Union has, like the Habsburg and Ottoman empires, inherited an incredibly complex patchwork of ethnic, linguistic and religious groups, often related to each other not as compact territorial groups, but as social strata. But unlike Turkey and Austria, it did not shed them in 1918 — to the regret of some Russians at least.

A number of plausible principles can be invoked to determine the ethnic-territorial organisation of the country. It could be that, in each region and district, the majority should decide. But there is also the consideration of historic and geographical continuity. There is the consideration that some local demographic majorities are the fruits of quite arbitrary, forceful and brutal transplantations of population in Stalinist times; others are the consequence of recent industrial migrations, and many nations feel that the link established with a territory by growing potatoes there or herding camels or breeding pigs, is weightier than the link established by producing pig iron or computers. In agrarian work, land and labour mix with each other, so to speak, and create a deep bond; industrial work fails to do this. After all, the latter distribution of industry and hence of workers is a largely arbitrary consequence of ministerial decisions. (For instance, it is claimed by some that the location of many new industrial enterprises in the Baltic region, with the consequent in-migration of Russian workers, is a result of the fact that the bureaucrats, charged with supervising the establishment of the said new industries, greatly preferred to be sent on their *komandirovki*, missions of inspection, to the Baltic, and take in a little mini-holiday by the sea whilst they were at it, rather than having to travel out to, say, Siberia.) This potato-and-pig principle may be odd — are not industrial workers human beings too? Have they no rights, no love of the land they inhabit? Marxism can hardly deny it; but all the same that principle carries much emotive weight. There is also the consideration that some ethnic groups are not in the majority in the territory which bears their name, and some are not in a majority anywhere. For all that, they feel entitled to their own, autonomous or independent cultural-political roof.

These various principles, each of them with its own plausibility, cut across each other and come into conflict in numerous situations. Naturally, many ethnic groups invoke the principle which happens to favour them, and feel outraged when a rival principle is invoked against them.

For all these reasons, the ethnic problem was highly prominent at the Congress. There is perhaps another reason: the Congress was the supreme expression of the transformation and loosening of the previous system, the dissolution of the previous political and ideological monopoly and centralism. It is not at all obvious what pluralistic institutions, what kind of civil society, is available to step into the vacuum so created. New institutions and associations do not emerge so quickly. But ethnic sentiment and cohesion are the quickest catalysts of effective new association. Nationalism steps into the space vacated by ideocracy.

The Congress was a time of excitement and optimism. Since then, further nationalist eruptions have occurred; and in reaction to them, certainly during the late summer, it feels as if the current had begun to flow in the other direction. Ominous warnings against nationalist excess may be found in the Soviet press and on television. In the second week of September, a televised speech by Gorbachev carried an undercurrent of menace. So did the pronouncement at the Party Plenum on nationalities later the same month. It is of course far too early to speak of all this with any confidence.

The present volume assembles the most interesting contributions made at the Congress and in the first sessions of the new Supreme Soviet on the nationalist issue. In so doing, it illustrates both the nature of this most remarkable political assembly, and the character of the ethnic problems which constitute one of the two main dangers for perestroika, for the very process of which the Congress was the expression.

Ernest Gellner
Moscow, September 1989

THE CONGRESS: DEMOCRACY AND ETHNIC ISSUES

At exactly 10 a.m. the table of the Presidium on the stage stood empty. The leaders of the party and government did not walk out from the wings in a previously arranged order. No deputies leapt from their seats in ecstatic gratitude. The youthful voices of the cheer leaders did not ring out, nor was there an outburst of thunderous and exhausting applause which left the palms aching and the conscience uneasy for long after. For decades such a cheap performance was considered obligatory for an event of such world significance. It was quite obviously inappropriate for this Congress....
Izvestia 26 May, 1989.

By contrast with the rubber-stamp sessions of the former Supreme Soviet the novel Congress was an event of historic importance. At the very least, it marked a considerable advance in the process of perestroika, glasnost and democratisation underway since 1985. Two months after the elections in late March, 2,249 'people's deputies' assembled in Moscow for the first ever gathering of this kind. Their tasks, as drawn up in the agenda, were to choose 542 of their fellows as members of a new permanently-sitting Supreme Soviet, to elect the Prime Minister, and approve the USSR Prosecutor General and the Chairman of the Supreme Court. It was rightly expected that Mikhail Gorbachev, 'the founding father of perestroika' as Sakharov called him, would be overwhelmingly approved as the Chairman of the Supreme Soviet or 'President' of the entire country.

In the event, the deputies sat for longer than anticipated, discussed many more issues than those on the agenda and were watched and listened to continuously in live television and radio transmissions by vast numbers of Soviet citizens.

A catch phrase of the day among radical reformers warned that 'democratisation is not yet democracy, glasnost is not yet freedom of speech, and the Supreme Soviet is not yet a parliament'. This is all true. Yet there has been nothing comparable to the recent elections in Soviet history since the ill-fated Constituent Assembly in 1918 (where the Bolsheviks won 25% of the vote).

Fifteen hundred deputies were directly elected to the Congress by the adult population. In 275 of these constituencies no candidate received the necessary 50% of the vote to be declared outright winner so second and (in 76 cases) third rounds were held. Turnout was genuinely high and in some areas (Georgia, 97.8%) it was astonishing. Still, 399 of the 1500 directly-elected deputies had no rival candidates. The first secretary of the Communist party in Kazakhstan, Kolbin, admitted that it "would certainly have been better" if the candidates opposing the local party bosses in his republic, for instance, had not almost all been refused registration.

The remaining 750 deputies were chosen from among 912 candidates by 'non-governmental' or public organisations: these included the Communist Party, Komsomol (Young Communist League), trade unions, women's committees, Unions of writers, artists, composers and so on. The total electorate in such bodies amounted to only 16,200. Genuine and open electoral contests did occur, however, in the Academy of Sciences which sent Sakharov, Shmelev and Karyakin to the Congress. In other cases the deputies were in effect nominated, though many such nominees played an active, constructive and vocal role in the Congress proceedings.

As a result there was a crude preponderance of the 1143 deputies who had either been nominated, chosen by a few thousand writers or artists or elected unopposed in regular constituencies over the 1101 who had fought contested elections. (Over 4000 candidates were officially registered but in 910 of the elective constituencies, it was admitted, there had been public protest at the refusal of the preliminary district commissions to register certain other candidates.) Thus while the Congress might be quite representative of Soviet society in one sense, it was not yet a democratically-elected body in the usual meaning of that term.

As far as the practice of democracy at the Congress itself was concerned there were often bursts of hostility, or demands to end discussion, in addition to procedural muddles and drawn-out voting. Academician Goldansky (nominated by the Soviet Peace Foundation) commented regretfully, on the tenth day of proceedings, that domestic discussion and debate had yet to catch up with the indubitable achievements of perestroika in international affairs and foreign policy:

> ... in the last few years our foreign policy has acquired a number of qualities that were formerly quite alien to it.
>
> First, the ability to listen to the arguments of the other side, even if they to-

tally diverge from your own. Second, the capacity to convince the other side of the rightness of your arguments. And I mean convince, not by applying force. Third, the ability to seek and find mutually-acceptable solutions to controversial problems, by striving to reach consensus and unanimity for the sake of being constructive.

These qualities are indispensable in international relations ... and just as essential if deputies are to work properly. ... For the time being we clearly haven't learnt these lessons.

The election of 542 deputies as members of the Supreme Soviet, with the exception of the Moscow delegation, was made almost entirely on the basis of one seat-one candidate nominations put forward by the republican and regional delegations. Subsequently a further 400 deputies were appointed to the Supreme Soviet's various committees and commissions. When the Congress closed, the remaining 1000 or so deputies for the most part returned to their constituencies, with still unclear rights of legislative initiative, the right to participate (but not vote) in sessions of the Supreme Soviet and its commissions and committees, and the prospect of entering these bodies through rotation in a year or more's time.

The ethnic debate at the congress

"After an interval of 66 years, frank discussions about national and ethnic relations in our country are being held for the first time since the 12th congress of the Bolshevik Party. This discussion shows that all the fears Lenin expressed and warned against in his testament have come true."
Klara Hallik (Estonia)

The new permanently sitting Supreme Soviet is divided, like its predecessor, into two Chambers. In one, the Chamber of the Union, the members are chosen according to a territorial principle, each representing 771,000 adults of voting age. In the second, the Chamber of Nationalities, each union republic has 11 seats while autonomous republics, regions and districts have smaller quotas.

At the Congress, however, these two principles were both represented. There were 750 territorial and 750 national-territorial deputies. Thus while Estonia's population only justified it having 4 'territorial' deputies it was allocated a further 32 'national' constituencies because of its status as a union republic. This attempt to represent fairly the complex federal structure and ethnic diversity of the Soviet Union, together with the procedural concessions extracted by the national republics, ensured that the voices of those nations would be heard throughout the country without the mediation and frequent distortions of the central Russian-language press and television. While the Baltic republics probably made the most effective use of this platform, many other nations and ethnic groups also took this opportunity to speak out.

Thus the theme which emerged most clearly and insistently from the Congress was not the state of crisis (the word many deputies used) in the Soviet economy and society with its dissatisfactions and rising crime rate, but the long-neglected problems of that part of the population which is not Russian. At the same time, the national self-identity of the Russians themselves, the largest of all Soviet nations, was an important issue and was raised particularly by deputies from the western border territories.

Chapter 1

TOWARDS DISINTEGRATION, DICTATORSHIP OR A NEW FEDERATION?

After the first few days of fierce debate at the Congress, and after the election of Gorbachev and of the 542 members of the new Supreme Soviet, calls began to be heard from all quarters for "consolidation". Some suggested this would be better done without the merciless attention of the TV cameras.

An Estonian academic, Victor Palm, did not convince many, though, when he told the Congress to get used to confrontation and conflicts of interest: these were, he insisted, an inevitable fact of political life. Yegor Yakovlev, editor of *Moscow News* and a bogeyman for conservatives, announced that the potential for consolidation between all the various groups was far from exhausted.

On what basis, however, were deputies and the different social, ethnic and regional interests they represented to reach such consensus? For apart from the mistrust and hostility generated by the "democratic minority", four of the Union's 15 major nations demanded on the fourth day that the terms on which they had been incorporated into the USSR be re-examined: the Georgians perhaps more as an emotional gesture, the Baltic nations as an official and urgent request from their own governments.

These critical, democratic and separatist tendencies evoked a strong reaction from the right. In one of the most dramatic (and alarming) moments of the Congress, a severely disabled Afghan war veteran expressed disappointment that Gorbachev had offered no political assessment of the Afghan war in his speech, attacked "political intriguers" in the Baltic republics and Georgia, and condemned remarks made by Sakharov. The retired Ukrainian major Chervonopisky concluded with an appeal to return to traditional values:

'More than 80% of those in this hall are Communists. Many of them have already spoken, but not from one of them have we heard the word communism. I'm a convinced opponent of slogans and show. But I believe the three things that we should struggle for with all our might are: the State (*derzhava*), Motherland and Communism.' (Applause,

1

many deputies stand) (155).

A suitably sceptical reply to this appeal for "traditional Soviet" values came several days later from Mariu Lauristin (herself daughter of a famous Estonian Communist): 'When you translate the Russian word *derzhava* into Estonian it comes out as "empire".' (156, 'inaudible' in transcript)

Imperial policy, imperial ambitions

Formally, the Soviet Union replaced an autocratic empire with a voluntary federation of equal republics. The only other comparable modern land empire, that of Austria-Hungary, fell apart in 1918. For a variety of reasons the Soviet regime avoided this fate. However, in Olzhas Suleimeinov's words, the process of decolonisation "was suspended in the 1920s". The Soviet Union became a highly centralised state that included, or subsequently re-incorporated, virtually the same area and nations as the former Russian empire. Naturally it inherited many of the practices and attitudes that went with it.

The country now stands, perhaps, before its next great transformation. The change from Empire to Union after 1917 was preceded by rapid political evolution but, in contrast to the present, was accompanied by equally rapid and destabilising economic development. At several moments during the Congress different speakers alluded to the stages on the long historical trajectory Muscovy had followed to reach its present position in the world: first uniting the various Russian principalities to throw off the Tatar yoke and fight back Poland-Lithuania in the West, before expanding eastwards to become first a vast empire, and ultimately a super-power. Evgeny Kogan, a Jewish deputy from Estonia commented, for example: "We don't need laws like those on language that divide us up into petty principalities if we want to remain part of a great power (and I think that's what the majority wants)." (147). The famous Russian eye surgeon Svyatoslav Fyodorov (148), criticised parochial concerns within the Russian Federation and regional chauvinism in the same terms: "I have just been listening to a few speeches and it seems to me that we are still in a country broken up into petty principalities, where each "is at war" with another, and therefore wants to elect its own ambassador who would defend the principality interests here in Moscow." Baltic deputies objected to this kind of talk.

Ilmar Bisher, professor of law at the University of Latvia, (148) politely demurred: "There was talk about petty principalities here. I don't think there are any but since we are a federal state there are union republics." Kazimieras Uoka of the Lithuanian People's Front declared more passionately: "I find it frightening when the concepts of region and republic are constantly confused here. If even in this Chamber [of Nationalities] there is no desire to listen to every deputy, I repeat every one, who represents the interests of a nation, then I consider I have the right to talk about the possibility of my native Lithuania leaving the union of Soviet Socialist Republics. It is a constitutional right. If things go on like this, I do not want my native Lithuania to be in such a bad Union ..." (159)

Representatives of the national republics, and the "democratic minority", instead proposed to radically remake the Federation, finally eliminating these imperial elements. Whether these were genuine desires for transformation or merely tactical moves to ease secession only time and the growing impatience of the people they represent can show. On the other hand, if perestroika or restructuring of the Soviet system was not successful, the immediate future looked very bleak to many speakers. The alarming warnings of imminent economic collapse from Nikolai Shmelev, threatened an unavoidable return to the command economy and, probably, the danger that force would then be used to keep order, and prevent the country breaking up: into principalities, republics, autonomous regions or whatever they might be called.

Some of the proposals for this new Federation are laid out in the following chapters, as are the sceptical and often hostile reactions of the traditionalists. However, the First Congress of People's Deputies naturally began by exposing and critically discussing all the Soviet Union's present sources of power and authority: the institutions, ideologies and forces that, in theory and practice, at present hold the Union together. Moreover, they did so in discussions of unprecedented frankness during which reactionary, conservative and democratic attitudes and policies were clearly outlined.

1 POLITICS AND IDEOLOGY
Gorbachev: Electing a President

> ... there came a man who disturbed the enchanted kingdom of Brezhnevite stagnation. He did not appear from outside but emerged from the depths of the system itself. ...

> However, the present paradox is that the waves of discontent have now turned back on the founder of this historic movement, Mikhail Gorbachev.
> *Chingis Aitmatov 146*

Gorbachev was the obvious candidate as far as all the republics were concerned (he and two other proposed candidates were all, naturally, ethnic Russians). Concern was nevertheless expressed from the outset about the unprecedented power his new post would give him. At the same time, the danger of his sudden removal was also mentioned, thus raising the question of his democratic credentials and the validity of his election.

Andrei Sakharov (Academy of Sciences) 146

I have repeatedly expressed my support in public for Mikhail Gorbachev (Applause). I still ...do not see anyone else who could lead our country. But my support is conditional. I consider it essential to have a discussion and speeches by different candidates: we must have a choice for all elections at the present congress, including that of the Chairman of the USSR Supreme Soviet. ...

Mariu Lauristin, journalism faculty, Tartu University (territorial deputy, Estonia) 147

The popular-democratic movement in defence of perestroika in the Baltic area has from the very beginning looked on Gorbachev as a democratic leader and we do not see any alternative to him now. But we have certain questions, to which I would like an answer, before I can with a clear conscience vote. First, what legal and political guarantees of the self-determination of the nation and of the republics sovereignty do you, as Chairman of the Supreme Soviet, consider essential to include in the USSR Constitution?

Second, do you personally consider the use of the army in our country for punitive operations against the civilian population to be compatible with the development of democracy and the rule of law? We are all very concerned about what happened in Tbilisi.

Third, who in the Politburo was informed ahead of time of the intention to use troops in Tbilisi? It would probably be very important for all of us to know when you yourself learned about this.

Dainis Ivans, chairman of Latvian People's Front (national deputy, Latvia) 147

We musn't forget that we are today not choosing a boss but a leader, our own colleague. Since someone has already mentioned courage then I think that Gorbachev's courage depends on our courage. At our forum of different nations in Latvia we suggested that to help Gorbachev we must be more Gorbachevian than he himself is.

Valentin Logunov, deputy editor-in-chief of *Moskovskaya Pravda* **(territorial deputy, Moscow) 147**

I support Gorbachev's candidacy but during the election campaign I frequently heard the following advice from the voters: to protect our people and the new Chairman from the partocracy and free him from party discipline, Mikhail Gorbachev should resign as General Secretary of the Party and as a member of the Politburo.

Evgeny Velikhov, vice-president of USSR Academy of Sciences, Moscow (Communist Party) 147

We talk about the combination and separation of powers. Of what powers are you talking? The Soviets as yet have no real power or authority! When we have given power to the Soviets and strengthened them, then the question will arise of separating party and state, and of the holding of more than one post. The issue today is the transfer of power. Let's resolve it first. (Applause)

Woman deputy 147

Yes, Gorbachev has made mistakes, with the cooperatives, women's issues and much else. (Commotion in hall) We women very much hope that Gorbachev will receive support from all. ... We have problems like no other country. But tell me, please, who first began to struggle against alcoholism? Who first began to struggle against those who thieve and steal from us? ... who first gave us all courage and opened our eyes to so much? ... Vote for him! And he'll understand all his mistakes, I think.

Vladimir Yavorivsky, writer, secretary of Ukrainian writers' union, Kiev (territorial deputy, Ukraine) 147

It would of course mark our progress towards democracy if we chose between different candidates when we vote today. I shall not praise Mikhail Gorbachev, now is not the time. The Ukrainian delegation will vote for him but we shall not forget Boris Yeltsin.

And let us tell the people that we are doing this for the last time....Let's think about all the people electing our president next time round.

Muhammad Yusuf, Tashkent (territorial deputy, Uzbekistan) 147

I am chairman of the Directorate for the Muslims of Central Asia and Kazakhstan. In the name of the millions of Muslims living in our country I call on you to vote for Mikhail Gorbachev, a man who has done a great deal for the people ...

As well as the predictable attempt to get Boris Yeltsin to run for this post, a non-party research worker, Alexander Obolensky, from the Leningrad Region put forward his own candidacy.

Anatoly Sobchak, professor of law, Leningrad University (territorial deputy, Leningrad) 147

For decades, any official post in our country has only been held by party members, from the chairman of the rural council to the Chairman of the Supreme Soviet or government ministers. ... This is why we must include Comrade Obolensky, who is not a party member, in the secret ballot list for the post of chairman. As a matter of principle.

Alexander Obolensky, Geophysical institute, Apatita (national deputy, Russian Federation) 147

I do not doubt that Mikhail Gorbachev will win and I shall vote for him myself. However, I hope there will be elections in the republics offering a real choice of candidates. Then I will not have set a bad example here.

689 voted to include Obolensky in the ballot sheet; 1415 voted against with 33 abstentions. Yeltsin was proposed by others but stood down. Gorbachev received 2123 votes (95.6%), with 87 against.

Only after election, did Gorbachev, now both head of the Party and of State, answer various questions. Thereafter he took a very active part in the Congress proceedings whether he or another member of the presidium were in the chair. For the first sessions he not only encouraged, directed and channelled discussion but also, usually standing not sitting, demonstratively voted himself.

Vilen Tolpezhnikov, hospital doctor, Riga (national deputy, Latvia) 149

We very much respect Mikhail Gorbachev. We don't know any other [such] leader in the country. However, I am categorically opposed to his interventions during other deputies' speeches.

Vladimir Zubanov, party secretary, steel factory, Donetsk (territorial deputy, Russian Federation) 149

We can all see, the whole country sees: the feeling among deputies today is that whichever way Mikhail Gorbachev decides to go that's how the whole hall will react. ...

Gennady Filshin, economist, Siberian branch of Academy of Sciences, Irkutsk (territorial deputy, Russian Federation) 149

Today we are making an exception and electing the first deputy chairman of the Supreme Soviet [Lukyanov] without a choice of candidates. Tomorrow we'll do the same for the Prime Minister [Ryzhkov]. Whenever will we do what we promised our voters?

First, we must not permit any more one-candidate elections for the highest posts in the country. (Applause) We're all tired, incidentally. Is that the hope, that we shall now vote everything through?

Mikhail Gorbachev (in chair)

I have to disappoint you. You may or may not agree with the nominations made by the Chairman of the USSR Supreme Soviet. However, I am fully empowered by the Constitution to make nominations to such posts, beginning with the first deputy chairman. ... So I offer the alternative candidates — after you have not rejected my first nominee.

Yuri Vlasov, writer (territorial deputy, Moscow) 153

Deputy Gorbachev's vague reply to the question of who ordered the reprisal raid in Tbilisi meant that we had to set up a commission. Yet it is impossible to believe, in the circumstances, that the head of state could not know all the circumstances of some action. If he really does not, then what kind of president is he? It is likewise impossible to conceive that members of the Politburo did not know, and do not now know, the answer.

... It is not a question of the concealment of important information from the Congress ... we must include an article in the constitution to permit impeachment, i.e. dismissal of the President, if he conceals the truth from the people. (Applause)

Turning the Supreme Soviet Into a Parliament

Formally, there are Soviets (or councils) at every level, from the local district, to the republican supreme Soviets up to the highest legislative body of all, the USSR Supreme Soviet. Only with the elections in March 1989 did the last body begin to acquire some genuinely democratic features.

The Congress, and the Supreme Soviet that continued sitting after the former dispersed, was an obvious second focus of consolidation. For the first time elected representatives of the people from every republic and region would regularly confer together instead of the highly formal 3-4 day sessions of the old-style Supreme Soviet. Yet deputies' rights were never clearly defined, and the lower level Soviets were still formed according to the old rules. This placed considerable responsibility and strain even on the people's deputies and those they elected to the Supreme Soviet.

The vague formula that ranking local officials elected to the Supreme Soviet would give up their jobs "as a rule" led to concern about the functioning of the new system. The suspicion was voiced, more than once, that behind the scenes the membership of various bodies had already been decided.

Yuri Afanasyev, rector of the historical-archives institute, Moscow (territorial deputy, Moscow region) 149

I have looked once again very closely at the qualifications of those we have just elected ... we have again chosen a Stalinist-Brezhnevite Supreme Soviet ... (noise in hall, applause) I am specifically addressing you, those I would call the aggressive obedient majority ...

Mikhail Gorbachev:

Quiet, comrades. This is a serious matter, I think.

Afanasyev

Don't clap or yell, please, because that's exactly why I asked to speak now. I'd like to warn the aggressive obedient majority of the following. And you as well, Mikhail Gorbachev. I can't decide whether you are attentively responsive to the majority or skilfully manipulating them. We can carry on like this but we must not for one minute forget those who sent us here ... to decisively change the situation in our country.

Nikolai Sazonov, party secretary at Kamaz truck plant (territorial deputy, Tataria) 153

Of course, we've been working 6 days and we're a little tired but I call on you to be very vigilant. This morning you received a questionnaire for signing up to the committees and commissions of the Supreme Soviet. But the structure of that body has not yet been discussed. ...

We've already permitted a grave miscalculation in elections to the Supreme Soviet. Of its members 231 are leading figures in the Soviets, the Party or bodies controlling the economy. They will be absent, as a rule, and as a result our parliament will not function continually.

In spite of these fears the Chamber of Nationalities proved extremely lively from the very beginning; almost certainly because the constituency each national group spoke for was much more clearly defined than those in the amorphous Chamber of the Union. And in the other Chamber, the Speaker Primakov's attempt to "do a Gorbachev" (intervening, commenting, guiding) was very quickly and firmly halted by Salambek Khadzhiev, the director of the Grozny oil refinery: "We made you speaker to organise our discussions, not to tell us what to do." (This polite but uncompromising reprimand did not find its way into the transcript, unfortunately.)

Thereafter the Supreme Soviet interrogated minister after minister, and some of them were visibly and audibly shaken by this quite novel experience. It rejected no less than 5 of them and gave only a conditional acceptance to several others.

The Party: politics, unity and careers

In the 1977 the dominance of the Communist Party was, for the first time, constitutionally defined in article 6, and given the 'leading role' in Soviet society. The only political party permitted in the country, it had for decades become inextricably intertwined with the state through the nomenklatura system, i.e. the exclusion of all but Party members from the highest (and also many comparatively modest) posts in every sphere.

Valentin Rasputin, writer, Irkutsk (USSR writers union) 159

I am not a Party member and quite consciously decided not to join after observing how many self-seeking characters were trying to get in. It was profitable to be a Party member then [under Brezhnev] , that's why the Party lost its authority. ... To resign from the party now is not courage ... but the same calculating approach that led people to join it before.

(Applause)

Evgeny Evtushenko, poet, secretary of USSR Union of writers (national deputy, Ukraine) 154

... There are about 100 million adult non-Party members in our country [and 20 million party members]. ... But there is not one non-Party USSR government minister in the country. Search as you may, you will not find a non-Party factory manager. There is only one non-Party minister in the republics, Raimond Pauls [popular music composer, Latvian Minister of Culture] and one, and only one, non-Party chief editor of a countrywide periodical, Sergei Zalygin [of *Novy Mir*]. I think they had better be registered straightaway as endangered species.

I could not understand what people mean when they say that the attacks on the Party at our Congress were organised by "sinister forces". Non-party deputies make up only 13% of the total: what takes place here is almost nothing more than an inner-party discussion! ... We've had enough of hunting for enemies! And neither should those 38 regional party leaders who lost in the elections to this Congress say this was an attack on the party.

Since 1985 the party has found itself in a quite different political situation. First 'informal' pressure groups of various kinds appeared, and then political People's Fronts (some officially recognised, others not) were formed openly in the republics and attracted mass support. (The 'people's fronts' set up in major Russian cities have so far tended to be more like political clubs than mass movements.)

The overwhelming majority of deputies to the Congress were still party members, though the proportion varied from 64% in Lithuania to 96% and 93% in Turkmenia and Tajikistan respectively. (A further 133 were members of the Komsomol, or Young Communist League.) The Party also had a guaranteed allocation of 100 nominated deputies. Yet there was a noticeable difference as to which type of Communist was elected (or nominated in the Party's quota): leading party officials in Leningrad and Kiev, even when standing unopposed, were rejected by the voters. The vast majority of those elected to the Congress, 88%, had never served in the USSR Supreme Soviet before.

The elections were a demonstration, therefore, of a kind of one-party democracy. In an interview after the Congress, Gorbachev's deputy Anatoly Lukyanov demanded to know "where and when a multi-party system has been more efficient and democratic" (Izvestiya 176). Moscow candidates during the election campaign usually declared in TV interviews that, in principle, they favoured a multi-party system. The examples of Hungary and Poland also began to make this idea less unthinkable in the Soviet bloc, although such small unitary and culturally homogenous states bear little comparison with the Soviet federal giant. (Yugoslavia offers a closer and less happy parallel.)

Yet in a country where all other parties, socialist or not, have been banned since 1921, and also fractions within the Communist party itself, the very suggestion of a distinct and organised radical or democratic grouping among deputies met with vocal opposition.

Gavriil Popov, professor of economics, Moscow University (USSR Union of scien tific and technical societies) 149

The Congress was elected by secret vote with alternative candidates. Now it has begun to propose the same number of candidates as there are vacancies.

We must therefore think of changing our tactics. What we are suggesting is the formation of an inter-regional independent group of deputies and we invite all deputies to join us. (Applause)

We believe this group should be able to present alternative reports following those to be given by Gorbachev and Ryzhkov next week.

Vladimir Stepanov, director of state farm (territorial deputy, Karelian ASSR, Russian Federation) 149

Your suggestion of creating a fraction, comrade Popov, is madness. Think what you're doing! ... You're introducing disorder into the work of the Congress and distracting it from the real problems.

Janis Peters, writer, chairman of Latvian writers union, Riga (national deputy, Latvia) 155

Although this is not a congress of Communists. A word about the party. Yes, the party triumphed in the elections but the party was also defeated. It is telling that the absolute majority of communists elected people's deputies were precisely those who supported the popular movements for democracy and the idea of national renaissance.

Why was Mikhail Gorbachev elected President of the USSR almost unopposed? The secret is very simple. The leader of the Soviet Union's communists resolutely took the side of the people.

So who won in the end? For the first time, after decades of subservience the winners were the people, democracy and the desire to begin building an association of independent and law-governed states.

Lenin and socialism

The congress proceedings were conducted beneath the brooding gaze of a bust of Lenin. He was quoted and referred to, even by the Baltic deputies: "We need new conceptions that take the best from Lenin's legacy and nothing from Stalin's," said Vytautas Lansbergis of Lithuania. Yet the traditional genuflections to the father of the Soviet state were much less evident here.

The Congress made its own contribution to the current re-assessment of Lenin, emphasising his historical role and legacy as a politician rather than the legitimating role of his cult. The latter was established by Stalin but especially revived after Stalin died to fill the gap left by his own departure. The approach at the Congress was thus in part an appeal for legitimation to the policies of the early 1920s.

However, there was an indignant reaction to one suggestion.

Yuri Karyakin, institute of the international Labour movement (USSR Academy of Sciences) 155

People persuaded me not to raise the next issue. But I will dare to do so. When I was still a child I learnt an almost completely forgotten fact: Lenin himself wanted to be buried near his mother's grave in Petersburg. Naturally his wife and sister wanted this also. This was yet another stage in our dehumanisation.

What would he himself have said? That mausoleum is not a Leninist mausoleum, it is still the same Stalinist mausoleum. One can think of thousands of ideological and political reasons against preserving it, and not a single human reason. I was warned, the people will not understand this suggestion. I'm sure they will!

Gennady Bykov, plant foreman (territorial deputy, Leningrad) 160

Today we have democracy, glasnost and pluralism of opinions. Each is free to say all he wants. But I was outraged to the depths of my heart and offended by deputy Karyakin's speech. No, the people will not understand. I am a worker and I do not support your proposal. We must keep Lenin buried on Red Square forever.

Nikolai Kasyan, osteopath, Ukraine (Charity and health foundation) 159

Leave our great leader alone, don't go searching in the archives. Millions of people from all over the world go to visit him. We live with him and perhaps when we visit the Mausoleum we think again of our mistakes and find ways to correct them. (Applause)

Gorbunov (chair for the day) 159

Now some very short but important announcements before closing today's session. First, it has been suggested that we all now go and pay our respects to Lenin and lay a wreath on behalf of our Congress in front of Lenin's Mausoleum and another by the grave of the Unknown Soldier. (Applause.)

Gorbachev (in chair) [after Lithuanian walk-out] 161

Just don't let's suspect that some are Leninists and others aren't Leninists. Otherwise who knows where we might end up ...

Under Brezhnev it was declared that the country and economy had advanced to the stage of developed socialism. Even then this was widely regarded as a poor joke —. Why did people live so much better, in that case, under Hungary's unqualified "socialism"?

A much more pragmatic approach is now being adopted to the ideal of socialism. Non-Bolshevik and non-Marxist forms of socialism in Russia are beginning to be discussed again. At the Congress democratic self-governing socialism was frequently opposed to "Stalinist" or "barracks socialism". Many speakers, however, simply preferred to appeal, as they put it, to the standards and values of the developed and civilised world.

Aitmatov in his speech confirmed once and for all the breaking of a 50-year old taboo by saying what all thinking Soviet people knew, that standards of living were much higher elsewhere.

Chingiz Aitmatov 155

About socialism, the holy of holies in our theoretical teachings. We must not turn socialism into an icon. ... Whilst we have been divining and discussing and laying down the law, what socialism could and couldn't be, other nations already have a socialist state ... and are enjoying its benefits. Moreover, we have performed them a very good service in showing how not to make a socialist society. I'm thinking of the flourishing societies of Sweden, Austria, Finland, Norway, Holland, Spain and, across the Atlantic, Canada. I won't mention Switzerland, it's the best model of all. In these countries a worker on average earns 4-5 times more than the Soviet worker. We can't even aspire to the level of social

security and general well-being of working people in those countries. ...
... Can Stalinist socialism get us anywhere? No, ... We must take all
that is positive in the experience of the leading civilised countries and
that suits our vast and unique country.

2 ECONOMY AND BUREAUCRACY

*The total number of employees at all levels of the administration is about 18
million. While 3 million are employed in the type of ministries (Foreign Affairs,
Health, Justice etc) familiar elsewhere, a great many administer the Soviet
command economy.*

*The economy is based around 50 Moscow-based bureaucracies, the produc-
tion-branch ministries that control enterprises scattered throughout the entire
country and compete for resources in the Council of Ministers or Soviet
government. They thus combine features of federal ministries with those of large
monopoly trusts. They, rather than the government (Council of Ministers) or
even the centralised Planing Commission (Gosplan), wield the greatest power,
under the overall but often confused guidance of the Party Central Committee.*

*Some branches of the economy are controlled at the republic level in duplicate
bureaucracies, but it is the central "all-union", i.e. countrywide, ministries that
wield the real power and override local interests and objections. In his speech
Ryzhkov announced a reduction in the overall numbers of these ministries at
both all-union and republic levels, and cuts in their staffing are already supposedly underway. As yet no real challenge to their monopoly, no serious
competition in the production of goods has so far emerged from the tiny new
cooperative, family business and leasehold (private) farming sectors.*

*The proposals made by Moscow and Baltic economists started from the
pragmatic observation that the present system simply does not work. Their
suggestions were considered sacrilegious, however, by several speakers.*

Vladimir Stepanov 149

The Moscow economists have misled all Russia with [the concepts of]
leasehold [private] farming, cooperatives and the like. Is it they, perhaps,
who suggested these ideas to the Politburo, and the government without
consulting the people first? (Applause) ... Moscow is not the whole
country. And I doubt that industrial workers in Moscow support comrades Afanasyev, Popov and others.

Kirill Mazurov, [former Politburo member purged by Brezhnev in 1978], Moscow (Veterans organisation) 154

Not only are there now ideas rejecting socialism and arguing for market relations of a capitalist kind, and even for a multi-party system, in Soviet society. Active propaganda for these ideas has also appeared. This is incompatible with our ideology but it is not repulsed as firmly as it should be. If we don't have the necessary laws ... or do not strictly enforce them, we shall have, not a flourishing democracy but anarchism and permissiveness.

Gavriil Popov 162

The experience of capitalist countries shows that those which are economically developed have a state sector that accounts for 30-40% of the economy. Considering our traditions [Russian as well as Soviet] and the public interests, I think it would be enough if 50% of the economy remained state-owned. The other half should be handed over to cooperatives and the private sector.

There must also be decentralisation of state property. Evidently about 20% should be concentrated in the hands of the local Soviets, a further 20% in the republics, and 10% in the hands of the Centre, of the entire Union.

Nodar Mgaloblishvili 162

I don't think we need to "kill off" the all-union ministries. They'll die by themselves, or shrink drastically, when each republic including the Russian Federation has economic sovereignty and resolves all its own problems ... We shall remain part of a single community, after all, ... Let's be patient and look at the results of the experiment in the Baltic republics at the end of 1990. If necessary we shall give them aid ... But perhaps they will be able to help us, like Finland?

3 FORCES OF LAW AND ORDER

Key Russian officials

Under Stalin and Brezhnev it was an established tradition that key posts in the republics were given to Russians or Slavic officials sent from the Centre, i.e. usually the Central Committee in Moscow. Thus the second secretary of the local communist party, the commanders of the military districts in the area, and the head of the republic's KGB were all usually Russian or Ukrainian (more rarely Belorussian).

This was most dramatically highlighted by the Tbilisi events, in April 1989. There the local KGB was headed by a Georgian, Gumbaridze (who subsequently replaced the former first secretary). Questioned on 14 July in the Supreme Soviet, Kriuchkov, the nominee as chairman of the KGB, admitted that the head of the Georgian KGB learned of the decision to clear the square in Tbilisi using the military only 10 minutes before.

Tamaz Gamkrelidze, director of oriental studies institute, Georgian Academy of Sciences (national deputy, Adzharian ASSR, Georgia) 152

In the investigations into the Tbilisi events the second secretary of the Georgian Communist Party Boris Nikolsky behaved arrogantly, not even appearing before the Georgian Supreme Soviet's own commission. In this connection it seems appropriate to put before the Congress the question as to what in general are the role and functions of the so-called second secretaries in union republics, who are sent out to us from Moscow.

Such a practice cannot be justified in today's circumstances. ... As a rule, these people do not know the national traditions, culture or language of the indigenous population of the republic.

Ion Drutse, writer, living in Moscow (national deputy, Moldavia) 153

I would like to protest against the claim by my colleague from Dnepropetrovsk that he comes from "the birthplace of Brezhnevite stagnation". Everyone knows this is not so. Brezhnev was First secretary of Moldavia in the 1950s and since then there have followed a whole chain of such appointments.

More recently Moscow sent us comrade Smirnov to be second secretary of the party central committee in Moldavia. Then we read that he had committed serious crimes [having been transferred from Central Asia, Smirnov came under investigation by the Gdlyan team, see Chapter 6]. After a time it was announced that he was quite innocent. Once again Moldavia is the centre of attention! I want to ask our leadership and Mikhail Gorbachev not to send anyone else to Kishinev: over the years we have grown up and we have enough worthy young people of our own.

Rafik Nishanov, 1st secretary of Communist Party in Uzbekistan (national deputy, Uzbekistan) 152

All is going well at the Congress. One is only disappointed by individual outbursts, the division of deputies into progressive and conservative wings, and attempts to turn the Congress against party officials.

Yesterday, for example, there was an attack on the institution of second secretaries. All this does not help our consolidation and destroys our unity.

Armed Forces, Police and KGB

The only one of these three that was continually discussed was the 4 million-strong army (together with the Air Force and Navy). Since practically all young men do military service, and even college students in recent time had to interrupt their courses to go into the army for two or three years, the subject concerned everyone. (One of the Supreme Soviet's first achievements was to postpone the drafting of students until after completing their studies.)

There were 80 military deputies at the Congress, 27 of general's rank and above, elected from non-governmental organisations and regular civilian constituencies. There were 120 Afghan war veterans among the deputies. As the highest political officer in the army admitted, it faced its own severe social problems, and had begun internal reorganisation but reacted sensitively to public criticism.

In one of its most tense debates, the Supreme Soviet later barely approved Dmitry Yazov as Minster of Defence.

Vakhit Diusembaev, miner foreman (national deputy, Kazakhstan) 154

There's a lot of talk about the army today. ... Yes, there are problems there as well. But the army is the child of the people and one must love one's child and not betray it! ... Because we today only live and survive because our army has kept the peace and protected us for more than 40 years since the war. (Applause)

Alexei Lisichev, General, head of chief political directorate of Army and Navy, Moscow (Communist Party) 159

We accept positive criticism, comrades, ... but prophets have appeared who say that we don't need an army. They talk of a volunteer army and there have even been demands, with no thought of the consequences, to split the army up between our national republics and regions. ... Enlisted men and their officers [serving in other republics] are often called occupiers and told to go home. They are not given apartments, and their registration as local inhabitants, treatment in local hospitals, and provision of work and schooling for their families meets with obstruction.

Today the army is being cut back by half a million, almost 150,000 of whom are officers; that involves more than 500,000 people including wives and children ... And among those who remain in the army more than 100,000 officers do not have adequate living quarters ...

In late 1988 special crowd control forces were set up under the police to deal with the increasing number of mass demonstrations and rallies throughout the country. Their role was touched on at the Congress. The problem of creating a locally-recruited police force was not raised, although it is a sore point in many republics: presumably sovereignty would begin to resolve this issue. With rising crime rates, moreover, there was little doubt that the police had a difficult job to do. There was much greater scepticism about the KGB which the latter tried to deflect by shifting part of its efforts to the fight against organised crime.

The budget and number of employees of the KGB are not known and there was one dramatic denunciation of the latter's past and present at the Congress by a former Olympic weightlifting champion.

Yuri Vlasov (Moscow) 153

To bring the arbitrary activities of the bureaucracy under control we must subject the KGB ... to public supervision. ... As we take our first steps towards democracy there is simultaneously a desire on the part of some to crush that democracy. Such a force as the KGB acquires particular significance in these circumstances since it is subordinate only to the bureaucracy ...

The KGB headquarters [the Lubyanka] should be moved from Dzerzhinsky Square: we cannot forget the bloody history of the main building where rests the "sword that defends the people" ... The very extent and, inexplicably, monumental vastness of these buildings seems evidence as to who really controls this country.

Not only is the size and unaccountability of the KGB disturbing: it is blatantly prominent in every major city and town, not just in the centre of Moscow. When Kriuchkov was being questioned later, Gorbachev mentioned his journey to Ufa after the rail catastrophe. There he noticed the superbly restored pre-revolutionary mansion in the centre of town that the local KGB had recently taken for themselves.

Kriuchkov identified the problem that the KGB locally was too subordinate to the party authorities, and had too few recruits from the national republics. Yet it was not clear if greater centralisation was the answer, and, naturally, whether it would be tolerated in present circumstances.

4 CULTURE, LANGUAGE AND HISTORY

Russian was the language of discussion at the congress and in the Supreme Soviet. We may note that the Baltic Assembly of People's Fronts that immediately preceded the Congress, however, conducted its proceedings with official simultaneous translations in all three languages.

While national-language schools exist in the republics, the pressure to learn and use (a kind of) Russian is very strong when the only prestigious higher education, medical training etc is concentrated in Russian-language institutions. Though Moscow, and to a lesser extent other republican capitals, have special secondary schools with extensive curricula in major foreign languages (in Moscow there are Mandarin Chinese, Hindi and Korean schools as well as schools for all the main internationally-used European languages), only very recently have experimental weekend classes in the languages of various Soviet nations (including Yiddish) been set up in the capital.

The formal institution of a national language as the official state language is a step recently taken to redress this imbalance. However, the sizable Russian-speaking (i.e. also Ukrainian, Belorussian, Jewish etc) communities in the republics were very uneasy about such proposals. Apart from anything else, there are as yet too few qualified teachers of such languages or adequate textbooks for Russian-speakers to work from.

Ion Drutse (Moldavia) 153

The question of language is today worrying almost all our republics. I must confess that the Russian-speakers take quite a jumpy attitude to this concern, whether in Moldavia or in the Baltic republics. ... The Russian language has suffered no less than our national tongues. Any educated person knows that the difference between the Russian of Chekhov and Tolstoy and that used in today's *Pravda* is about the same as that between a Tsarist rouble and our present paper rouble ...

A debased form of Russian with vulgarities and obscenities has flooded into the language we use in the republics, to form something that the Belorussians wittily called *trasyanka*, a mixture of straw and hay.

That's the language we now speak in almost all republics, and in Belorussia, Moldavia and the Baltic republics.

Boris Oleinik, Ukrainian writer, deputy speaker of Chamber of Nationalities (USSR Communist Party) 160

As a representative of the Chamber of Nationalities, I think it is quite important in discussing this candidature [for Chairmanship of the Committee for People's Control], that comrade Kolbin learnt to speak Georgian when he was in Georgia [for 9 years]. Then working in Kazakhstan, he took up the study of Kazakh. I think this is quite important in our multi-national state.

Ilmar Bisher, professor of law, University of Latvia, deputy speaker of Chamber of Nationalities, (Latvia) 163

Since we are a multi-national state consisting of a number of republics I do not think there can be one [official] state language. In practice we already have 15 state languages in which all our laws and decrees are published. Unfortunately, the decrees of the USSR Council of Ministers are not published in these languages although it was specified in the Treaty on the formation of the Union of Soviet Socialist Republics in 1924 that the decrees of the union's government would also be published in the languages of all the republics.

At the same time I consider it quite natural ... that Russian has become the lingua franca of our country.

In the Transcaucasian republics of Georgia and Armenia there is no such need to assert the primacy of the language (and attempts to down-grade Georgian in the late 1970s led to serious riots). Moreover, they have preserved their own ancient scripts. Elsewhere, but especially in the southern Muslim areas, Central Asia and Azerbaijan, the preservation and extension of literacy has had a dramatic history.

First, following the example of Turkey, a Latin script replaced Arabic in the 1920s; then in the late 1930s Cyrillic was hastily introduced. This resulted in a harmful, though perhaps politically convenient, form of induced cultural and historical amnesia, a subject the Latvian Peters also raised...

Yet even when teaching is conducted in the mother tongue there are still problems.

Shalva Amonashvili, director of education and research institution, Georgia (USSR trade unions) 155

Often we say that in our [Georgian] schools we are teaching in our mother tongue. This is true. ... But education in, say, the Georgian language still does not at all mean that our school is a national, Georgian school. If we consider that all the remaining content of what is taught is no more than a translation from Russian into Georgian.

For instance, what history are we teaching our children? For the most part we study the history of the USSR. Our children know more about events in Russia than in Georgia itself. The history of their own country is barely squeezed into the schedule and there was actually a ban on devoting more hours to this subject.

Dmitry Likhachev, Academician, Chairman of Cultural Foundation (Soviet Cultural Foundation) 152

The low cultural level of our country adversely affects our public life, the functioning of the state and our inter-ethnic relations. For one of the reasons for enmity between nations is the lack of culture. A cultured person is not hostile towards other nations or different opinions, and is not aggressive. (Applause) Ignorance of the most elementary logic, basic legal principles, and the absence of public tact and politeness have a negative effect even on the working of our Congress.

Janis Peters (Latvia) 155

This is what the writer Chingis Aitmatov defined so precisely as 'Mankurtism'. A Mankurt, let me remind you, is a person who has lost his memory and therefore is prepared to shoot his own mother because he does not recognise her.

Today all the world is waiting to see whether the Latvian will not shoot his mother Latvia ... Everyone is waiting for our commission [on Molotov-Ribbentrop pact 1939] which must restore our nations' historical memory.

5 AUTONOMY, INDEPENDENCE OR SECESSION?

Of the four nations which demanded that the legal grounds for their inclusion in the USSR be re-examined Lithuania, Muscovy's historical enemy in the West, was politically and intellectually (and demographically) the most prepared to fight unremittingly for its full sovereignty. Several references by others to the impending unification of Western Europe in 1992 did not deter or dissuade the Baltic republics from their 'retrograde' demands for autonomy. In the later Supreme Soviet debate about Estonia and Latvia's own proposals for economic sovereignty the experienced political commentator Fyodor Burlatsky would argue that the Baltic republics themselves knew they were far from ready economically to go it alone.

From benches [Nikolai Medvedev, Lithuania to Venglovskaya, Ukraine] 163

What do you think about a law defining citizenship in the union republics and autonomous regions? We think that this would help, first, indirectly to replace extensive with intensive development and, second, to regulate migration.

Janis Peters (Latvia) 155

We must admit that for decades the Soviet government and the government of Latvia have been infringing article 76 of the Constitution, ...:
    "A union republic is a sovereign Soviet socialist state which has joined together with other Soviet republics in the Union of Soviet Socialist Republics." ...
    It's clear to any schoolchild that sovereignty is almost a synonym for "independence". So why are we so afraid of the word? Why is Russia afraid of becoming independent of the all-union diktat? Why is official Latvia afraid of this (when unofficial Latvia is already not afraid of anything or anyone). ... Why are we afraid of what we ourselves wrote in the constitution (article 80): "A union republic has the right to enter into relations with foreign states, make treaties with them and exchange diplomatic and consular representatives, and also participate in the activities of international organisations"?

Vytautas Lansbergis, professor at Lithuanian conservatory, 154

We need new conceptions that take the best from Lenin's legacy and nothing from Stalin's. If the moral and intellectual renaissance of our nations is strengthened and produces material results then it will again acquire the form of true nations, including Russia. Once again there will arise self-governing people's states. And then they can decide for themselves, what mutual agreements and unions they will sign and enter into as nations and states. Such a conception could embrace and unite entire regions of Eastern or Northern Europe and offer a much more feasible future for our trumpeted "common European home". And who knows, it might even pave the way for a cultural convergence of Europe and Asia, Christianity and Islam.

Then, of course, our European home would cease to be like a dormitory controlled by a supervisor who knows best and suspects everyone. Instead it would be more like a peaceful village where no one fears anyone else and where we can simply share the work, what we produce, help one another and sing songs of good neighbourliness. (Applause)

Chapter 2

THE BALTIC REPUBLICS AND MOLDAVIA: IN SEARCH OF SOVEREIGNTY

> We Soviet historians are not ashamed to say that Russia con-
> quered Central Asia or even the North Caucasus. ... But we still
> continue to write, in our official historical works and elsewhere, that
> Estonia, Latvia and Lithuania voluntarily joined the Soviet Union.
> This is not true.
> *Roy Medvedev (Moscow) 154*

The three Baltic republics of Estonia, Latvia and Lithuania presented the clearest demands to the central government at the Congress, with considerable parliamentary skill and massive popular backing from their own people.

The areas now constituting Estonia and Latvia were incorporated into the Russian Empire early in the 18th century, while Lithuania was acquired at the 3rd Partition of Poland. After the Revolution they broke away (as also did Finland and Poland) and for the first time became independent states. According to the August 1939 Nazi-Soviet pact, however, they fell within the Soviet sphere of influence and were soon occupied by Soviet troops.

The Baltic republics have relatively few natural resources apart from an educated and industrious population. A great deal of industry was sited there after the war and the large-scale migration of Russians and Belorussians has led in Latvia and Estonia to the most drastic changes in ethnic balance anywhere in the post-war USSR. When the liberalisation of perestroika and glasnost arrived all three republics became highly active politically and broad-based People's Fronts were established in each. Legislation was passed or proposed on issues of language, economic sovereignty and electoral rights. In reaction rival organisations, the largely Russian-speaking Interfronts were set up in Estonia and Latvia and the Unity movement in Lithuania. It should be noted, however, that there are also articulate and active Russian deputies among the People's Front groups in the Supreme Soviet.

The previous history of Moldavia is very different. It is an Orthodox

25

Christian area, speaking a Romance language like that in neighbouring Rumania, and passed from Turkish to Russian control in the late 18th century. This contrasts with the Baltic republics: before coming under Russian rule, the Estonian and Latvian territories were ruled from Sweden and hence are predominantly Lutheran Protestant in faith. Lithuania was for long part of the extensive Polish state and is predominantly Catholic.

After the Revolution Rumania gained control of Bessarabia while Moldavia in the 1920s and 1930s was part of the Ukrainian SSR. In 1940 Bessarabia was taken back from Rumania and together the two became a full union republic. Until recently it was a largely rural and agricultural area.

Although Moldavia differs economically and culturally from the Baltic republics, the influx of Russians and Ukrainians has led to a similar series of political conflicts about official languages, and concern about environmental pollution: by chemical fertilisers in Moldavia, by atomic power stations, industrial plants etc in Baltic republics. (In Moldavia there are also demands for a return to Latin script.)

In Moldavia a People's Front, soon opposed by the Russian-speaking Unity, also emerged. A language law led to strikes among the non-Moldavian population (very many of them Ukrainians). A third element here was the presence of the Gagauz ethnic group, Turkic-speaking but traditionally Orthodox, who began to claim the right to autonomy within the republic.

On 14 May the three Baltic People's Fronts held a joint Baltic assembly and their evidently coordinated and single-minded pursuit of their own objectives at the Congress, while an example to others, often provoked irritation.

The total number of Baltic republic deputies at the Congress was 157. Moldavia had 55 deputies.

PROCEDURAL MATTERS (1ST-3RD SITTINGS, THURS-FRI 25-26 MAY)

Kazimieras Antanavicius, Institute of Economics, Lithuanian Academy of Sciences (national deputy, Lithuania) 146

In the temporary statute [of Congress, 146] we have received today, none of the corrections introduced yesterday have been included.

For example, it was agreed that declarations, announcements and appeals put before the Congress by no less than 20 deputies would be circulated by the Congress as official Congress documents.

Then a correction was made concerning the termination of discussion. Deputies from a union republic have the right to demand the continuation of discussion on issues that affect the republics, if no less than two thirds of that republic's elected deputies support such a motion.

Yuri Boyars, Senior lecturer at University of Latvia (national deputy, Latvia) 146

The small delegations, in particular, from the Baltic republics, are concerned that they may not get the chance to speak at all on the major political issues among this very large number of generally constructively-minded comrades. Therefore yesterday we made a suggestion ... (noise in hall) No comrades, this is a serious matter. Each delegation, each republic should be guaranteed a minimum of three contributions in major political discussions.

Yesterday we more or less agreed, and a number of comrades from the Russian Federation and Moscow made the same suggestion, that each delegation would propose its own representatives for the Supreme Soviet. We are proposing our list and will stand up for it. By what right should I interfere in the affairs of the Russian Federation and decide who should represent it? I would even consider it immodest.

GERRYMANDERING IN LATVIA?

V. Alksnis, Lieutenant-colonel, Baltic military district, Interfront (national deputy, Latvia) 147

The Chairman of the Credentials Committee has misled the Congress. Yesterday I made an official inquiry as a deputy. Permit me to read it. "During the holding of elections in Latvia there was a gross infringement of the Election Law. Article 17 reads that electoral districts should all contain an equal number of voters. In Latvia this varied from 29 to 127,000 while the average number of voters should be approximately 62,000. These small electoral districts were mainly formed in rural areas. This considerably limited the chances for industrial workers and members of the Russian-speaking population to be elected. Typically it was specifically in these areas that many leading members of the Latvian People's Front were elected: ten of the 11 members of the Front's council."

On 11 May I sent a similar letter of complaint to the Presidium of the USSR Supreme Soviet and they, in the best tradition of the Brezhnev years, sent it back to those I was complaining about.

We have approved the deputies credentials but I appeal to the Congress to set up a commission to investigate. I see a real "Watergate" here.

ELECTIONS TO THE SUPREME SOVIET (3RD SITTING, FRI 26 MAY)

Ilmar Bisher, Professor of law at University of Latvia, Riga (national deputy, Latvia) 148

The Constitution specifies that each union republic has 11 seats in the Chamber of Nationalities. Since we have roughly one per cent of the USSR population the suggestion that we should have 3 seats in the Chamber of the Union suits us.

How should these seats be allocated? Since they've been allotted to the republic, the republic should decide.

There was talk about petty principalities here. I don't think there are any but since we are a federal state there are union republics. They are members of the Union and must be respected as such. If we all vote together for the Chamber of the Union the Russian Federation, with more than 1000 deputies, may "outvote" the Latvian delegation with its 50 members. I think that will not only be undemocratic but not in accordance with the Constitution.

Then someone here said that this would help defend the ethnic minorities in the Baltic republics. If you look at our list of candidates you will see that all nationalities in our republic are represented: there are Latvians, Russians and one Jew. We compiled this list democratically and discussed a great many candidates.

Anatoly Lukyanov, deputy chairman of Congress presidium (Communist Party) 148

After long discussion we decided to preserve the following principle. Deputies who gain more than 50% of the votes, and then those among them who gain more than their fellow candidates, will be considered elected to the Supreme Soviet.

Vytautas Lansbergis, Professor at Conservatory, Vilnius (national deputy, Lithuania) 148

I am forced to explain the position of the Lithuanian delegation and, as far as I understand, that of the Latvian delegation as well, concerning the voting procedure [for elections to the Supreme Soviet]. A number of deputies from several delegations have tried to explain that we do not have the right to vote for and elect people whom we hardly know. We don't have the right to vote "in the dark". It would be possible if each candidate spoke here and explained his platform. But that would demonstrate the mistakes committed earlier by a *reductio ad absurdum*...

Since this cannot now be corrected we consider we have no right to interfere, say, in the affairs of Tajikistan when it chooses its deputies. ... we will not usurp the sovereignty of Moscow as represented by its group of deputies. Neither do we want others to vote for us, not knowing us.

Roy Medvedev, Writer and historian, Moscow (territorial deputy, Moscow) 148

I have no idea what the representative of Lithuania meant when he referred to the sovereignty of the city of Moscow. Moscow has no sovereignty and if you don't like someone on the Moscow list — and it includes many people famous throughout the USSR — you can cross out his or her name [Medvedev was himself elected by 1293 votes to 856]. I ask the Lithuanian delegation to withdraw their ultimatum.

Sergei Zalygin, writer, chief editor of *Novy Mir*, secretary of USSR Union of writers (Union of Writers, Moscow) 148

I think that our Lithuanian colleagues will now discuss this among themselves. But perhaps it would be interesting for them to know the opinions of other deputies.

Perhaps all the ideas of perestroika, all the new changes of these last years, came to us from Lithuania? They actually came from Moscow, from here. So we should somehow value what we've received.

A 30-minute interval was announced to permit the Lithuanian delegation to confer.

Lansbergis (Lithuania) 148

We regret that my words were not correctly understood and interpreted. We shall not take on ourselves the right to make decisions for other republics as to who should represent them. We thought it necessary before voting to explain to our fellow deputies the reasons behind the voting of one or other of our deputies.

THE ROLE OF THE MILITARY IN TBILISI AND THE BALTIC REPUBLICS (TUESDAY 30 MAY, 6TH SITTING; FRIDAY 2 JUNE, 9TH SITTING)

Vitas Tomkus, journalist, Vilnius (territorial deputy, Lithuania) 152

The Lithuanian nation was particularly disturbed by the events in Tbilisi. The reason is that the same almost happened last year in Vilnius on Gediminas square. On 28 September troops and special forces [of the Ministry of Internal Affairs] were also brought in against defenceless people. Only at the last minute was a skirmish between the troops and the people avoided although some were injured nevertheless. I consider both these events and what happened in Tbilisi to be acts of provocation. I say this because nowhere in the Lithuanian press was it stated that the meeting had not been permitted. So people went there although the troops had already been brought in. As we have now learned from the USSR Ministry of Internal Affairs, a request for permission to deploy special forces was made from Lithuania two days before these events. So we may say that preparations for these events were being made beforehand …

Therefore I suggest that we reject the proposed commission, the membership of which was compiled anonymously by "higher authority", and form one that includes representatives of small nations as well.

Tomkus subsequently became a member of the commission investigating the Tbilisi events, 152

Boyars (Latvia) 152

Honourable deputies! I would advise you not to be so hasty in applauding speeches like that of General Rodionov [in charge of Tbilisi operation]. … I am obliged to tell you, unfortunately, that at the very same time it is possible that exactly the same was being prepared in Latvia. We were then making amendments to our republican constitution, to the electoral laws, in the Presidium of the Latvian Supreme Soviet. The leadership of our People's Front was invited to a meeting with our generals. I was among those invited but when I got there, or rather on my way there, I saw armoured personnel carriers on the streets of Riga. If there had been a demonstration or an unsettled situation then it is quite possible, I believe, that something similar might have happened. Therefore, comrades, I would like to ask General Rodionov if he knows what international humanitarian law is and how soldiers should behave towards women and non-combatants? Did he explain this to his soldiers before they set out to put down this conflict?

Sergei Chervonopisky, 1st secretary of Cherkassy Komsomol, Ukraine (Komsomol) 155

As someone who has seen his brothers-in-arms dying, I deeply hate war and death — God forbid that any of you should experience the same. Among those I lost were Belorussians, Lithuanians, Gagauz, Tatars, Dargints [ethnic group from Daghestan] and Russians. Today I am still unable to express a definite opinion about what happened in Tbilisi, evidently the most disgraceful and shameful piece of provocation in our recent history. But there is something that makes me particularly dubious. The same paratroop regiment from Kirovobad deployed in Tbilisi was one of the last to leave Afghanistan. I'm convinced that lads who even during battle saved Afghan women and children could never become murderers and executioners. (Applause) Yet this is what the political intriguers from Georgia and the Baltic republics called them, when they themselves have for a long time been training their own storm troops (Applause), and we know very well what role such forces played in the history of other states. And today they are not wearing their deputies' badges but display the symbols of their own People's fronts. (Applause)

I of course support the idea of republican cost-accounting. However, when goods in shops are only sold to people with domicile registration for the Baltic republics then, in my view, this could be called republican nationalist egotism. (Applause)

Nikolai Medvedev, Kaunas institute of Radio Instruments (national deputy, Lithuania) 155

We protest most strongly against the offensive attacks made about the delegations of the three Baltic republics from this high tribune and, therefore, against the nations they represent. We censure the chairman of that sitting [Anatoly Lukyanov, Deputy Chairman of Supreme Soviet] for failing to condemn such insults. We consider that such attacks are aimed at dividing and disrupting the Congress. We came here to work together but the whipping-up of anti-Baltic chauvinism could make such cooperation impossible.

I can only add that I am myself a 'storm-trooper'. Unlike the usual voluntary militia [delegated to assist police on a regular basis from all institutes and factories] we may be got out of bed any time of the day or night. We hurry to provide assistance as soon as we learn that someone somewhere (a Russian, Lithuanian, a Jew or a Tatar) is being mistreated. We are armed from head to foot: our weapon is the word. We have unlimited rights: we can deflect the blows, emotional and physical, on to ourselves when someone is being mistreated. Perhaps that's why we sometimes have meetings of up to 200,000 people which do not have to be patrolled by the police and which our respected first party secretary Brazauskas and second secretary Berezov, attend. We argue and reach agreement, go home and then gather again. We are only seeking the truth. There are never any drunks or hooligans at these rallies. And we hold them only at the weekends. (Applause)

MOLOTOV-RIBBENTROP PACT 1939 (MONDAY 29 MAY, 5TH SITTING, FRIDAY 2 JUNE, 9TH SITTING)

Egidijus Bickauskas, investigator for particularly serious crime, Lithuanian public prosecutor's office, Vilnius (national deputy, Lithuania) 150

Perhaps my question to you, Comrade Lukyanov, will not be understood by the majority of deputies. Your answer, however, will certainly do much to explain what is going on in the Baltic republics but is clearly not fully or correctly reflected in the central press. It will also explain the position of the majority of Lithuanian deputies. The answer is exceptionally important for all the Baltic region and for our voters; and it is exceptionally important when we are establishing a state governed by the rule of law ...

Before they vote [to elect you Deputy Chairman of the Supreme Soviet] the Lithuanian deputies and, I think, a number of those from other republics would like to learn what your position is regarding the Molotov-Ribbentrop pact and the additional secret agreements between the USSR and Nazi Germany. As a consequence, Lithuania and the other Baltic republics were occupied and incorporated into the USSR thereby losing their sovereign statehood. (Applause)

Anatoly Lukyanov, candidate for Vice-President (deputy Chairman of Supreme Soviet) secretary of Central Committee, candidate member of Politburo (Communist Party) 150

This is a very complicated issue that affects not only the fate of Lithuania, Latvia and Estonia but also western Ukraine, and other areas, and the fate of our country as a whole. Therefore the Party's Central Committee has now set up a commission to consider this question.

Endel Lippmaa, director of Estonian Academy of Sciences' institute of chemical and biological physics (national deputy, Estonia) 154

The issue of the 1939 treaties between the Soviet Union and Nazi Germany has been raised in many speeches and by many delegations here. We propose the following draft decree. The Congress of People's Deputies decrees: first, that a commission be set up "to provide a political and juridical assessment of the Nazi-Soviet non-aggression agreement of 1939, the 'Molotov-Ribbentrop pact', and of its secret additional protocol, i.e. the protocol concerning territorial and political reorganisation in Eastern Europe, and the Baltic republics and Poland in particular [a suggested membership of 20 is listed: it includes Lansbergis, Lauristin, Bisher and 7 others from Baltic republics]." In addition, we would like one representative each from the Ukrainian, Belorussian and Moldavian delegations. We did have some suggestions ourselves although this is, of course, the business of the delegations to choose. However, our suggestions were Professor Shinkaruk (Institute of Philosophy, Ukraine), Vasil Bykov (writer, Belorussia) and Ion Drutse (writer, Moldavia). As a chairman we suggest the writer Chingis Aitmatov, Frunze [Kirgizia].

Second, the USSR Ministry of Foreign Affairs and other government departments and archives are obliged to put all the essential materials at the disposal of the commission.

Third, the commission will present its conclusions to the USSR Supreme Soviet by the end of June this year and will make the results of its activities public.

The question remains why is there such a hurry? The answer is that 23 August this year marks the 50th anniversary of the agreement with Hitler about the partition of Europe. Therefore we must do something immediately. Moreover, there were suggestions to repudiate this pact from the moment of its signature. This isn't a bad suggestion but many of our deputies here do not know this text and, secondly, repudiation is not enough. We must draw conclusions. To declare the pact invalid is insufficient. There are a great many consequences and therefore a commission must be set up. This draft decree was put together by deputies from the Estonian delegation with the active participation of Lithuania and Latvia. It was, however, mainly the work of our presidium [of the Estonian Supreme Soviet].

Vladimir Yarovoi, director of the Lenin engineering works controlled by a Moscow union ministry, Tallin (national deputy, Estonia) 154

Comrade deputies! there is a lot of talk about this pact in the country as a whole and particularly in the Baltic republics. For the last one and a half years this pact has been used to work up the indigenous population and arouse their suspicions. As a result the non-Estonian part of the population has been transformed into 'occupiers' and 'colonisers' and who knows what else. I think that the commission put together on the initiative of the Estonian deputies should not be permitted to examine this issue: they are themselves interested parties. (Applause).

Zhores Alferov, Academician, director of Leningrad physico-technical institute, (Academy of Sciences) 154

Like many others I consider this pact was a shameful episode in our history. But do we need to discuss whether it is still valid or not? It was invalidated on 22 June 1941 when the war began. (Applause)

Vyacheslav Ivanov, Academy of Sciences institute of Slavic and Balkan studies, Moscow (Academy of Sciences) 154

This is an extremely important issue, perhaps one of the most important we shall discuss at the Congress. Naturally we can vote as a majority to reject this proposal and thereby subject ourselves to yet another major conflict within our federal state. I suggest that we use the method of consensus and assent, which we are in general making much too little use of. (Applause)

Vladimir Berezov, 2nd party secretary of Communist party in Lithuania, Vilnius (national deputy, Lithuania) 154

I am myself a Russian. I ask you to support this commission. This is the most sensitive issue for the Baltic nations. And solutions must be found. It is not just a question of the Molotov-Ribbentrop pact. The appeal of the Lithuanian Supreme Soviet has been circulated to you all. The real issue is the secret agreements reached by Molotov and Ribbentrop. All the time it is being said that they don't exist, they've been lost and so on. This only whips up emotions. We deputies from Lithuania, Latvia and Estonia cannot return home without having resolved this question. I ask you very much to support this commission. (Applause)

Igor Gryazin (Estonia) reads secret protocols to Congress.

Edvins Inkens, Senior editor of news and documentary broadcasts, Latvian government television and radio committee, Riga (national deputy, Latvia) 154

All the world knows perfectly well that such protocols existed. The unwillingness to discuss them here is simply like stuffing your fingers in your ears when someone tells the truth. One more point. This treaty has not been invalidated. Although the war had already begun in 1941 the Soviet Union concluded a special agreement with the Polish government in emigration (in London) about the partial repudiation of the pact. So, unfortunately, it does still have a certain validity. Most important of all, the pernicious part of the agreement refers to the period from 1939 to 1940. And that was when the Baltic republics were annexed.

Mikhail Gorbachev (from Presidium) 154

May I speak out of turn here to clarify certain matters? While we carry on a scholarly discussion in certain departments, all these documents, including the secret annex to the treaty, have been published everywhere, including the press in the Baltic republics. All attempts to find the original of the secret agreement, however, have met with failure. I touched on this in my discussions with representatives of the Polish press and intelligentsia.

Only copies exist and from what original we do not know. The signature of Molotov is written in German script and this particularly arouses our doubts. I'm sure Chancellor Kohl will not mind my telling you that in our private conversations during his visit here I asked him if the West Germans had the originals of this agreement and the addendum. He said yes and I asked him to send them to us. We sent our representatives from our Ministry of Foreign Affairs there but the originals could not be found. Isn't that so, Eduard Ambrosievich [Shevardnadze]?

Gorbachev accordingly suggested that the composition of the commission be widened, and the secret protocol be formally excluded from the title. He expressed doubts that the incorporation of the republics into the USSR was entirely involuntary, or that a clear statement could soon be made. Since Shevardnadze (like all ministers) was not a deputy it was suggested that Politburo member Alexander Yakovlev who is also responsible for international relations be included instead.

The Commission (155), headed by Yakovlev, finally had 26 members (incl. chairman) of whom 11 were from Baltic republics, 5 from Ukraine, Belorussia and Moldavia. It was to report back to the autumn session of the Congress.

Lansbergis (Lithuania) 154

In my view, Gorbachev himself has no doubt that such secret agreements existed.

LARGE AND SMALL NATIONS IN THE SOVIET FEDERATION (TUESDAY 6 JUNE, 10TH SITTING)

Alexander Mokanu, Chairman of the Moldavian Supreme Soviet's Presidium (territorial deputy, Moldavia) 154

Perestroika makes it essential to find optimal forms of national-state organisation ... ... We cannot do without exact criteria when we discuss the provision of new political structures for those nations and ethnic groups which live in compact territories and do not have other national formations in the country. For example, the Gagauz living in our republic are asking ever more insistently for autonomy.

Much here will depend on how effectively the Supreme Soviet's Chamber of Nationalities works. It is important that it should not duplicate the Chamber of the Union, as it did until quite recently. Naturally, the fundamental role in implementing national policy should belong to the highest authorities of the USSR and, of course, to the republics.

Anatoly Lukyanov (in chair) 155

The Presidium has received a considerable number of written suggestions from deputies on issues of inter-ethnic relations. Some deputies from the Abkhazian autonomous republic consider it essential to set up a full commission to study the situation there. Deputies Ivans, Lakis and others from Latvia (ten deputies in all), have made several suggestions about restoring historical justice as far the Soviet Germans and Crimean

Tatars are concerned. We've just been discussing that today. ... Deputy Fargiev asks the Congress to consider setting up a Chechen autonomous republic ... Deputy Anufriev has suggestions to make about the position of the Gagauz in Moldavia.

The following speech, printed in its entirety, is probably the clearest statement on the subject made at the Congress. It was delivered just before the first sitting of the newly elected Chamber of Nationalities by a Russian specialist in the field from Estonia.

Klara Hallik, research associate at Estonian Academy of Sciences institute of sociology and law, Tallin (national deputy, Estonia) 158

After an interval of 66 years, since the 12th congress of the Bolshevik Party, frank discussions about relations between nationalities in our country are being held for the first time. This discussion shows that all the fears Lenin expressed and warned against in his testament have come true. The causes have already been named here. They are the flaws of state-bureaucratic socialism and the abnormal and anti-democratic nature of the still tenacious habits of imperial administration. This system damages the interests of all nations, including the most numerous of all, the Russian nation.

When perestroika began neither its chief architects nor the public as a whole were prepared for the possible emergence of national movements. Even now not everyone accepts it as proper. We appreciated this in Estonia after our Supreme Soviet made its famous declaration of sovereignty on 16 November 1988. We were supported on the one hand by democratic public opinion but were branded, on the other, as proponents of creeping counter-revolution, separatism, nationalism and anti-socialism. The authors of the document handed out today [Kogan and others] were already in effect calling for the introduction of direct rule by Moscow in Estonia when the Congress was beginning its work. Last November they said, "Keep your national concerns out of it: we'll carry through perestroika and then you'll have your turn". At the Congress also appeals have been heard that "We'll first deal with affairs of state and then turn to national matters". We now understand that the state should have no affairs that are not also the affairs of its nations.

As we analyse our nationalities policy we uncover many bitter truths and many people are not psychologically prepared to grasp them. Nevertheless it is essential to try and sort out the reasons for the present ethnic tensions. Only this way will we be able to find a place for the national-democratic movements in perestroika.

The first and main reason for today's national conflicts and tensions is that Lenin's attempt to organise a federal union did not succeed. Stalin restored the empire and was not above using the methods of imperial foreign policy. A unitary state in a federal shell was created, without local self-administration, in which the peripheral areas were subordinate in every respect to the centre. It is this reality and none other which explains both national injustices and, as a reaction, the constant repro-duction of centrifugal aspirations. How then must we act when the country is democratising? We have been reminded, in alarmist terms, of the state's primacy. I think everyone already sees, however, that it is impossible to preserve the integrity of the state using the methods that were employed in the past. These methods will meet an ever greater resistance from all the nations. We have no solution other than to genuinely restore the rights of nations to self-determination and to give the Union both the form and substance of a union of equal and sovereign states. Nations without their own state structures must be assured of wide powers of national self-government both territorially and cultu-rally. It is precisely this right to self-determination and not the gift of residual rights by a powerful centre which must become the source of the republics' sovereignty. And a [ratified] treaty must become the source of federal law. In other words, we must carry out a constitutional reform of the Union in order to return to Leninist ideas of federalism.

In this connection I shall say a few words about the other side of the "Russian coin", a theme already raised by Boris Oleinik and Vasily Belov. The Russian national state is truncated in its structure and the Russian Federation is administered not as one country but as a conglom-erate of regions. This leads to a dilution of national self-awareness and substitutes for it an all-Soviet identity. Today this slows down the [Russian] national renaissance and, as a result, many there perceive the struggle of other republics against bureaucratic centralism as a struggle against Russia itself. If Russia were provided with all the same political institutions then the majority of union ministries and organisations would become unnecessary. They would be replaced by direct, mutually beneficial and equal links between the republics. And then perhaps we might be able to calculate how many "Russian" nations there are in this country: one, fifteen, i.e. in the union republics, or 35, taking the auton-omous republics into account? This lack of clarity is a source of ethnic tensions in the republics. Incidentally yesterday's *Sovetskaya Estonia* showed how little support certain comrades who claim to represent all the non-Estonian (or, as they say, "Russian-speaking") population of the republic actually have.

Constitutional reform of the Union has the task not only of resolving the nationality issue but also of leading socialism towards a self-governing, democratic society. Everyone needs this equally; large and small nations alike.

Second, we have begun recently to stop considering ourselves the most wise and far-sighted, and started to pay attention to the experience of other countries (though still selectively). That experience shows that modern civilisation is moving towards international integration, but not by centralising and subordinating. Free nations can integrate when their interests as sovereign subjects are coordinated but not subordinated. The centralism and subordination that has taken shape in our country is in profound contradiction with the objective tendencies towards integration at the level of national structures. Russia, let alone Moscow, cannot consider itself even the centre of Slavic languages, not to speak of the Turkic, Baltic or Finno-Ugrian groups. As we can see the church and religion still play a major role in the modern world. In this respect the centre of the state coincides only with the centre of the Russian Orthodox church. For those who are Muslims the religious centres are located beyond the bounds of the state, just as they are for Catholics and certain other Christians. The culture of the Latvians and Estonians, for example, leans towards that of the Scandinavian nations and the rest of the Baltic region. The closest linguistic relative of the Estonians, as we all know, is Finnish. What I mean to say by this is that the uniqueness and originality of our nations are not only the result of their inner self-development but also of the richness and diversity of our inter-national and inter-ethnic ties. As we open up to the world in the hopes that our state will take its proper place in the the world economy, the protection of the environment and the development of universal human culture, we must also concede this right to all our nations in accordance with the distinctive features of their history and culture.

The uneven socio-economic development of nations and countries is a reality everywhere in the world. In the world's political vocabulary it is denoted by the concept "North-South" and "East-West". This polarity is also represented in our state in as much as there are institutes studying the USA and Canada and the countries of Asia and Africa, but none studying Central Asia and the ethnic groups of the Soviet North and East. This problem has never been seriously considered although Lenin and the resolutions of the 10th Party Congress [1921] directed national and ethnic policy towards a thorough consideration of such realities.

Since the subject of relations between nationalities entered perestroika later than others, we are still not ready to analyse them in universally-accepted terms and concepts. More often we make use of metaphors and invocations such as "our common home", "indestructible friendship", "a strong centre" and "strong republics". Incidentally, what is this strong centre? Has a 16th republic appeared? If so, then it happened in secret and was not put to a vote by all the other fifteen. I would like to add my own humble contribution to these concepts and introduce and develop deputy Sokolov's suggestion of our "common blanket" [which will not cover us all if we pull it to our side of the bed: see Chapter 5]. One does not need to be particularly perceptive to see that this "common blanket" is a bedspread made up of patches of varying strength and that the draughts have already blown through it for a long time. Perhaps it would all the same be better if each had his own blanket: a down quilt in the North, and a light blanket in the South?

And a third aspect of national relations. What must we do so that national resources are directed towards the widening of perestroika and the renewal of socialism? The answer is to take those measures which will make the society viable again. First this means transcending the destructive consequences of the "class struggle" against the peasantry and the intelligentsia. It is the peasantry that has always been the guardian of the national sources of culture, and of balanced and solicitous attitudes to nature. We must halt the alienation of the nation from its past and from its natural environment. And only nations can do this, not populations, even if the latter do have distinctive ethnic characteristics. Second, the sway of the [central ministerial] monopolies in the national republics and regions has led to the disruption of the social integrity of a number of nations. As a result of the monopolist economy some of them are no more than a social stratum employed in agriculture or in other subsidiary branches [of the economy]. The unrestrained extensive growth of industry also threatens the population structure of the Estonian nation. It is being transformed into a nation without a complete social structure. In order to halt this process it is essential to make a drastic shift in ideas of how regions and republics are to develop economically. The national consequences of all these economic measures must be weighed up. This, incidentally, is the national meaning of our concept of republican "cost-accounting".

The small nations of the North and East deserve particular mention. Over the centuries they adapted to the severe and, at the same time, fragile and easily disturbed natural conditions of these regions. They created unique and solicitous traditions of human interaction with nature and preserved for present generations, and the country, a viable natural environment. By way of thanks our state repeated one of the greatest disgraces of European civilisation when the American Indians were exterminated. And we did so on the threshold of the 21st century in a country that calls itself socialist. While there is still time the state must perform a penance before the small ethnic groups of the North; and not just of the North. A special body should be set up in the Chamber of Nationalities for the protection of small ethnic groups. A government programme should be devised and the public aroused so that these groups can once again lead a normal and productive life and, thereby, restore both their human and national dignity.

I have here an Appeal from the Small Ethnic Groups that was approved at the international meeting of writers from the Finno-Ugrian nations, and also from the Kurds, the Crimean Tatars, the Gagauz and some others. It should be added to the documents of the Congress.

I believe that cultural policy should lead to the restoration of the cultural variety of our country. This is a difficult task because the integrity of the cultural systems of many nations have been disrupted. In a number of cases this happened because the national languages were forced out of science and scholarship, politics and higher (or even secondary) education. Even the languages of certain nations that number millions are turning into village dialects that city-dwellers are ashamed of. The experience of this country and elsewhere shows that when culture loses its national and ethnic sources it is defenceless against the onslaught of commercial culture. This leads to a growth in philistine amorality and undermines the moral foundations of human community.

The present state of national relations in the USSR cannot be explained as the result of particular mistakes and individual miscalculations, though there are many of those as well. It grows out of the entire system of administrative-state socialism. The attempt to do away with nations as historical subjects was destructive not only for them, but for society as a whole. In its struggle with the national and the ethnic, society wasted vast amounts of energy. To make our society viable again our nationalities policy must be fundamentally changed. If this does not happen the [Stalinist] structure of administrative rule will be preserved to a great extent and, as a consequence, so will the basis for anti-perestroika forces in the centre and at the local level.

International pacts concerning the rights of nations must underly the renewed national policy. All the world quotes Mikhail Gorbachev's words that each nation must have the right to its own historical choice. Our state is also a distinctive kind of "united nations organisation" which can only develop as a civilised society if there are political guarantees of national rights and liberties.

In conclusion I would like again to support the appeal made yesterday that we seek for peaceful political and democratic ways of resolving all the national contradictions, which have grown up over many years in our country.

ECONOMIC SOVEREIGNTY OR REPUBLICAN "COST-ACCOUNTING" (1ST JOINT SITTING OF BOTH CHAMBERS OF SUPREME SOVIET, WEDNESDAY 7 JUNE; 12TH SITTING OF CONGRESS, THURSDAY 8 JUNE)

The phrase "cost-accounting" (khozraschet) means a shift from the present system where material resources are allocated according to a central plan and prices are arbitrarily determined, often bearing no relation to production costs.

Mokanu (Moldavia) 154

The transition to regional cost-accounting is of fundamental importance. ...The diktat of union ministries here give rise to serious problems. We appreciated this in the case of our cement works. We built them and then they were taken out of our control, in spite of our firm objections.

It is difficult to make the transition to territorial cost-accounting without a balanced price system. ... In Moldavia the Agro-industrial complex potentially occupies the leading position in the republic's economy. But it is pulling the other way in financial terms. There is a substantial disparity between the prices paid for agricultural products and those for the agricultural machinery needed by the Agro-industrial complex. Thus it is those enterprises not dependent on the resources of the republic and its natural and climatic potential which are 'profitable' for Moldavia. We don't object to all-union bodies preserving the right to lay down strategy in pricing. At the same time, union republics' rights to establish and regulate prices must be greatly widened. And not only for its internally sold products but also for that which it exports ...

Voice from hall 160

Comrade Ryzhkov! I would like to ask a specific question and, at the same time, make a request the satisfaction of which will, to a large extent, determine the attitude of many inhabitants of Lithuania towards you. As you will be aware, an expedition is planned this summer to various parts of Siberia with the purpose of bringing home the remains of those who died there during Stalin's deportations in 1941-53. Preliminary work has already been done: there is a list of those who died, the places of burial have been ascertained, and expenses and so on have been allowed for. Only the question of transport remains to be solved. We have already applied to you and received a negative answer. So far I as know, this question was raised in the Politburo but we received no definite answer there either. Can we rely on your help in solving this problem which is very important for the inhabitants of Lithuania?

Nikolai Ryzhkov, candidate for post of Prime Minister (Chairman of Council of Ministers), (Communist Party) 160

Of course, the problem of transport is not the main issue here, I think. We all understand the tragedy that took place in our country then. It affected both Lithuania and all the union republics, all the cities and all our people. We must only evaluate this question in those terms. The Politburo actually takes a definite line on this issue. We must commemorate those who died and today a great deal is being done directly at the local level, i.e. in all parts of the country. That's our position. And it applies to Lithuania as much as anywhere else.

Kazimyra-Danute Prunskene, Rector of Lithuanian Council of Ministers' Institute for advanced economics training, Vilnius (territorial deputy, Lithuania) 160

I have two questions, Comrade Ryzhkov. First, you have several times asserted that Lithuania receives more than it gives to the USSR economy. Do you believe that this is true today, if we take into account the shortcomings in the system of pricing and subsidies, and in the tax system and economic management as a whole?

Second, 109 deputies have signed a draft law concerning the economic independence of the union republics. It has been submitted to the Congress. If you have studied this draft law then how do you assess it and the prospects of its being accepted?

Ryzhkov

Let me answer the first question. I never talked of republics "living at the expense" of others. You may check any of my official statements; there are no such words there. There were and are economic calculations and these can be presented to the deputies. They were actually made to obtain an objective picture of what is really happening in our republics, all 15 republics. We took the imports into the republic (and this meant every conceivable kind of finished good, commodity, raw and semi-processed materials etc) and the exports from that republic. In the case of Lithuania such economic calculations show that the republic imports more than it exports. We asked that the calculations be made in world prices because I agree that present Soviet prices do not give an objective picture... And not only for Lithuania but for each republic. And quite an interesting picture emerges ...

Kazakhstan could just as well say, for example, that it is continually running at a loss since it is a large republic producing raw materials but we pay low prices for them ...

I never intended to say that someone is supporting someone else. We live in a single economy ...

The second question about territorial cost-accounting. I shall speak in rather more detail about this since it worries many people. For two years we were searching for and outlining the principles of our economic reform.... by June 1987 these principles had been formulated [in the Law on the State Enterprise]. ...

Even then we were profoundly convinced that it was insufficient to reform only at the level of the enterprise... In November 1988 we saw that the development of regional cost-accounting was progressing and the Baltic republics were preparing their model, and other republics as well. The central economic bodies also were not idle and also prepared their own definite model. In view of all this, we gathered together the Prime Ministers of the republics [Chairmen of republican Councils of Ministers] and their Gosplan chairmen and discussed all one day how to organise economic cost-accounting [rather than administrative planning]. A special commission of 17 members was established, the fifteen heads of republican state planning commissions, deputy chairman of Gosplan Sitaryan and Head of USSR Gosplan Masliukov.

In January this year they finished their work. We thought that the main principles had been correctly formulated. The matter was examined by the Politburo and the Supreme Soviet and it was decided to publish the main principles in the press. After waiting a little while we indeed received documents from Estonia and Lithuania that differed from the principles we had laid down and published.

Evidently we must sit down again together and thoroughly weigh up all the pluses and minuses. ... There is much that is constructive in the suggestions published and discussed by the Supreme Soviets of the republics [Estonia and Lithuania].

In my view there are also a number of suggestions that, if they are taken as they now stand, will not be to the advantage of these republics. Our policy is one of integration. But certain of their propositions lead in the opposite direction. ... I would describe what's outlined in the Lithuanian and Estonian documents in the following way: there are both positive aspects and constructive proposals, but there are also suggestions that contradict the Constitution and sometimes run counter to our living in a single economy as we understand it now.

Kazimyra Prunskene 160

Honourable President! honourable deputies!

Many years of partial economic reforms have convincingly proved their inadequacy when the management of the economy of the super-power that the USSR now is, remains hyper-centralised. This gigantic economic organism must undergo a cure: it must be stirred from its immobility and stagnation and emerge from recession. Yet all this is unthinkable if we retain the old methods of remote control from the distant centre of this super-power, no matter how powerful and wise that centre might be.

The Baltic republics conception of economic reform embodies the principle of localising decision-making. Problems must be tackled at the level where economic and social processes are taking place, where there is genuine information and those involved are the interested parties. We see the economic independence of the republics as the primary and essential condition for the restructuring of the economic management both of individual republics and of the Union as a whole. The necessity for this is determined by a long succession of circumstances.

First. The decentralisation and democratisation of the economy can only take place at all its levels. It cannot be selectively introduced, i.e. by striving to make the enterprises independent but leaving the republics as a whole and their local Soviets without any rights. Otherwise the appeal [of the Bolsheviks in 1917] to give "All power to the Soviets!" loses its meaning.

Second. The so-called unity of the economic complex is established through the centre and according to its will. Everyone knows the results. It must be replaced by direct links between the republics, and primarily between their enterprises. Nothing so unites nations and their economies as the market.

Third. The development of the economy of any republic or region must take the principle of regionalism into account. By this I mean the century-long traditions of economic thought and motivating behaviour of a particular nation, and the nature of its interaction with a specific social and natural environment. Disregard for this principle and the attempt to try and find and then adopt comprehensive decisions at the centre brings enormous losses to all the nations of the Union which are not compensated in any other way. Such an approach destroys the natural development of an inter-national division of labour in which each nation makes its own inimitable contribution. Isn't that what has led to the dying of the Aral Sea and many other ecological catastrophes?

Fourth. Perestroika can only be carried out by individuals who are themselves motivated and are not simply the workforce of an enterprise or ministry. Such motivation as there is on the factory floor is one-sided: it does not embrace the ecological, socio-demographic, cultural and national aspects of life. Yet these all can and should be controlled within a socially-manageable territorial community. Examples are the small republics that could become masters of their own lives and direct the development of the economy in the service of the individual, the nation of that republic, and the Union as a whole.

Fifth. Perestroika is proceeding unevenly both in particular republics and regions. And some are more ready than others to become self-governing. This unevenness is natural and it should be acknowledged. We can sense it at the Congress also. Artificial restraints on social, political and economic activity will lead to an under-use of the republic's and region's potential. It will do nothing but harm each of them, and the Union as a whole. The only direction in which we can march in step is towards the abyss. Only by unleashing initiative can we break the routine of stagnation and immobilism.

Sixth. The right of the republics to independently manage their economies is as natural as the individual or nation's right to existence and self-determination. The effective absence of rights in the economic sphere, and not there alone, makes the restoration of these rights, in our view, the most acutely felt and urgent issue. We might not even touch on those specific circumstances linked to the deals between Stalin and Hitler about the Baltic republics. Yet if we do not acquire these rights then democratisation itself and the idea of a law-governed state and Union will become merely wishful thinking.

Finally, people and enterprises must be protected by laws and guarantees, and be able to trust in those laws. This is essential if people are to be encouraged to invest their labour and capital in private peasant farms (even in the leasehold system, which has little future in the Baltic republics), if they are to acquire shares, and if the economy is to be de-monopolised in other ways. It is much easier to restore people's lost confidence in the laws and the authorities at the republican level than that of the Union as a whole. Today the Lithuanian peasant is already prepared to trust his deputies. But will he have confidence in the vote of the Congress? That's the big question. For the moment we cannot persuade him of that ourselves without violating our own consciences, for what is already quite obvious to the majority of people in the Baltic area is still not obvious or acceptable for many deputies from other republics. Yet can all Lithuanians or Estonians or any other nation be wrong, irrational or emotional? And who would be prepared to make such a judgement?

Some brief remarks about the actual details of economic independence outlined in the draft law presented to the Congress and already distributed to deputies. Let me emphasise that this law is a total conception. If certain parts of it are put into practice or excluded but not the whole then the mechanism simply will not work. According to the draft, republics will take charge of legislation concerning the economy of the republic. They will own, use and dispose of the state property of the republic and this means the decentralisation of state property itself. The republic will become full legal master of its own land, mineral resources, forests and other resources which were not just created during the period of Soviet rule. In this way the republic, at last, will become a self-motivated property-owner. The state authorities of the republic and other republican bodies will regulate all spheres of activity, including the credit and financial system, the republican and local budgets and foreign economic activities. These authorities will determine the basic principles regulating wages and salaries, pensions and allowances. They will determine the sequence of price-formation, and of the principle of economic activities of enterprises in all sectors of the economy, including the cooperative sector. The flaws in the latter are actually caused by the state of the economy itself and the lack of a proper market.

One of the arguments used by the central authorities in Moscow and other opponents of the idea of republican economic independence is the concern that regional differences could be intensified. I think it's better to live differently and well, rather than all live equally and badly. (Applause)

We have already experienced what such levelling means. It not only holds back the more developed: it helps to prolong the enfeebled state of those that lag behind. Many deputies from the Baltic republics are amazed, to put it mildly, by the repeated statements of Comrade Ryzhkov, which provoke antagonism towards us from other republics.

Supposedly, we have been provided with more favourable conditions and, by using cheap raw materials, appropriate the final product for ourselves and thereby profit greatly. (Noise in hall) Using unrealistic price estimates, Lithuania is 'condemned' to have a deficit in the inter-republican commodity balance. Apparently we are therefore living at the expense of others. I cannot believe that the prime minister does not know the real situation, and who acquires a considerable profit from industry in the final analysis. After all, almost 95% of the deductions from the profit of enterprises subordinate to union ministries are accumulated by the Centre. The prices for agricultural products are extremely low, and Lithuania is obliged to supply half of what she produces here to the central reserves. Is it not a paradox that if the republics provide more for those reserves their debts to the union treasury are increased, when they already run into thousands of millions? If only we produced less, it seems, we wouldn't run into debt. It's not us, after all, who fix prices, the level of state procurements, production quotas and who controls the other ways of exercising economic power. These are all decided by the Centre itself behind closed doors. Say, Lithuania does not fully recompense Uzbekistan or Tajikistan because prices for their cotton are now set unjustifiably low. If all republics were economically independent agreements would be made at mutually-beneficial prices. And this cannot result in any splitting up of the economy, of which certain leaders are so alarmed. It will merely lead to the correction of the irrational and at times distorted structure and links imposed by the centre. Integration will at last acquire a natural foundation.

We realise that in present conditions of scarcity a certain amount of time will be needed to establish an effective inter-regional market. The necessity for direct intervention by the state in trade deals between enterprises will then disappear. Our conception envisages the support of the existing inter-republican ties during the transitional period. It is intended that they will be implemented through mutually beneficial agreements and contracts between individual republics. And also between them and the union administration which here represents the particular interests of producers and consumers in the form of aggregate supply and demand of the republics in equivalent commodity exchange. When all republics and regions have become economically self-governing the establishment of independent and self-financing enterprises, interacting on the all-union market, will also be considerably accelerated.

The economic independence of the republics is in no way consonant with the present principle by which the Union budget is formed, nor with that now proposed by the USSR Council of Ministers. The relationship should be organised from the republican budgets upwards to the Union budget, for the Union does not unite economic enterprises but sovereign republics. They have the right to know and jointly determine what budget we need, how it is formed, and how much and on what we spend it. The last item includes the unproductive activities of the ministerial bureaucracies, the excessive demands of the armed forces, the space programme and so on. The disastrous conditions in which our people live oblige us to be reasonable and thrifty and decide all questions concerning the budget, of the Union as well as the republics, as the people wish us to.

The nation of my republic, like many other nations, is capable of working fruitfully and imaginatively; it is hard-working and wants to live better. It does not want to take unfair advantage of the labours of others or live on handouts from the centre. And anyway, where does the Centre get things from in the first place? We insist on the universality of the principle that if you work better, you have a right to live better. This is not a selective right, it is universal and applies to all nations. Failure to recognise this in relation to Lithuania or any other republic is a renunciation of that which is most sacred for the individual and the nation: the right to free self-determination.

We have boldly taken the initiative in transforming the Union from a super-republican, strong republic-ruling centre into a community of sovereign republics with an inter-republican administration that they have devised and which represents *their* interests. This also refers to economic relations within the Union. We shall be able to judge how wise the centre is and how strong is its desire to democratise and restructure by the way it reacts: whether it is able to transcend a selfish interest in its own self-preservation and help the process of democratisation, or intends to carry on the tradition of deciding everything for large and small nations, even in minor economic matters.

This is part of the "Baltic problem" which, even as the Congress has been sitting, has inevitably been transformed into the universal problem of the structure and future of the Union. In the meantime we do not see shifts towards a recognition of the republics' need for economic independence, either in Comrade Ryzhkov's speech or in the actions of the government. Instead there is only talk of expanding certain rights for those republics when their people have already stated quite specific wishes in this respect. The resolution of this problem cannot be postponed even to the autumn. A nation cannot long be in a state of political tension, exacerbated by obstruction and delay on the part of the Centre which conceals its inaction behind talk of defending the achievements of socialism and internationalism. The economic models developed by the Baltic republics are very close to the proposals of the Moscow economists and sociologists and there is much more socialism in them than what we have today. The Baltic republics are prepared to take the responsibility (which they bear to their own people, and not to the super-power centre) and be the experimenters, if you like, who shift the economy onto a normal and healthy path of development. We simply have no other way out and, it seems to me, neither does Moscow. Thank you. (Prolonged applause)

REFORM AND SUPERVISION OF THE CONSTITUTION

Anatoly Gorbunov, Chairman of Latvian Supreme Soviet Presidium (territorial deputy, Latvia) 152

One of the most complex problems of the restructuring and democratisation of the Soviet political system is to provide it with legal foundations. As soon as any major changes in one or other sphere are proposed, they each time come into conflict with out-dated laws. A paradoxical situation is developing. We can work inefficiently but in accordance with the clearly outdated norms of the existing law. We can wait passively for the new Soviet constitution; more than one year will be spent drafting it. And in this case we certainly cannot rush. Yet there is an alternative: to advance the restructuring without waiting and simultaneously make use of the more decisive measures that have ripened in the field of legislation. There have been assertions at the Congress, it is true, that people will not understand if we start introducing amendments to the USSR Constitution as we go.

The deputies from Latvia take a different view. Our voters will not understand us if the Congress, after working for two weeks, still does not introduce a single amendment to the Constitution. At least in those articles that clearly hinder progress. For instance, in developing our Federation so as to promote a qualitatively new political and economic sovereignty of the union republics. (Applause) The legislators of the republics are actively drawing up new laws without which the further democratisation of our political system will be impossible ...

I am deeply convinced that we cannot work today if we are constantly referring back to the outdated union laws. ... Therefore I am offering for the Congress's consideration a draft law for the USSR as a whole, concerning changes in the Constitution. The proposed changes affect only a few of the articles which, in our view, are the most important.

... No one now needs persuading that the rebirth of the union republic's sovereignty ... not only requires the re-examination of old dogmas and a grasping of the new situation. It demands quite specific practical measures.

We could take the economy of Latvia. Many examples might be given where the unjustified centralisation of administration leads to a total lack of correspondence between certain industries and factories, on the one hand, and the interests of the republic where they are located and of the nations whose needs they were set up to meet, on the other. For instance, we can give no explanation whatsoever to the inhabitants of Latvia as to why when there are 4 large works producing agricultural machinery in the republic, our farmers cannot get the most elementary equipment, a decent plough or seed-drill. ... The unjustified construction of large-scale or simply enormous industrial plants has often taken no account of the ecological and social consequences. When there was no local energy, raw materials or labour resources this led to excessive and unregulated migration. The result was not only a catastrophic shift in the national and demographic composition of the population in a number of union republics and regions but also a degradation in the society's socio-cultural infrastructure.

Today one can frequently hear comments about centrifugal tendencies, and accusations of separatism. At times any mention of such words as economic independence, sovereignty and independence are immediately presented as appeals to secede from the USSR. I think there are a great many misunderstandings here, and unnecessary suspiciousness or simply ignorance.

So what kind of independence are we talking about? what do we mean by this word?

First, the recognition that our state is made up of sovereign union republics that have the right freely to determine their own domestic and foreign political status without any external pressure. ...

Second, the recognition that the powers of the state must be distributed in such a way that the union republics can exercise the full measure of authority in their own territory. (Applause) Here we base ourselves on the proposition that the union republics are primary and the federation is derivative ... and not the reverse.

Third, a republic cannot be recognised as a sovereign state if it cannot independently control the use of its own territory and resources. ...

Fourth, and last, a sovereign state cannot be limited in its legislative activities. ... The present Constitution gives us the right to pass laws on any subject at the Congress. But if one thinks for a moment this contradicts the principle of the republics' sovereignty. We would like to think that the Congress and the USSR Supreme Soviet will restrict themselves in their legislative activities to the level and issues of federal relations, and leave all the rest for the law-makers of the republics. (Applause)

... So we shall not forget that sovereignty is the inalienable right of the nation, and will take a reasonable and respectful attitude to this right.

If we're to be honest, we must acknowledge that sometimes we do not show a reasonable and respectful attitude here. It is this that lies at the heart of the inter-ethnic tension in Latvia, which at times acquires a nationalistic or chauvinist colouring. However much we condemn these shameful manifestations, they will remain if we do not abolish the social roots of inter-ethnic tension.

So economic and political independence is not an end in itself but a way of improving the environment in which not only the Latvian nation but also the entire population of our republic lives. ...

Thus the main question is how we shall arrive at mutually acceptable decisions? Using ultimatums and strikes or through a political dialogue based on mutual respect? The Central Committee of the Communist Party in Latvia and the Latvian Supreme Soviet have firmly declared ... that political issues must be resolved only by political means. (Applause)

We consider that the sovereignty of Latvia in union with the other republics is in the interests of people of all nationalities who have linked their destinies with that of our republic. ... (Applause)

Yarovoi (Estonia) 159

Many speakers have offered their models for getting the country out of its present complex economic and political situation. ... Some see the solution in radical economic reform, others see the root of all evil in the existing bureaucratic apparatus. Yet others put the sovereignty of the republics first. ... I would not be honest and principled if, in the name of my constituents, I did not focus the attention of the deputies on the situation in our common home, the Union of Soviet Socialist Republics, and show the necessity of protecting it from a possible division into separate national states. Then the application of any of the suggested models will be impossible. You may ask, is there really such a danger? Are you not over-dramatising the situation? No comrades. Let me tell you that this is what my voters think, and they work for the major industries and enterprises brought together in the United Council of

Workers of Estonia (of which I was elected chairman).

Just look how rapidly the pressure in the country's political barometer is falling. New regions where the situation is tense and unstable are constantly appearing. First here and then there, conflicts erupt, mainly on ethnic grounds. The chorus of voices submitting ultimatums to the Centre grow continually louder and clearer: they demand that the state structure of the country, and the Constitution ... be re-examined. Even at our Congress a representative of the Lithuanian delegation tried to organise a demarche during discussion of elections to the Supreme Soviet. Shielding behind perestroika and confusing democracy with demagogy numerous extremist groupings and organisations are acting with increasing openness and brazenness. ... they try to sow mistrust towards the existing system, the party and the government and instil enmity towards the population that speaks a different language. But from whom do they wish to free themselves? From the ukases of central ministries? or from a part of their own nation which speaks in a different language? The legislative acts passed in the [Baltic] republics indicate that the latter is intended. Not satisfied with success in their own republic, these new missionaries actively propagandise their views and aspirations in many parts of the country. And here also at the Congress...

... The constant concessions of the [Estonian Party and Soviet] authorities who have lost the initiative means that perestroika in Estonia is now a one-way street. And there is no place there for the majority of the non-Estonian population which does not support the cult of the [Estonian] nation's priority. (Applause)

... The republic first violated the Constitution (Article 74) on 16 November last year when the Estonian Supreme Soviet adopted its famous amendments to the Constitution and its Declaration of sovereignty. The Presidium of the USSR Supreme Soviet declared them invalid ... [but] the republican leaders did not abolish the anti-constitutional articles. They merely noted the Presidium's decision. That legal conflict ... has not been resolved to this day. On 18 May 1989, moreover, the conflict was exacerbated when the Estonian Supreme Soviet adopted a Law on the Principles of Cost-Accounting in the Estonian SSR ... A paradoxical situation emerged whereby we, citizens of the USSR, do not know under which law we are living. ...Can we seriously believe the assurances of the Estonian leadership as to the socialist character of these changes and of their striving to strengthen the socialist federation when we can see the opposite happening: the artistic unions, non-governmental organisations and voluntary societies in Estonia are breaking their ties with their own central bodies in Moscow.

The Young Pioneers [for 9-14 year olds] organisation has ceased to exist in the republic, the Komsomol is about to be disbanded and there is constant talk of the Communist Party of Estonia becoming autonomous.

... The Central Committee of the Communist Party and the Presidium of the Supreme Soviet [in Moscow] know very well what's happening in the Baltic republics. But they do not respond to numerous appeals from the workers and primary party organisations ... expressing concern and worry for the future of Estonia. ... Can that be the right policy when we remember the sad experience of Sumgait, Karabakh, and now Tbilisi and Ferghana?

... Indeed there are no direct clashes, pogroms, refugees, tanks, armoured personnel carriers or black berets [special riot-control forces] on the streets of Estonia. However, there is a real confrontation and growing alienation ... Strike committees are being set up ... and civilian committees that demand secession from the Union. Ever more frequently voices can be heard suggesting that a separate administrative and territorial unit be established in northwest Estonia where most of the non-Estonian part of the population are concentrated. Is that really what we should be striving for?

(Yarovoi spoke immediately after the Russian writer Rasputin, see Chapter 5.)

Election of the Constitutional Review Committee (Thursday 8 June, 12th session)

While a commission to work on a new Constitution was established with more or less full agreement (161), the proposal to set up the above committee led to a dramatic confrontation.

Romas Gudaidis, writer and literary adviser to Lithuanian union of writers, Vilnius (national deputy, Lithuania) 161

A suggestion that we do not set up a Committee of Constitutional Supervision will probably be seen by you, honourable deputies, as obstruction or an attempt to slow down the earlier mentioned scenario for the closure of this Congress. All the same, I must express the will of my voters and of the citizens of Lithuania. The hasty creation of this committee will immediately become a means of exerting pressure on the national renaissance of the union republics, and a restraint on their sovereignty.

Neither are we reassured by the high professional qualifications of the

Chairman [Academician Kudryavtsev] and members of this committee … when the centralised unitary state is still being justified, and the most important features of the Stalinist imperial model are preserved. You may try to reassure us by saying that the Committee will not become the "legal" guarantor of those forces which wish to curb national movements with an iron hand. You may try to reassure us by saying that the Committee will not oppose the drawing up of new democratic constitutions in the republics …

To test this we might make an amendment to Article 127 of the USSR Constitution: "The Constitutional Review Committee is elected from among legal specialists and has 15 chairmen and 15 members from each union republic. They will work in strict rotation. If the sovereignty of a union republic is infringed it has the right of veto."

Let this be material for reflection in the future. The present formulation is unacceptable to us. The overwhelming majority of the Lithuanian delegation and also a large group of deputies from Latvia and Estonia make the following declaration to the Congress.

"One, the Congress has exposed a constitutional crisis. There are internal contradictions between the [1977 Brezhnev] Constitution of the period of stagnation and the necessity of establishing not supervision over observance of the out-dated constitution but the drawing up of a new USSR Constitution;

Two, the actual law concerning constitutional review procedures in the USSR does not yet exist;

Three, the mandate of the Committee as it is presented in the Constitution … permits the infringement of the sovereign rights of the union republics by that body;

Four, the population of Latvia, Lithuania and Estonia in mass protests already held in autumn last year collected about 4 million signatures expressing their disapproval of the latest undemocratic amendments and supplements to the USSR Constitution;

Five, now the electors have mandated us to protect the sovereignty of our republics;

We therefore do not consider elections to this Committee to be advisable and will not take part in them". Thank you. (Applause)

Evgeny Kogan (Estonia) 161

One of the deputies from the Baltic region here claimed to speak for all the three republics and all their voters. We can clearly see a desire to shorten the reach of this Committee before it is even set up so that it cannot intervene in the affairs of the union republics. ... But it seems to me that the Committee is being set up precisely to ensure that nobody's rights are infringed in our country. In this connection, ... the rights of many inhabitants of these same republics are already being infringed. Such are the laws that have been taken there and I would like the Committee to begin its work with the Baltic, and Estonia in particular. (Applause)

... I would like this Committee to investigate the legality of our "laws" about language, where education in one language [Estonian] is guaranteed, while in another it is only tolerated. Moreover, knowledge of the language is also made the basis on which work contracts are concluded and prolonged. ... Finally I would like to draw your attention to the following documents which seem to me work for the Committee itself.

[Quotes from recent newspapers of the Baltic republics] ... The newspaper Atmoda for 29 May 1989: "For the first time the leadership of the Latvian People's Front discussed the creation of voluntary militia to preserve public order". ..... Next ...

Gorbachev (in chair)

Your time has run out.

Kogan

Just a few seconds more. ... Finally I make an official request that a group of independent jurists be set up that will investigate all these matters. ...

Andris Plotnieks, Professor of University of Latvia, Riga (national deputy, Latvia) 161

We announce that we have the fullest confidence in and respect for the candidates [for membership of this committee] including Academician Kudryavstev, its future chairman. At the same time, however, the circumstances under which this question is being decided are very unusual. Proposals by the deputies on changes and amendments to the USSR Constitution have as yet not only not been worked out but the Constitutional Commission [for reform of the Constitution] is not yet even in existence. The 1977 USSR Constitution is still in force ... and abounds in contradictions and omissions.

The drafting of a new Constitution still lies before us. At the same time, to advance the cause of perestroika in the union republics major changes must be made in republican constitutions in the shortest time-span. This is going on in all the three Baltic republics and in other union republics....

You may object and ask me, what's the hurry? We'll adopt a new Constitution and then start on the constitutions of the union republics. Such an approach, however, is fraught with many dangers.

First, the all-union market and republican cost-accounting, the transition to economic methods of management, satisfying the market demand for commodities and many of our immediate daily needs ... require decisions. The economists offer various cures for these economic ills but without change in the constitutions of the union republics these treatments will be ineffective and a cure impossible.

Second, logically the renewal of the constitutional legislation in the socialist federal state should begin at the level of the republics. The most successful formulations should then be generalised at the level of the USSR Constitution. We suggest the following very short decree:

"The Congress of USSR people's deputies decrees: that the constitutional review committee envisaged under Article 125 ... has the right to halt the implementation of normative and legal acts that contradict the USSR Constitution or a Union law but are not applicable to the Constitutions of the union republics." (Applause) ....

Our disquiet is not without foundation, especially after Comrade Ryzhkov's speech yesterday outlining the immediate tasks of the USSR government. He actually laid stress on the unitary, not the federal, organisation of our state. The majority of deputies from the Baltic republics (and not only from there) promised their voters that they would stand up for the 'restructuring' laws of their own republics: they want to keep their word, and will do so. ... How should we behave? Vote against, abstain, leave the hall ..? However, we are for the suggested membership and for the Committee itself. (Applause)

Yuri Golik, Dean of the law department, Kemerovo University (territorial deputy, Kemerovo, Russian Federation) 161

We have been trying to establish such a Committee for many years and so I consider the attempts here, masked by apparently democratic slogans, to torpedo its setting up to be intolerable. (Applause) ... After all, we are being choked to death by the regualations issued by every ministry and department. The sooner we put an end to such legislative activities the easier we shall breathe.

Alksnis (Latvia) 161

There have already been many representatives of the Baltic republics on this tribune talking loudly of a return to Leninist principles of federalism. I would like to clarify that while speaking in favour of federalism what they are actually suggesting is confederation.

I would like to request the legal experts to provide deputies with information about the basic distinguishing features of confederation and federation. ... Furthermore, on 31 May 1989 when our Congress was already in session the Council of the Latvian popular front made an appeal to all members. Until then [it says] "the Front, in accordance with its foundation congress, had relied on the first alternative, the federal principle. However, the events of the last few months show ... it has met with ever-growing counter-measures by the Centre and internal reactionary forces even to the point of using violence as the tragic events of 9 April in Tbilisi show.

"The course of the Congress is evidence that a conservative majority has emerged there, opposed to the aspirations of the union republics. In this connection the executive of the People's Front's council puts forward for discussion a question of vital importance for our nation: the beginning of the Front's struggle for the complete political and economic independence of Latvia." For the first time, in other words, the mask has been discarded and the main aim of the Front has been shown: secession from the USSR. ...

... From this high tribune I appeal to the representatives of human rights organisations, including international bodies, that they come to the Baltic republics and evaluate whether these laws [recently passed in Latvia] meet the standards of international law. (Applause, in which many People's Front deputies show enthusiastic approval of the latter suggestion.)

Andrei Tsirulis, Chief editor of the newspaper *Padomiu Yaunatne*, **Riga (national deputy, Latvia)**

I understand the indignation. When you listen to representatives of the Interfront what they say really does appear awful. I would indeed be an unhappy man if what they said was true. ... But it's very difficult to judge what's happening in Latvia, Lithuania and Estonia, and about life in the other republics, if we only read the central newspapers and watch the Central TV channels. A very wide range of opinions should be represented, after all.

I very much liked comrade Alksnis' suggestion of inviting international representatives to check what's happening. They are much needed in the Baltic and would only bring benefit. We very much need glasnost. And we would be very thankful if this happened. (Applause)

Mikhail Gorbachev 161

Now we must decide in principle whether we are going to form this committee or not. ... Those in favour? Those against? Comrades, we probably don't need to count here: a clear minority.

Chief Teller

43 deputies voted against, and 61 abstained.
The deputies from the Lithuanian delegation did not participate in the voting. 50 deputies.

Gorbachev

Out of a total of ...?

Chief Teller

Comrades, how many deputies are there in the Lithuanian delegation, 58? No? Then, excuse me, can I ask you to raise your hands so that we can count how many are present.

At this the Lithuanian deputies stood and left the hall.

Gorbachev

Comrades, please keep calm. This is a far from simple matter. There's no need to simplify ... We must now consult as to how we can carry on.

An interval is declared for consultation with the Lithuanian delegation.

Gorbachev

We have agreed to meet with the Lithuanian delegation after today's session.

It was agreed as a compromise to set up a commission to draft the law concerning such a Constitutional review committee (162).

POSTSCRIPT: ELECTIONS TO POSTS IN THE SUPREME SOVIET

Prunskene was proposed by Anatoly Sobchak (Leningrad) as an alternative to the Speaker, Primakov's, preferred choice of deputy from Kazakhstan in the Chamber of the Union. But she herself, recently elected deputy chairperson of the Lithuanian Supreme Soviet declined, partly on the grounds that her views differed from those of Primakov.

In the Chamber of Nationalities, Klara Hallik was proposed as deputy speaker but stepped down in favour of Evdokia Gaer. Ilmar Bisher, the speaker Nishanov's second nominee, was elected without opposition.

Kazimieras Uoka, Secretary of Sajudis (Lithuanian Popular Front), (national deputy, Lithuania) 159

If even in this Chamber [of Nationalities] there is no desire to listen to every deputy, I repeat every one, that represents the interests of a nation, then I consider I have the right to talk about the possibility of my native Lithuania leaving the union of Soviet Socialist Republics. It is a constitutional right. If things go on like this, I do not want my native Lithuania to be in such a bad Union …

Voice from benches

Weren't you afraid after the speech by our comrade?

Uoka

Who do you mean exactly?

Voice

The factory director [Yarovoi]…

Uoka

Oh, the factory director! Fine, then let's remember that over 90% of the workers at that factory are not Estonian. The director himself organised things so that Estonians would not go and work there. And he didn't ask the agreement of the Estonian nation to do so.

Voice from benches:

Don't you think there will be some kind of Karabakh in Estonia?

Uoka

I'm from Lithuania, not Estonia. Moreover, let me say that the Russians who live in the other republics have their own native land, Russia. But the nations of these republics have no other to go to.

This exchange is wrongly attributed in the official transcript to the phlegmatic investigator Bickauskas, not to Uoka.

Chapter 3

THE CAUCASUS IN TURMOIL

> Before we begin our [first] session I ask you to commemorate those who died in Tbilisi. (All stand and observe a minute's silence).
> On the instructions of my voters I am putting an official question as a deputy: I demand that we be publicly told here and now, at the Congress, who gave the order to beat peaceful demonstrators in Tbilisi on 9 April 1989 and to use poison gases against them ... (Applause)
> *Vilen Tolpezhnikov (Latvia) 146*

The use of the military to break up a large unofficial demonstration in the Georgian capital Tbilisi, soon after the March elections to the Congress, was a dramatic and disturbing response by the authorities to the spread of unsanctioned meetings and rallies throughout the country. As discussion at the congress revealed, ethnicity and politics were thoroughly intertwined. The question of who took the decisions, locally and in Moscow, was raised but not answered.

Undoubtedly the recent cycle of ethnic strife and violent clashes in the USSR started with the Nagorno-Karabakh autonomous region. A part of the Azerbaijan republic although its population is 75% Armenian, its grievances surfaced into the whole country's view in 1988. Deep historical roots fed the re-emergence of a long-standing and neglected problem.

The three main nations of the Caucasus contrast markedly. Almost all Georgians live in Georgia (but still only account for two thirds of the republic's population). Armenians, in contrast, are to be found all over the Soviet Union and throughout the world in the Armenian diaspora while the Azerbaijanis are separated by the river Araks from the much greater number of their brethren who live in western Iran.

The Georgians and Armenians belong to two ancient Christian nations later surrounded and at times subjected by Muslims: Abkhazians, Ossetians, Azerbaijanis and Turks. Both sought an ally against the Turks (and Persians) in Russia, and came more or less willingly under the latter's protection by the early 19th century. The Georgians belong to an independent Orthodox church, but the Armenians are Monophysite and pride themselves on being the first state in the world to officially adopt Christianity. In contrast, the third of the Azerbaijani nation now in the

Soviet Union was incorporated after capture of the region from Persia in the 18th century. More than half of the population are Shiite Muslims, the only significant concentration of this Islamic confession in the USSR. Baku before the Revolution produced half the world's oil, and with its multi-national workforce was an important centre of Bolshevik activity.

Following the 1917 Revolution, all three republics had a brief and troubled period of independence until Soviet rule was established 4 years later.

The relaxation of the government control caused by perestroika immediately resulted in eruption of spontaneous and organized local conflict that soon grew to involve the entire nations of Azerbaijan and Armenia.

The call by Armenians for secession of Karabakh from Azerbaijan and unification with Armenia was supported by continuous strikes in Karabakh and Armenia and mass rallies involving hundreds of thousands. While the authorities were hesitating the tension inevitably developed into violence. Numerous bloody local skirmishes and fights in villages and towns produced ugly rumours in Azerbaijan and in February of 1988 crowds of excited Azerbaijanians went on a bloody rampage in the industrial town of Sumgait ransacking homes of Armenians, raping and killing women, children and men. Similar riots though on a smaller scale occurred in other Azerbaijanian towns and villages. The authorities brought in troops to stop the riots but, Armenians claim that it was intentionally done too late.

Some say that it was the Karabakh infection that Georgia had caught and indeed the Georgian nationalist movement grew prominently in the wake of the Armenian events. The major factor in the recent troubles was the proclaimed intention of the Abkhazian Autonomous Republic, administratively a part of Georgia, to secede. (In contrast to Karabakh, the mainly Muslim Abkhazian population are now a clear minority in Abkhazia.) The news infuriated Georgians and a period of mass rallies and parades in Tbilisi, the capital of Georgia, followed. The demonstrators carried virulent anti-Russian and anti-Abkhazian slogans and called for Georgian independence but no violence was involved initially. The Georgian party and government leaders, alarmed by this mass outpouring of nationalist sentiment, secretly ordered the paratroopers recently returned from the Afghanistan war into the city.

Georgia had 91 deputies at the Congress, Armenia 53, and Azerbaijan 72.

THE FIRST ACCUSATIONS: EVENING SITTING, DAY 1

Eldar Shengelya, director Georgian film studios (USSR union of film-industry workers) 147

A commission of the Georgian Supreme Soviet started work immediately after the events of 9 April. I ask your permission to circulate the documents of that commission, and the findings of the medical and chemical investigations.

Second, we are putting three official questions to Yazov, Minister of Defence, Kochetov, first deputy minister of Defence and Bakatin, Minister of Internal Affairs [in charge of police and riot-control forces]. We ask that they give us an official answer when this issue is discussed here.

Third, we have made a video which, I believe, you must all see in order to understand for yourselves what happened. ... I would ask Mikhail Gorbachev and the Presidium also to watch this cassette.

Lastly, as a consequence of this punitive action by armed forces 21 people died, more than 4000 applied for medical treatment ... This action was directed by General Rodionov. I do not think that such a deputy should sit among us at this Congress.

Vitaly Vorotnikov, Chairman of Russian Federation Supreme Soviet's Presidium, Politburo member (Communist Party); chairman of sitting

This is a very important question that disturbs not only the Georgian people, but all the Soviet nation. So there is a suggestion that the Presidium be entrusted to set up a special commission, to be confirmed by Congress, to discuss these questions and report back to The Congress.

Mikhail Gorbachev (from Presidium)

Let the presidium work on this and present the membership of this commission for confirmation by the Congress. We must set up a commission that we all trust.

Genrikh Igityan, director, Modern Art Museum, Armenia (USSR Union of Artists) 147

...As a deputy I went to Tbilisi and studied the evidence. It was, indeed, an awesome tragedy, violent and brutal... But I want to draw attention of the Congress to the events in Sumgait [in February 1988]. Gorbachev had made an appeal to the nations of Azerbaijan and Armenia and demonstrations in Armenia were held under the slogans "Lenin, Party, and Gorbachev". They were answered by the horrifying massacre in Sumgait which claimed many lives. Only in time of foreign invasions has anything of that kind happened in this country. People were raped and killed, crosses were burnt on their bodies, and their homes were ransacked. This outrage continued for several days only a 30-minute car-ride away from Baku, the capital of Azerbaijan. No political analysis of these events has yet been made. I think this is the beginning of a barbarity that will go very far if we do not put a stop to it now.

We lived through the Second World War and we were all brothers then. We should not fail to pass political judgement on this vandalism in the time of perestroika when the party appeals to all nations of the country... I believe that all union republics will support us in this. Moreover, I must say that we have not seen the progressive part of the Azerbaijanian public or their intelligentsia condemning these acts of violence. If Armenians had done this I would stand up and ask forgiveness from the entire Soviet people and the world community. Somehow we have not heard anything of the kind. We have only heard the 1st Secretary of the Azerbaijanian Communist Party Central Committee talking about *namuz*, about conscience. Can one talk about conscience after committing acts of such brutality? I ask all Soviet republics and all honest Azerbaijanians to support me in this call.

Muslum Mamedov, 1st Secretary, Baku City Committee of the Communist Party (national deputy, Azerbaijan)

I must answer the irresponsible speech by deputy Igityan. His words, which I would not like to repeat or to address to anybody in this hall or to any representative of another Soviet nation, are slanderous. They are a slur on my nation, on the proletariat of Baku... Everything that was done in Azerbaijan demonstrates that we had never sought confrontation. We never looked for excuses for hostility between our nations. Everything shows that it is we who are trying to find a compromise. I condemn what happened in Sumgait but surely Igityan knows that not a single one of the 165,000 Azerbaijanians who lived in Armenia have remained there? Surely Igityan knows how many Azerbaijanians were murdered in Armenia?

Vitaly Vorotnikov (in the chair)

I urge you to stop. I think this is neither the time nor place for mutual denunciations of this kind. We have gathered here as one family, representatives of 65 Soviet nations and nationalities to unite and together work out a programme for further advance, progress towards perestroika… We must show restraint and our statements must be responsible…

WHAT HAPPENED IN TBILISI 6TH SITTING (EVENING), TUESDAY 30 MAY

Anatoly Lukyanov, candidate for deputy Chairman of Supreme Soviet, 150

Violent methods like those that were used in Tbilisi are unacceptable, in principle, in dealing with inter-ethnic problems. Like my comrades in the Politburo I learnt of their use 6 hours later.

Roy Medvedev (Moscow) 150

When Mikhail Gorbachev had only just returned from England dramatic events took place in Tbilisi which violated the Constitution. Martial law was introduced by the local authorities and not the Supreme Soviet as the Constitution requires. Someone was in a great hurry … we still do not know who in Moscow gave approval for this action … If it wasn't either Lukyanov or Gorbachev, as they tell us, then there are probably people in this hall who knew what happened in Tbilisi but are today keeping quiet.

Tamaz Gamkrelidze, director, Georgian Academy of Sciences Institute of Oriental Studies, Tbilisi (national deputy, Adjarian Autonomous Republic, Georgia) 150

I speak for a group of Georgian deputies who are not satisfied with Comrade Lukyanov's reply that the Presidium of the USSR Supreme Soviet [sic] … only learnt of these events 6 hours later …

A fundamental restructuring of the social and economic life of the USSR depends on major changes in the entire political structure. In this light Georgia puts the following basic questions. That the annexation of democratic Georgia in February 1921 be condemned as a gross infringement of the treaty of 7 May 1920 signed by Lenin and concluded between equal and sovereign states, Soviet Russia and democratic Georgia.

All inter-ethnic issues in Georgia must be resolved by examining the interests of all nations living in the republic … (this, evidently, is where the issue of the Meskhetian Turks which you raised, Comrade Lukyanov, belongs).

D

In view of the demands of the voters Georgian deputies consider that the time has now come to let conscripts from Georgia who want to perform their military service in their own republic to do so. (Applause)

Gamkrelidze 152

... The Congress began by paying its respects to the innocent victims of 9 April 1989 ... And this was quite natural since the Tbilisi tragedy was a terrible blow against universal human values... the social and political consequences of which are hard to foresee.

... We must learn the full details of the tragedy. Only then can we have some legal guarantees that it will not be repeated elsewhere in future.

... At 4 a.m. troops were used in Tbilisi for an unprecedentedly brutal attack on innocent people on the pretext of breaking up a rally that had not been allowed officially. Up to 10,000 people were participating in a rally which was entirely peaceful, without any violence or calls for violence. When tanks and armoured cars made their appearance without any warning in the square before Government House, the people, feeling threatened, stood with lighted candles, sang ancient hymns and prayed. The available video recordings and photographic evidence, supported by the affidavits of numerous injured persons and other participants, enable us to establish precisely what took place.

In addition to clubs, the troops used small sapper's spades and toxic gases: this was officially established by the special commission of the Health Ministry of Georgia and by independent experts from Moscow, Leningrad, Switzerland, West Germany, France and USA.

This military action supervised by Colonel-General Rodionov, Commander of the Transcaucasian Military District, was evidently conceived not as the dispersal of a peaceful rally but as a specially-planned punitive operation aimed at murdering people. The troops gave no warning of any kind before starting. Soldiers blocked the passages, surrounded demonstrators and hit them with clubs and sapper's spades. They did not spare the hunger strikers lying in the square who included young girls and old women; they attacked doctors and Red Cross workers; and they pursued those trying to escape, continuing to hit the wounded, snatching them from the hands of the medics. They even attacked the local policemen who tried to save lives.

According to official figures 16 people were killed there and then. Fourteen of them were women, the eldest 70 and the youngest 15. Three persons died later in hospital.

The reports in the central and military press, and even in [the schoolchildren's daily] *Pionerskaya Pravda*, later read as though Georgian men had been killing their own womenfolk and children while the troops tried to save the victims from the enraged men. It is disgraceful that the mass media, especially central press and television and the [nightly TV news programme] *Vremya* ... asserted that the people killed were somehow the victims of a "crush that occurred" for unintelligible reasons. On the whole, the reports in the national mass media were biased and amazingly primitive and incompetent...

An especially ugly fact was the use of poison gases against peaceful demonstrators... It was a crime against humanity. ... no less serious was the prolonged denial by the military that they had used poison gases, thus hindering the medical treatment of the casualties...

Over 3500 people were treated for poisoning and 500 of them had to be hospitalized...

More tragic events followed after 9 April. The public was informed about the curfew in Tbilisi only a few minutes before it became effective. Half an hour later a youth was shot by troops at point-blank range through the windshield of his car, and several persons were wounded including a 12-year old boy who was riding his bicycle.

In the aftermath of the tragedy the tension in Georgia is so high that it may give rise to unforseeable actions at any moment. Only the fullest glasnost and the punishment of those responsible can prevent this tragedy having a catastrophic influence on the moral state and the behaviour of our fellow Georgians throughout the USSR...

The Georgian nation regard these events as a calamity whose significance lies outside the national boundaries and concerns the basic principles of human rights and freedoms. The Tbilisi tragedy revealed a complete failure of the legal system in the USSR whereby the fate not just of individuals but of entire republics is at the mercy of the reactionary forces hostile to democratization and progress...

If those responsible are not identified and punished the public will take it as evidence that the party apparatus and the military high command have unlimited power...

General Rodionov justifies this punitive action by referring to the sadly-familiar Decree of 28 July 1988 "On the duties and rights of the special troops of the Ministry of Internal Affairs". The tragic events in Tbilisi have given vivid proof how dangerous this decree is when freely interpreted. ... This is, in particular, linked to the question of the legal status of the "special" divisions, professional killers who distinguished themselves in the Tbilisi operation by their especial cruelty and inhumanity.

We see it as a manifestation of the utmost cynicism, and cruelly offensive to the feelings of the Georgian nation, that General Rodionov is still sitting in this hall as a representative of his Georgian constituency though his voters have already recalled him, following the proper constitutional procedures. (Disturbance in hall) General Rodionov has neither a legal nor a moral right to remain a People's Deputy from Georgia...

The Patriarch of the Georgian Orthodox Church Ilia II said in his audience to Academician Sakharov "It was ordained that the Georgian nation had to bear this heavy cross thus saving other nations from similar ordeals. It must never happen again." (Applause, some deputies stand).

Rafik Nishanov (in chair)

There have been some calls from the hall for General Rodionov to say what he thinks about the Tbilisi events. An official question was put to the Minister of Defence. I thought that there would be an answer, or shall we listen to General Rodionov?

Igor Rodionov, commander of Transcaucasian military district (territorial deputy, Georgian) 152

I think it necessary to make a political assessment of the Tbilisi events. Otherwise we shall not be able to interpret its consequences correctly, and the consequences were severe. ... I quote from the daily newspaper of the Georgian Communist Party: "Leaders of the extremist groups used people including women and teenagers not only for the propaganda of their anti-Soviet, anti-state and anti-Socialist views but also, what is more dangerous, for carrying out their subversive anti-state activities". Those who are talking now about the peaceful nature of the rally forget that, at the same time, vile calls to assault communists were heard in the central street of Tbilisi and anti-Russian and nationalist feelings were being stirred up. (Noise in hall) I was not allowed to address the [Georgian] Central Committee session after the tragedy... And why? Because it was outright [counter-revolution: Rodionov did not complete the cliche but this is almost certainly what he wanted to say, tr.] ... (Noise in hall). I continue to quote from the [Georgian Communist Party] daily, from the assessment made directly after the events. Groups of well-trained organized people penetrated factories and prevented hundreds and thousands of people from working... defiled monuments... disseminated trouble, confusion and unrest throughout the republic. There was a danger of the vital installations being occupied. A meeting of party activists decided that the situation was fraught with unpredictable consequences... All possible measures had been exhausted and only the use of force remained ... It was not the sending of troops that led to a deterioration in the situation: the deteriorating situation demanded the deployment of troops. Some relevant facts... A mass rally (of up to 6000) led by the Tseretelli society on 6 April approved an appeal to the US Congress and NATO countries to support the independence of Georgia including, in particular, deployment of the UN or NATO troops for this purpose. Let me quote some of the slogans disseminated in Tbilisi (some of them in English). "Down with Russian communism". "Russian invaders, get out of Georgia." "Down with the rotten Russian Empire." "Down with the Communist regime". "The USSR is a prison of nations"... Such is the Georgian version of perestroika... It is only this version that will satisfy those who signed the address to the Congress in the name of the Georgian people. The latter, incidentally, go on living and working honestly and do not take part in this mayhem though the evil forces do everything to draw the working people into it... We did everything possible to avoid casualties... The situation was very complicated... We made some mistakes but we had to hurry since we had had the experience of Sumgait, Kirovobad, Nakhichevan and Zvartnots where there had been victims. This is why the early morning time, 4 a.m., was chosen for the operation. Only officers carried firearms... Not a single shot was fired in the square. We warned the demonstrators to disperse through loudspeakers. We did not expect such heavy and stubborn resistance: barricades and armed vigilante detachments. 172 military personnel were injured, and 26 of them had to be hospitalized though they had protective shields, helmets and bullet-proof vests...

... You should come to Tbilisi and see for yourself how such rallies are conducted ... Out of the 16 bodies found on the site of the tragedy not a single one had stab wounds or cuts... It is all rumours and emotion ... When I listened to the previous speaker I was so outraged I kept on repeating to myself our Russian magic [four-letter] words...

Since there were no wounds they started talking about gases. What gases could be used in two hours when the troops themselves had no gas masks or no protective gear? They try to represent the events as if it were a folk festival with lit candles and prayers... It was provocation...

Yes, three persons died in hospital and one of them had cuts on his head. But he was a 34-year old man, he could have been attacking the troops. Many did ...

I am particularly indignant about the charge that special chemicals were used ... To avoid heavier consequences, a tear-gas-type chemical was employed but by the special forces not by the army ... Only 19 persons were later admitted for hospital treatment with slight after-effects following exposure to them...

I would like to ask the investigating commission to give me an answer to the following questions. 1. Why did the mass media reverse their initial evaluation of the events? 2. Why were the victims, early on in the investigation, referred to as innocent and why was the anti-Soviet riotous assembly that went on for several days described as a folk festival? 3. Why were the heads of the government and party in the republic dismissed at the beginning of the investigation while the new heads declare that everything was done without them and they knew nothing? ... For instance, the new First Secretary of the Central Committee of the Georgian Communist Party Gumbaridze was at that time the Chairman of the Committee of State Security [KGB] of Georgia... Who will tell the truth here?

The former leaders keep silent, the new ones deny everything. After a quick perestroika the mass media started to distort the reports and mislead the public. It turned out that the special forces and the Soviet Army on their own initiative invaded the square where people were praying, singing psalms and dancing, and then brutally assaulted them... What did the Georgian deputies do to prevent us from taking these extreme steps?...

I took command of the forces in Transcaucasia a year ago. Azerbaijan and Armenia were already in turmoil but everything was quiet in Georgia and everybody was happy. It was a result of a year of your work that we reached the point of taking extreme measures.

... We now talk of Stalin's reign of terror in 1937 but today things are harder than in 1937. The mass media can vilify you in any way they please but they give you no chance to reply. I wrote an open letter to my constituency after the tragedy but we had to distribute it as we did in the last war over the enemy-occupied territories: dropping leaflets from aircraft. Where the military authorities attempted to paste them to the walls the local police immediately tore them off...

In a recent slanderous and provocative article in the Georgian youth paper, the responsibility for the events is attributed to the top political and military leadership of the country. I believe, on the contrary, that it was itself the target of this provocation... (Prolonged applause).

The membership of the proposed commission prepared by the Presidium was then announced. The majority of its 13 members came from public organisations

in Moscow (8), and this provoked demands from Georgian and Baltic deputies
for more representatives of other nationalities, such as Lauristin, Tolpezhnikov
and the Belorussian Ignatovich. Shengelaya particularly requested that Polit-
buro member Alexander Yakovlev head the commission: "he was in Tbilisi a
little while back, in February when things were also difficult and tense, and his
speech on television was approved by all the official and unofficial organisa-
tions".

Ales Adamovich, Belorussian writer, director, Cinematographic Art Institute, Moscow (USSR Union of Film Workers)

The speech of the Comrade General would have appeared convincing to me if there had not been the events in Minsk [Kuropati demonstration, see Chapter 5] where no such slogans had been heard, no calls for secession of Belorussia from the USSR, but gases were nevertheless still used and then followed with big lies... We see here how easy it is to succumb to emotions. The Georgian deputy spoke and we applauded, the general then spoke and the applause was even louder... The commission on Tbilisi must be absolutely disinterested, absolutely objective...

Nikolai Petrushenko, Lieutenant-Colonel, Agitprop Instructor of the Political Section, Army unit, (territorial deputy, Kazakhstan)

...As a career officer, I see from the speeches and publications by General Rodionov, under whose command I have served, that the tragic events have been exploited to sow discord between the army and the public. We do not like carrying out police functions. But neither do we, the military, want to be reproached about being too late to prevent such tragedies... The Tbilisi commission must include army officers since such is the dialectics of democracy, unfortunately. I nominate also deputy Miroshnik who is the Chairman of the State Security Committee of Kazakhstan... An experienced eye is needed to penetrate the secrets of the forces that have planned this provocation which, I feel, had far-reaching goals...

WHO TOOK DECISIONS AND BEARS THE RESPONSIBILITY

Djumber Patiashvili, former 1st Secretary of the Central Committee of the Georgian Communist Party, (territorial deputy, Georgia) 152

I shall tell all the available truth on the Tbilisi tragedy... Attempts have been made to misinform the investigators... Everybody tries to avoid responsibility but I do not, and will not. I was accused of making a mistake in charging General Rodionov with the overall supervision of the operation... But it was done only after Rodionov with the First Deputy Defence Minister, General Kochetov visited me and informed me that Rodionov was in charge... 20 minutes before that the Minister of Defence, Yazov telephoned to tell me they were coming... The Bureau of the Central Committee passed the resolution to clear the square in front of the Government House and Rodionov was put in charge of the operation...

Unfortunately, there are no minutes of this meeting... When the investigators ask us why there is no documentation we have to answer that nobody thought of it at the time... Notes made by the army general who acts as the secretary of the Defence Council have assurances that no casualties are envisaged since the troops carry only shields and clubs... Half an hour before the beginning of the operation the commander reported to me and I suggested putting it off because I had information that a great number of people were in the square. The commander assured me that he saw no complications... Unfortunately, instead of dispersing the rally the troops surrounded the crowd and brutally assaulted them... Though their task was only to clear the square, they pursued and beat people a long distance from it. Some demonstrators were killed or injured at distances of up to a kilometre away from the square... Over 3000 people were poisoned. When I received the report of the first two deaths at 5 a.m. I submitted my resignation... I did not know at the moment about the troops using spades and gases, otherwise I would not have resigned but would have accepted all responsibility... The military admitted using spades only on the third day. It was only after Soviet and foreign experts gave their evidence that the military, at the end of April, confirmed the use of gases... [The speaker is often interrupted by cries and noise in the hall]. Our rally was the same as the rallies that happen here and elsewhere. Therefore,...

I admit my responsibility, I will be punished, but the point is that... I do not accuse anybody, I just say that the operation was carried out in a wrong way, that the information was wrong... I also have a question to ask. Who ordered the use of spades and gases? Who determined the extent of violence towards the public...? [Commotion in the hall, cries].

Mikhail Gorbachev

We must not simplify this issue... This is a profound political problem that involves the very basic principles of our society... The prosecutor's office is carrying out an investigation. The local investigation commissions produced some material... The available information is still highly controversial... We must get to the roots of the matter in the interests of the entire country and the Georgian nation. At this moment we cannot raise doubts about this or that piece of evidence. We must find the truth whatever and whoever is involved...

In November of the last year the situation in Georgia was also very tense... I love this nation and, I hope, they respect me. When I was informed then that the Georgian authorities had started sending telegrams to Moscow asking for the imposition of a curfew I directly asked Comrade Shevardnadze to convey verbally my words to the Georgian intellectuals and public asking them to resolve this problem. I realized that if we embarked on such actions in Georgia it would insult the nation who then would never agree to it... By 4 a.m. (the same timing, you understand) the problem was resolved... So the tendency to discuss, to make contacts, to maintain order was there as early as November last year. This is why I say, we must take stock of things. The question is how can we maintain a dialogue in this country, how can we protect and preserve the democracy to which we have aspired for decades...

The following day the new composition of the commission was announced, now including 6 representatives of non-Slavic republics and 2 military men. However, the proposed chairman Nurlustan Nazarbaev, soon to be 1st party secretary of Kazakhstan, immediately provoked demands for his resignation by saying that the video film of the events presented little additional factual evidence. Eventually Roy Medvedev was chosen to chair the commission.

A Lithuanian deputy dramatically announced that he would not participate further in the Congress as long as Rodionov remained in the hall, and walked out.

Taras Shamba, party committee secretary, Central Committee Academy of Social Sciences, Moscow (national deputy, Abkhazia)

I have been asking for a chance to speak for more than 5 days now. ...

The events we are discussing are linked with the Abkhazian issue. Therefore I ask, and insist, that a speaker from Abkhazia be allowed to clarify how much the Abkhazian people are "to blame" for what happened.

Anatoly Lukyanov 154

...Several speakers suggested the responsibility of the highest authorities in this country for the Georgian events... I shall read to you some documents that will give you an objective picture of the events of those days... Mikhail Gorbachev has already told you about the trouble in Georgia in November 1988 when the Georgian authorities asked for the imposition of a curfew in Tbilisi. After Gorbachev's address and a night of talks the tension was relaxed. Here are three recent telegrams. First telegram dated 7 April, time 8.20 p.m., states that owing to the Abkhazian calls for secession from Georgia the extremist forces in Georgia are whipping up nationalist sentiment, calling for strikes and civil disobedience, and discrediting the party and government bodies. Extraordinary measures must be taken. Criminal proceedings must be started against anti-Soviet agitators. A curfew must be imposed in Tbilisi and additional special police forces and regular army troops brought into the city. Political and administrative measures must be taken to stabilize the situation. The mass media must be prevented from publishing any reports that make the situation more complicated. Signed by the First Secretary of the Georgian Communist Party Central Committee, Patiashvili. This is the original telegram [The speaker waves some official-looking paper].

Next day, 8 April, time 8.50 p.m. Six hours are left before the tragedy starts. "Situation in Tbilisi remains tense. Many thousands taking part in the rally outside the Government House calling for Georgia's secession from the USSR, etc...

"Three thousand Georgians in Abkhazia held a rally protesting against the suggested secession of Abkhazia from Georgia. Some university students started a hunger strike in support of the demonstrators. On the whole, the republican and local party and administrative bodies have the situation under control and are carrying out measures to stabilize the situation... Workers' voluntary public-order squads comprising 4685 members have been set up in Tbilisi for maintenance of discipline and order. Special plans have been worked out in coordination with the police and military authorities to maintain law and order and forestall unlawful activities. No additional measures by the USSR government and Central Committee are required at present". Signed: Patiashvili.

The last telegram. 9 April, time 10.25 a.m. "Despite all the measures taken by the party and administrative bodies and the law-enforcement agencies the rally outside the Government House started getting out of control on the night of 8 April ... Apart from the anti-Russian, anti-Soviet and anti-Socialist slogans, extremists called for physical assaults on communists, top officials and the members of their families. Demonstrators who included many under the influence of drugs and alcohol called the entire population of the republic to strikes and civil disobedience... Messengers were sent by extremists to outlying districts of Georgia. An attempt was made to occupy the metallurgical plant in the town of Rustavi. The leaders of the so-called national-liberation movement announced plans for seizing power in the republic.

"Under the circumstances a decision was taken to use force for clearing the square... Top party and government officials, as well as the Patriarch of Georgia Ilia II, repeatedly appealed to the demonstrators to leave the square peacefully.... But the organizers of the rally called on the participants to sacrifice their blood and lives resisting the forces of law and order ... Police and troops did not employ any weapons. The rule on the careful treatment of women and minors was strictly adhered to. Owing to the fierce resistance of extremists who used stones and sticks the crowd became unmanageable as the first lines of demonstrators were pushed back... Many provocateurs in the crowd used steel weapons. In the resulting stampede 16 persons were killed - 13 young women and 3 young men... The wounded were given emergency medical treatment... The square has been cleared of demonstrators and is now guarded by troops. Measures are being taken to arrest the instigators of the disorders and to prevent further rallies and demonstrations... To prevent mass rioting we ask for permission to introduce a curfew in Tbilisi starting today". Signed: Patiashvili. I do not want to add any comments to it. We knew how the Georgian nation might respond to that...

Mikhail Gorbachev

We were right to set up the investigative commission... Everything should be carefully analysed... We see that the situation there was critical, it was not a folk festival as some people here have tried to picture it. Or, perhaps, everything is wrong? Here are the telegrams. We were right to show them here to prevent people from thinking that there is something sinister in all this. No, we really intend to get to the roots of these events. We shall make everything clear and report to the Supreme Soviet and then formulate the decisions. This is a correct attitude, in my opinion.

THE ABKHAZIAN ROLE IN EVENTS

Vladislav Ardzinba, Director, Abkhazian Institute of Language, Literature and History, Sukhumi (national deputy, Abkhazia) 155

I cannot agree with the statements made by some deputies at this congress that the universal problems of the USSR have priority over purely regional problems and that the latter can wait.

None of the problems faced by the whole country can be solved without taking into consideration the problems and interests of all the regions. I stress this point since here we have heard only a few speeches concerning small nations or, to be more exact, nations that have numerically small populations. Deputies have spoken mainly about the Union Republics, the expansion of their rights and the restructuring of their relations with the central authorities in Moscow. The suggested concept allowing the widest possible independence of the Union Republics, the principle of "strong Republics", gives cause for concern to all those nations that have failed to be listed among the 15 "strong ones", and there are representatives of 65 nations here. The total number of nations in this country is much larger still [the latest official figure is 127 and many believe it an underestimate]. Some of them have some form of national statehood while others even lack any form of cultural autonomy. In addition, numerous problems arise for the ethnic groups that reside outside their national territories. If relations between nations in the USSR are not restructured to cover the entire spectrum of issues then serious difficulties and dangerous ethnic conflicts will be unavoidable. The present Constitution gives an autonomous republic a status that leads to a practical inequality of nations in legal and other spheres. The classification of nations by seniority is a direct product of Stalinism and the Stalinist command system and gives rise to a unitarian approach to nations that particularly badly affects the autonomous state units. A suitable illustration is the statehood of the Abkhazian nation and its history.

Soviet rule was established in Abkhazia on 4 March 1921 when the Soviet Socialist Republic of Abkhazia was set up. In December 1921 under pressure from Stalin Abkhazia had to sign a pact of union with the Georgian Soviet Socialist Republic and the pact remained in force until 1931. Legally this union meant a federation of two sovereign republics enjoying equal rights... But in reality it marked the beginning of the erosion of Abkhazian sovereignty.

In 1931 Abkhazia was transformed into an Autonomous Republic within the Georgian Union Republic. Abkhazia is, apparently, the only republic in the USSR whose status was scaled down, rather than up, according to Stalin's wishes.

... Between 1937 and 1953 the very existence of the Abkhazian nation was in question. This is shown by the systematic persecution of the Abkhazian nation which lost its elite: all prominent party and state leaders and practically all its intellectuals. Numerous peasants were arrested. After 1940 the term "Abkhazian nation" was no longer used. Broadcasting in Abkhazian was discontinued in 1941. Abkhazian-language schools were closed in 1945-46 and the Abkhazian teachers lost their jobs. Practically no Abkhazians were left in the senior Party and administrative positions. Families of Greek, Turkish and other origins were deported from Abkhazia [to Siberia] and their houses were given to settlers from inner Georgia. The settlers were brought against their will in great numbers and at great expense to the government even in the difficult war years of 1941-42 [the invading German army was then within a day's march of Abkhazia, the official justification for the mass deportations of "unfriendly locals"]. As a result, the Abkhazians became a minority in the ancient land of their ancestors. [Georgians often question the Abkhazians claim to their "ancient" homeland showing some evidence that Abkhazians were relatively recent newcomers to the disputed area of the Black Sea coast.] Even the ancient names of the Abkhazian villages were forbidden and in 1948-1951 the total of 147 villages were renamed in a suitable [Georgian] style. When Eduard Shevardnadze was First Secretary of the Georgian Communist party he admitted that "the policy towards the Abkhazian nation in this period was ... chauvinistic. It was against the interests of both Georgian and Abkhazian nations and contradicted the Leninist friendship of Soviet nations".

But official criticism of Stalinism did not lead to an elimination of its heritage which is still felt. Representatives of all classes of the Abkhazian nation (workers, intellectuals and peasants) sent numerous petitions to Moscow in 1947, 1957, 1967, 1978, and 1988 complaining about serious distortions in the policy [of the Georgian authorities] towards the Abkhazian people.

Some improvements were made after such petitions but later the reasons for complaints sprang up again.

In late 1988 this situation deteriorated when calls for the liquidation of even limited Abkhazian autonomy were made at unofficial rallies in Tbilisi. A programme issued by an unofficial Georgian society claims that "the rule of the separatists and the violence of the Abkhazians towards other nations in the Abkhazian Republic was discontinued in 1936-1954". These Georgian "democrats" thus admit that for them the best years were when the Abkhazian nation was being exterminated. Envoys of these "democrats" frequent Abkhazia fuelling anti-Abkhazian feelings among the local Georgian population and organizing rallies and parades.

Not only Abkhazians but other citizens of Georgia were also alarmed about the suggestion that Georgian be used as the only official language in the republic, compulsory for all its citizens... This was yet another reminder of the brutal suppression of Abkhazian rights in the recent past...

On 18 March 1989 an officially sanctioned mass rally was held in a field near Lykhny village where Abkhazians from time immemorial have traditionally decided their historical problems. The rally approved a petition addressed to the heads of the USSR Communist Party and Government and other Moscow authorities. About 32,000 Abkhazians signed it, including a number of senior local Party and administrative officials and the deputies of the Soviets at all levels. The petition was also signed by more than 5000 Russians, Armenians, Georgians, Greeks and people of other ethnic origins. It asked for the restoration of the Soviet Socialist Republic of Abkhazia [for its independence from Georgia], the status Abkhazia had in 1921 when Lenin was alive.

Despite assertions to the contrary this does not mean secession [from Georgia]. It restores the union between Abkhazia and Georgia that, under the pact of 1921, allows Abkhazia to determine its future independently if the other republic in the union [Georgia] decides to secede from the USSR: the Abkhazian nation believes that the only way to preserve its national identity is to stay in the USSR (applause). Such a pact could serve as a model for regulating the relations of other autonomous units within the Union Republics.

Claims by the Georgian Supreme Soviet that this petition is in conflict with the decisions of the 27th Congress and the 19th Conference of the Communist Party are absolutely invalid. It seems that the Abkhazian nation has no right to its own opinion and the authorities of [Georgia] have decided the future of the Abkhazian autonomous status long before the Plenum of the Central Committee of the CPSU. The campaign [against Abkhazian demands] was stimulated by the official [Georgian] attitude and the [Georgian] press keeps it up even in the days of this Congress.

Georgian intellectuals who met the [Moscow] officials after the April tragedy in Tbilisi tried to represent the Lykhny petition as the cause of those events. Their causes and goals were quite different. We deplore the tragedy, deeply sympathize with the victims and ask for a comprehensive investigation and punishment for the guilty.

On 26 May 1988 celebrations were held in Abkhazia to mark the 70th anniversary of the restoration of the Georgian state [after the collapse of the Russian empire in 1917 Georgia was an independent state with a highly unstable mainly Socialist government until 1921 when the Red Army led by the Bolsheviks overran it]. Historians will pass their judgements on this event. For the Abkhazian nation, however, it was this Georgian state that drowned the Abkhazian Bolshevik Commune in blood in 1918 and later terrorized Abkhazian villages. Numerous messages we receive these days show that the situation in Abkhazia is very alarming. If nothing is done urgently irreparable damage might be done.

The Abkhazian deputies addressed the Central Committee and the Council of Ministers on 25 May but received no reply, unfortunately. We urgently suggest that a special commission of deputies be set up to analyse the national problems in Abkhazia... The extremist forces are presently concentrating their efforts on Abkhazia to stir up conflict and then to blame our nation for it later. It will not be hard to accuse us of being responsible for any conflict since the mass media give only biased information while the Abkhazian representatives lack the right to make their views known... A decision to establish such a commission will restore some calm in people's hearts and a belief in the ultimate victory of justice.

THE LOCAL OFFICIAL VIEW

Givi Gumbaridze, 1st Secretary of the Georgian Communist Party Central Committee, (national deputy, Georgia) 161

... Though we have strong personal feelings about the Tbilisi tragedy we must overcome our emotions and analyse the events in a broad political context since they concern not just the authority of our state but the prestige of perestroika as a whole. We have boldly revealed the rotten foundations of the authoritarian regime: this is precisely why we must build our new political model on the finest humanitarian and moral principles on which Lenin's theoretical concepts were based.

It would be wrong and, at least, politically naive to describe the rallies and parades in Tbilisi in April as "folk festivals". It was a political action and the demonstrators attempted largely to link it to the question of national self-determination. It would also be wrong to state that no extremist slogans and calls were heard there.

But all this cannot justify the bloody tragedy of that night. One can easily charge a seventy-year old woman or a ten-year old boy with extremism and we have seen what such charges can lead to. It is also an irresponsible attitude to charge an entire nation with anti-Russian feelings. Such feelings or Russophobia [a term currently popular with Russian nationalists] do not exist and never existed in Georgia. We know that the Russian nation, Russian intellectuals, as well as all fraternal nations grieve with us over the Tbilisi tragedy. One must not confuse a revolt against bureaucratic rule and the anti-Russian attitudes.

...We are sure that the investigating commission will reveal the truth and that those responsible, whatever their positions, will be punished...

Public order is the concern of society. For extreme cases we have police and special public-order forces. Deployment of paratroopers for this kind of civil operation is hard to explain, let alone justify, though some people are trying to do it.... Even the introduction of the curfew, announced 4 minutes before it became effective, produced serious consequences.

It has been said here that the army must not be used against the people. In my opinion, we must take care of our army and not encumber it with the political problems we failed to resolve...

One would think that General Rodionov who referred to the tragedy as the "Tbilisi provocation" would be prompted by simple ethical considerations to find in his vocabulary some words of sympathy to the victims... [applause]. There can be various opinions about his speech. But how can one justify the brutality, the unnecessary eagerness? Were they the reasons for the subsequent lack of honesty and even disinformation? How can one justify one's action with quotations from the official paper reports of the period when the military rule was imposed and the distorted information was fed even to the higher authorities?... The use of sapper's spades and poison gases at first was stubbornly denied even before two Politburo members who came to Tbilisi to investigate. Perhaps, it is not common knowledge but I must say that it was only their determination and the integrity of Mikhail Gorbachev that made it possible to reach the truth...

When the principles announced by perestroika remain mere declarations, the public initiative brought to life by them gives rise to open protests if it is not given a natural outlet. Consolidation, reasonable compromises and integration of all potentialities of the society are the only means for avoiding unnecessary intellectual and physical losses as we carry out our revolutionary reforms...

Perestroika has broadened the framework and opportunities for expressions of national sentiment and attitudes and we must get rid of the dated ideological stereotypes in this sphere... The simplest approach to such events as those in Tbilisi is to explain them away as a surge of nationalist sentiment. But are they not, to a certain extent, a result of the well-known deformations of the Socialist principles, and particularly of the federal principles stipulated by the Constitution? The thousand-year-old traditions and concepts of Georgian statehood were being eroded ...

We must make an objective appraisal of our history, particularly of the recent years, without making political issues of historical research and controversies.

POSTSCRIPT: ELECTIONS IN THE SUPREME SOVIET

The new speaker of the Chamber of the Union proposed a Georgian as one of his deputies. However, the latter's frankness about his own political views, though welcomed by many members of the Chamber, led to his not being elected.

Nodar Mgaloblishvili, architect, president of Georgian architects union, Tbilisi (USSR union of architects) 162

Perhaps I shall say a few words first ... because it's important for other members to know where the person they're electing stands. ...

About the Congress. ... First, I'm very discouraged when the well thought out and thoroughly prepared proposals of our Baltic colleagues are met with uncultured barracking ... by a certain section of the Congress. (Applause)

Second, I feel ashamed when two of the most outstanding people in our country, and in the whole world, are rudely ... abused: Gorbachev and Sakharov ... (Applause)

Finally, third, I was simply frightened when that same part of the Congress almost gave Rodionov an ovation after he'd talked about the supposed presence of anti-Russian slogans for which women and young girls were cruelly killed. ...

Victor Kulikov, Marshal, inspector-general, Ministry of Defence, Moscow (War and Labour veterans organisation) 162

Did he himself see what happened in Tbilisi then? ... Why do you already talk of some intentional action, thereby putting others in an awkward position and whipping up emotion? I shall vote against you.

From benches

I have just returned from the Ferghana valley and have an urgent question to ask. ... In the final years of the war the Meskhetian Turks were treated barbarously: without any formalities they were expelled from Georgia [to Central Asia]. Now those of them living in the Ferghana valley have suffered a second tragedy ... What do you think: can this nation which was illegally exiled from their own country (where they had lived for thousands of years) resettle again in Georgia? ...

Mgaloblishvili

This is a very complicated question. ... Everything should be settled justly. ... As I understand it, those Turks who want to live where they used to live should be able to do so. But it's very difficult to fix any timetable for this. These Turks migrated there in one century, then they left ... I think such an issue should be settled in the same way as for the Crimean Tatars, the Germans and so on.

Sergei Akhromeev, adviser to chairman of Supreme Soviet Presidium (i.e. Gorbachev), Moscow (territorial deputy, Moldavia)

It really is good that this candidate has frankly stated his position. I shall vote for this candidate since you have proposed him, Comrade Primakov. ... But he should be more tolerant of the views of other deputies ...

Mgaloblishvili received 128 votes in his favour, and 116 against. Since this was less than 50% of the full membership of the Chamber he was not elected. The post was later filled by a Moldavian.

ARMENIA AND AZERBAIJAN: THE KARABAKH ISSUE

Throughout the Congress the issue of Nagorno-Karabakh was repeatedly raised by Armenian deputies. Replies from the Azerbaijanians inevitably followed; and they even took opposite sides, for instance, in discussing the candidature of Evdokia Gaer in the Chamber of Nationalities.

The official figures for casualties in the Sumgait events of February 1988 were more than 30 killed and hundreds injured though Armenians give much higher figures. After this the escalation of violence could not be stopped though the government established military rule throughout the region.

Another belated measure was to put Karabakh under the direct rule of the Moscow authorities. The head of the Direct (or 'Special') Rule Committee, Arkady Volsky, an important Central Committee official, claimed that all the ethnic trouble in the region was fuelled by organized crime networks that were afraid of their future under perestroika and therefore tried to subvert it. In his estimate organized crime had yearly earnings in Azerbaijan of around 10,000 million roubles while in Armenia they were even higher. At the same time the leaders of the peaceful Karabakh movement in Armenia were arrested and brought to a Moscow prison. This simplistic approach failed to resolve the situation. Armenians fearing for their lives fled from Azerbaijan and the number of refugees on both sides quickly reached the 100,000 mark. Mass strikes and rallies grew into everyday reality and sporadic violence has taken its toll. In the aftermath of the terrible Armenian earthquake at the end of 1988, in which over 25,000 people died and hundreds of thousands were made homeless, there was a chance that the long-standing enmity would be, at least, softened as a wave of sympathy towards Armenia swept throughout all the Soviet nations as well as the entire world community. Unfortunately, the Party and government officials in Moscow, Armenia and Azerbaijan and the mass media under their control bungled this opportunity. After a lull the conflict raged once again.

Sporadic strikes, mass rallies and ethnic violence are the order of the day. The road links to Karabakh are in effect cut off and deliveries of essential supplies are made in convoys heavily guarded by regular army troops. Despite regular patrolling by special forces violent clashes between Azerbaijanians and Armenians, often involving the use of firearms, are reported almost daily from Karabakh.

Much time was taken up at the Congress in clarifying who exactly had proposed the two candidates from the autonomous region, an Armenian and an Azerbaijanian, to the Chamber of Nationalities. Two deputies from Leningrad even offered to surrender their seats in the other Chamber so as to allow two more representatives from the region to be chosen, restoring the ethnic balance. In the end deputies voted again, this time with three candidates for the two seats.

THE PRESIDIUM SPEAKS

Piusta Azizbekova, director, Azerbaijanian History Museum, Baku (national deputy, Azerbaijan) 154

...Each of the union republics comprising the USSR has its own peculiarities which are reflected in its economy, social conditions, and culture. Clearly, the republics must not copy each other in developing their political institutions or economic models... But we do need comprehensive legislation to coordinate the interests of the USSR and those of the union republics...

Frequent calls are heard now for what will essentially mean disintegration of the constitutional foundation of our multinational state. But all those who make such calls represent the interests of narrow groups, rather than those of the entire nation. Our descendants will not forgive us if we allow a deterioration of the links between the Union and the republics, and between the republics themselves that will result in weakening of the Union and the republics, and national self-isolation...

Recently we have seen grievous events caused by nationalist outrages in various regions of our country including Transcaucasia... Unjustified demands for the absorption of Karabakh by Armenia destabilized the region and produced ethnic conflicts. The traditional economic links and friendship ties have been broken. The tragic events will shape the destinies of an entire generation... About 300,000 in Azerbaijan and Armenia lost their homes. Now 50,000 Armenian refugees have returned to their homes in Azerbaijan and we are happy about that. We would like the 165,000 Azerbaijanian refugees from Armenia to return to their homes, too. Refugees present a terrible problem and it is not just our regional problem. The non-indigenous population of any republic where ethnic conflicts are brewing may become refugees. We urgently need special legislation for refugees, to restore justice and protect their human and property rights...

Despite all complications and obstactles, the Karabakh problem can be resolved. Direct rule in Karabakh is contributing to stabilization and helps to find compromises for overcoming the ethnic disagreements and tensions. The Direct Rule Committee has done much in that respect. Yet its activities are efficiently hindered by forces that openly oppose perestroika: they organize strikes and obstruct the implementation of the decisions taken by the Moscow authorities. Though the country faces a critical economic and financial situation 500 million roubles were allocated for the economic and social development of Karabakh. For unclear reasons, however, this aid has been, in effect, rejected. What is lacking is goodwill and a sincere desire to cooperate in normalization of the conditions in the region...

The nations of Transcaucasia in the past lived through tragic events provoked by obsessed nationalists. In such periods leaders emerged who succeeded in bringing peace to the nations that can live in friendship for ages. I am proud to say that one of them was my grandfather Meshadi Azizbekov [a prominent Communist, one of the 25 Baku commissars executed by the nationalist Socialist government in Baku in 1918]. To continue this tradition, I call all those who have forgotten about the ancient brotherhood of our nations to make peace. It would be naive to think that the conflict will resolve itself. Careful hard work by the healthy patriotic forces of both nations, political guidance by the party organizations, and combined efforts of people's deputies will be able to do that, despite the blackmail by the forces opposing perestroika...

Victor Ambartsumyan President of Armenian Academy of Sciences (national deputy, Armenia)

...Esteemed Deputy Azizbekova painted a picture of the Armenian-Azerbaijanian

friendship in her speech. This friendship has, indeed, a long history but she forgot to indicate how this friendship can accomodate the Sumgait events... Every day for the last year and a half we have heard disturbing news from Karabakh. For many decades since it was illegally and forcibly separated from Armenia in the 1920s the people there have been oppressed ... The situation in Karabakh can be finally normalized only if the Karabakh people are allowed to exercise their right to self-determination. It was Lenin who formulated this principle and experience shows that it is the only viable method for solving such problem2as a wholes in the spirit of perestroika...

We ask the USSR government to bear in mind that not only the USSR as a whole, but individual republics may have interests of their own, both economical and political, and in the sphere of foreign policy... Foreign Minister Molotov stated in the name of the Armenian nation that it relinquished its claim to the Kars district and to the territory where Armenians were subjected to genocide in 1915. As all the world knows, he was lying. He brutally suppressed the interests and feelings of a nation belonging to the Soviet Union. The Armenian nation is for peace. Nobody suggests using force to resolve this problem but we hope that a peaceful solution will be found in future...

THE VIEW FROM ARMENIA

Suren Arutyunyan 1st Secretary, Armenian Communist Party Central Committee, Erevan (territorial deputy, Armenia)

...Any regional problems, if they are not resolved in time, inevitably expand their scope and affect the entire country...For the last year and a half the Karabakh problem has been producing convulsions throughout our republic and the entire Transcaucasia, and the tremors of it are felt throughout the USSR. It provides a tragic illustration of the acute ethnic issues. For decades we repeated Lenin's maxim that all nations in our country were equal. And for decades we steadily cut, to the officially approved size, the live tissue of ethnic relations.

Even now some try to avoid an honest analysis of the problem by replacing it with standard phrases about ancient friendship and brotherhood of nations, trying to reduce the ethnic problems to the conspiracy of extremists and organized crime...

Biased mass media reports aimed at manipulating public opinion, and calls for mutual understanding unsupported by real actions, only make the problem more acute... What we are dealing with are the consequences of the Stalinist anti-democratic attitude to nations. If such consequences are regarded as being sacred, it means justifying the regime that brought severe distortions into socialism. If we rehabilitate individuals who were illegaly persecuted in the past why can't we do the same for entire nations? [applause]

...For decades the Azerbaijanian authorities insulted the national dignity, and ignored the social and cultural needs, of the Armenian popultion of Karabakh... It was an open injustice that led to the crisis in the region... Unfortunately, even now, when it is especially important to calm ethnic enmity and distrust, steps are often taken to set in opposition the interests of Armenians and Azerbaijanians in Karabakh.... We strive for normalization, for dialogue, for constructive approaches but encounter various obstacles in establishing normal links between Armenia and Karabakh. Any economic, social or cultural issues are elevated to the rank of political problems. Armenian officials and intellectuals have difficulties in visiting Karabakh....

In Armenia the Karabakh problem is the concern of the entire nation. Even the recent catastrophic earthquake failed to uproot it from the hearts of the people. The Direct Rule Committee was a compromise prompted by the realities. Unfortunately, the Committee failed to develop an administrative system directly governed from Moscow. The loss of confidence in the Committee led to an increase in tension in Karabakh and, hence, in Armenia. The authority of the Committee must be enhanced, it must be given a real right to administer independently all the vital functions in Karabakh.

The Karabakh problem remains an unhealed wound... This Congress has the right to conduct referendums. I suggest that the Congress exercise this right for Karabakh. Let the population of this autonomous region decide its destiny by its own free will...

The Sumgait tragedy which still awaits proper analysis gave rise to the terrible plight of refugees. At the moment Armenia has accepted 200,000 refugees from Azerbaijan. Tens of thousands of Azerbaijanians fled from Armenia. If you recall that 530,000 people were left homeless after the recent earthquake you will realize the full extent of the problem. Almost a third of the population in Armenia are homeless and many of them have lost their jobs.

Another cause of concern in Armenia is the repeated mass poisonings of industrial workers that occurred in the last few months because the law enforcement agencies and numerous investigation commissions failed to find those responsible for them.

The delays in solving urgent problems disturb the people in the republic, and produce a feeling of social and national vulnerability and a crisis of confidence in the republican leadership....

The heavy confronation between the Armenian and Azerbaijanian nations is a sad fact that cannot be ignored. Our nations will have to live side by side in the future. It is extremely important, therefore, to prevent the crisis from deepening. Both republics and, primarily, their communist parties must make use of all opportunities to overcome animosity and to restore the atmosphere of mutual understanding and trust...

Many difficulties in ethnic relations are due to the lack of relevant legislation and the inconsistencies in the USSR Constitution... The Congress must work out guidelines for modifying the Constituion in accordance with present-day realities, particularly in the field of ethnic relations... The fundamental principle in this sphere, that must protect us from wrong decisions and extremist measures, is the strengthening of the Soviet state as a federation of sovereign republics....

A KARABAKH DEPUTY SPEAKS

Boris Dadamyan Director, Stepanakert Transport Enterprise, Stepana-kert (national deputy, Nagorno-Karabakh, Azerbaijan). [unsuccessful candidate in the Congress re-vote: 726 for, 1382 against] 158

... In 1921, according to Stalin's wishes, the Armenian nation was divided into two parts. The Karabakh district with 95% Armenian population was included in the Azerbaijanian republic with the purpose of "establishing peace between Armenians and Muslims". The division was carried out in such a way that a 5-kilometre corridor separated the two parts so that Karabakh did not have a common boundary with Armenia...

Those who did this knew very well what they wanted to achieve! Was it an error of judgement or the policy of "divide and rule"? The result was continued discrimination against the Armenian population in Karabakh by successive Azerbaijanian governments. Discrimination in the economy, education and culture drove Armenians from Karabakh. The total number of Armenians who have left Karabakh is about 300,000. Only ten per cent of Armenians born in Karabakh in 1970-1979 remain in the district. Any attempts to establish cultural and spiritual links with Armenia were severely punished. They tried to rob Armenians not just of their present but of their past, too. Armenian schools were not allowed to teach Armenian history. Ancient Armenian monuments were destroyed and defiled... They went as far as trying to convince Armenians that they were not Armenians at all but Armenianized Albanians. The aim of this historical and ideological aggression is to prove that Armenians are newcomers and foreigners in this land of Karabakh.

... Karabakh Armenians have before their eyes the tragic destiny of Nakhichevan, an ancient Armenian territory that was given to Azerbaijan in response to Turkish demands in 1921. At present practically no Armenians are left in this autonomous republic which is part of Armenia but governed by Azerbaijan... Over the last six decades the national liberation movement in Karabakh has been ruthlessly suppressed ...

New hopes were brought by perestroika. In February 1988 the Karabakh Soviet addressed the Supreme Soviets of Azerbaijan and Armenia and the USSR Supreme Soviet, asking for reunification of Karabakh with Armenia. It is sad but true that in this country it is typical to select not the very best solutions when complicated problems arise. Another golden rule of the stagnation period is to put the problem aside without trying to resolve it.The same happened with Karabakh. The USSR leadership regarded the Karabakh problem as a dangerous precedent that could impede perestroika... This is why their first response was negative...

The delay in the solution of the problem led to a sharp deterioration of inter-ethnic relations in Karabakh and elsewhere in Transcaucasia. Only many months later was the issue recognized as a real problem caused by the discriminatory, even inhumane, to use Gorbachev's words, attitude towards us by the former Azerbaijanian leadership.

Some tried, and still try, to substitute the economic issues for the political problems of Karabakh. The Karabakh economy is, indeed, in a very poor state... But nothing can be done in the economy without first solving the political problem in the framework of self-determination. It is confirmed by the fact that the 450 million roubles that were allocated by Moscow for Karabakh development projects are held in Baku and we have yet to see them...

Do we still recognize Lenin's principle of the self-determination of nations?... Now, in the late 20th century, the clearly expressed will of the nation for reunification of Karabakh with Armenia, fully valid under international law, is still regarded here as an illegal wish to change the state boundaries, as something antisocial and basically evil....

Must we understand this attitude as a practical rejection by the party of the principle of self-determination?... 85% of those sitting in this Hall are communists. Let us ask ourselves what higher principles demand that the Armenian people of Karabakh must suffer? What kind of self-determination is it when a smaller nation must ask permission from a larger nation? And the larger nation may graciously allow it or haughtily prohibit it. It is high time our Constitution be changed in accordance with Lenin's concept of self-determination!

...I would like to draw your attention to the prevailing practice of selective de-Stalinization. We get rid of the Stalinist heritage in various spheres but retain intact the arbitrary structure of the federal state established by Stalin. The existing status of the autonomous republic or region is, essentially, a semifeudal institution which formalizes the concept of national hierarchy. Under such a structure the very concept of national equality becomes fictional.

...What did Karabakh get instead of self-determination?... The Direct Rule Committee was hailed as a compromise that would stabilize the situation without infringing anybody's interests... all forms of local government and party committees were, in effect, suspended. In fact, direct rule is based on massive military involvement but, unfortunately, it does not prevent the Azerbaijanian leadership from even heavier discrimination against the Armenian population which contributes to worsening of the ethnic conflict. Do we realize that the Azerbaijanian government is trying to achieve a "Cyprus-model" development in Karabakh? The district is split into two communities opposing each other on ethnic grounds. This development must have been predicted long before instead of whipping up fears by talking about "unforeseeable consequences".

...A political analysis of the Sumgait crimes is necessary and important for both Armenians and Azerbaijanians. We do not put responsibility for this outrage on the Azerbaijanian nation and we strongly deplore that the real instigators and organizers of it have still not been found out...

I must pass on the demands of the Armenians from Karabakh to the Congress. 1. To restore immediately local government and party structure. 2. To repeal the decision of 1921 about inclusion of Karabakh in Azerbaijan. 3. To set up a commission of the USSR Supreme Soviet on the reunification of Karabakh with Armenia.

Chapter 4

AUTONOMOUS REPUBLICS, DISPOSSESSED NATIONS AND MINORITY GROUPS

> I'd like to register some degree of protest at the Presidium's disregard of the autonomous republics, regions and districts. We've been debating for 2 days and no one from the autonomous republics has yet spoken.
> *Nikolai Sazonov (Tataria) 153*

> So far 89 deputies have spoken at the Congress: 32 from the union republics, 20 from regions of the Russian Federation, 27 from non-governmental organisations, and from the autonomous republics (we have received complaints that these were very few) 7 deputies, and 2 from autonomous regions.
> *Brazauskas (in chair) 161*

Apart from the 15 union republics, 38 of the estimated 127 different nationalities in the Soviet Union formally have a degree of territorial and cultural autonomy. In the past, some of them advanced up the existing 4-tier system to improve their status. For instance, 5 autonomous republics became union republics before 1941. During the war, however, several nations and ethnic groups were deported en masse, chiefly to Central Asia and Kazakhstan. Some were rehabilitated after Stalin's death but others then became victims of the subsequent immobility in national policy. Only now are these and other long overdue and complex problems beginning to be tackled.

The incongruities are glaring. Some autonomous units have quite as much population, territory and industry as the smaller union republics and yet are clearly inferior in status. Moreover, those nationalities without any form of autonomy included several million Soviet Poles and Germans (and, effectively, the Jewish population).

With the exception of Abkhazia and Nagorno-Karabakh, representatives of these nations only began to make themselves heard in the new Chamber of Nationalities.

93

THE 20 AUTONOMOUS REPUBLICS

> It's time to abandon the Stalinist interpretation of the distinction between au-
> tonomous and union republics. I believe that the overwhelming majority of
> our autonomous republics should become regular union republics ... (Ap-
> plause)
> *Gavriil Popov [Greek in origin, head of Greek association] 162*

> Comrade Bisher, I must say that I'm very dissatisfied with your answer that
> everything depends on whether an autonomous republic is mature enough
> to become a union republic. What does that mean? That you share the Sta-
> linist idea that republics are distinguished by their population or by whether
> they are on the borders or in the middle [of the country]?
> *Tufan Minullin, From benches 163*

*Hitherto the formal criterion of geographical position has probably been the most
important criterion in defining this status: that the right to secession could not
be given to those sharing a border with a foreign country.*

*Historically, the majority of these republics were nations and states enveloped
by the eastward and southward advance of Russia, so that 16 of the autonomous
republics are in the Russian Federation. Five of the most heavily populated are
clustered around the upper Volga and in August 1989 1100 years of Islam was
celebrated there in Kazan and Ufa. Apart from the originally Muslim Tatars
and Bashkir, the Finno-Ugrian Udmurts, Mari and Chuvash were early con-
verted to Orthodox Christianity. In most cases, Russians now form the majority
of these republics' population.*

*Today resentment at their second-class status and progressive assimilation
mirrors that of the 15 republics. It was revealed by the new head of Soviet TV,
that they are allowed only 3 hours daily of local television, compared to the 6
hours of the union-republics.*

*Each autonomous republic had a quota of 11 national seats at the Congress,
thus accounting for over 200 of the Russian Federation delegation, for example.
In the Chamber of Nationalities they were allocated 4 seats each but they lost
out in elections to the Chamber of the Union.*

**Vitaly Vorotnikov, Chairman of Russian Federation Supreme Soviet's
Presidium, member Congress presidium (Communist Party) 149**

When we discussed the list of candidates for the Chamber of the Union
from the Russian Federation with the representatives of the regions and
autonomous republics ... candidates from 4 autonomous republics were
not included: Buryatia, Mari, Tuva and Kalmykia. Our explanation was
that since we were giving much more than 10 seats to Moscow [28], and

since there was a quota of one deputy for 712,000 voters, the candidates from a great many regions and from these 4 republics were excluded. ... We explained that there are only 535,000 voters in Mari, ...the same applies to Buryatia (which even has 660,000 voters), Kalmykia and Tuva.

Tufan Minullin, secretary of USSR union of writers (national deputy, Tataria) 159

Many of our deputies were elected in rural areas. Of course, villagers are more patient than city people. They've quietly tolerated a great deal and will continue to do so. "Anything, so long as there isn't a war".... Thanks to the sensible foreign policy of our state the threat of war does not today loom over us and we can in all seriousness examine our domestic affairs.

During my meetings with voters I talked about the law-governed state. They listened attentively, agreed with me, and in unison demanded that gas be piped to their villages. If I can help to bring gas to a few villages in each district they promised to elect me for a second term.

... They are worried by the moribund state of the Volga, and the construction of an atomic power station on the Kama river. It is being built in the centre of a densely populated industrial area of Tataria. Despite numerous protests by specialists ... construction continues.

... The voters are patiently waiting for this issue to be resolved. Just as they also want the republic to become economically self-sufficient very quickly so they can live on the money they themselves earn.

The nationality issue was also included in the election platforms of deputies from Tataria. The child-like invocation of the "friendship of nations" is today coming up against the real conditions in which the nations of our country live. ... As a result of dogmatic attitudes, and the failure to follow the Leninist national policy, our own policy in this field has been flawed. ... One of the chief reasons, I believe, is that the equality of nations has not been respected.

We all know that only equals can be friends. ...

Why, for example, are 32 national deputies elected from the union republics but only 11 from the autonomous republics? Why does one type of republic have 11 members in the Chamber of Nationalities and another, only 4? ... Even at our Congress the union republics are given special opportunities to speak while we are allotted the role of audience. ...

It is not just a question of prestige. Such inequality .... is chiefly noticeable in the sphere of national culture. A territorial-administrative concept of culture has given some nations privileges. Why does the 7 million Tatar nation not have its own film industry? ... The republic now produces 23,000 million roubles worth of goods. ... Why are the television and radio services of Tataria, Bashkiria, Chuvash and Mari republics all allowed far less broadcasting time than the union republics?

... 120 kms from the capital people cannot watch their local television programmes. Technical and economic explanations are offered but I am forced to see other causes here and look at this fact from a political point of view. And if we turn to publishing; but I don't want to arouse feelings of pity. ...

How do we propose to overcome this demeaning situation? ... I believe it is essential to give equal status to all republics. (Applause)

The destructiveness of the administrative-territorial concept of culture is especially clear for my own nation. Only a quarter of the Tatar nation lives in Tataria. The rest are almost entirely cut off from the region where the mainspring of national culture lies and where the nation's thoughts and views are formed. The natural desire of those living outside the republic to preserve their distinctive culture was earlier regarded almost as rabid nationalism. While our efforts to link them to their culture was seen as an interference in the domestic affairs of a foreign state. ...

As I sit here Moscow's Tatars are constantly appealing to me. There are more than 160,000 of them and they have been asking for several years to have their own cultural centre in Moscow. The city authorities listen to their demands but do nothing. Tatar Muscovites demanded that I mention this at the congress. ...

There is another problem that does not have administrative or territorial limits, and it concerns all nationalities. ... the necessity of knowing one's native tongue. There is no need to prove that we must know Russian as the language of inter-ethnic communication. But how can the two be accommodated?

Inter-ethnic relations are not as strained in our republic as in other regions but that gives us no right to be smug. ... one of my voters asked me just before I left for the Congress, why none of the six deputies elected in our capital Kazan was a Tatar? It was a very difficult question ...

David Kugultinov, chairman of Kalmyk union of writers, Elista (national deputy, Kalmykia) 159

I have talked about my own nation which has been rehabilitated and the Kalmyk republic which has been restored. However, I would here like to talk of other nations that have not yet returned. I left on my seat a folder stuffed with telegrams from Crimean Tatars, Germans from the

Volga republic, Turks who were exiled from the southern borders of Georgia and many nations who appeal to each of us ... that when we talk of the equality and brotherhood of all nations we remember those ... who have not yet been given back their land. Those whom Stalin condemned to long years of grief as second-class nations. ... I want to suggest that we do something now, at this Congress. We must pass a law re-establishing Crimean autonomy, ... restoring the German Volga republic. ...

A few words about Kalmykia. .... Do you remember Pushkin, "Farewell, my kind Kalmyk maid." Do you remember? (Stirring in hall) ...

And today this kind Kalmyk girl with her little child is suffering from AIDS ... [one of two notorious cases of mass infection in a children's hospital through unsterilised needles occurred in the Kalmyk capital Elista.] All our deputies yesterday went to visit the only hospital in the USSR where AIDS victims are being treated and we were amazed by its wretchedness. It's a run-down, second-class hospital ... Of course, I understand, my time's run out. Still when I'm talking about mothers and children suffering from AIDS I feel disconcerted when deputies shout "Time!" (Applause)

Discussions in the Chamber of Nationalities: Nishanov's candidacy

M.M. Safin, collective farm chairman (national deputy, Bashkiria) 159

Frequently we asked for time to speak at the Congress but only one representative of our republic (and there are 4 million living in Bashkiria, for better or worse) spoke there. And now only the Baltic republics are asking questions. You seem to be favouring them somehow ... That's a question to you, I think, Comrade Gorbachev.

Second, a question for Comrade Nishanov. We only have 4 representatives in the Chamber of Nationalities but there are 4 million of us. Union republics have 11 seats. ... What's your position on this question.

Rafik Nishanov, candidate as Speaker of Chamber (Communist Party)

This is a constitutional question ... Probably, if it is being raised, there is a problem and we must sort it out in a calm atmosphere ... Of course, I understand that Bashkiria and Tataria are large republics. There are 3.6 million people in Tataria.

Gorbachev (in chair)

Comrade Ivashko [2nd party secretary] says that there are 52 million in the Ukraine and they also only have 11 seats.

Nishanov

But there are 4 million living in Bashkiria.

Gorbachev

And I shall not say a word about Russia.

Nishanov

There are more than 147 million in the Russian Federation, and in our republic [Uzbekistan] 20 million. …

David Kugultinov (Kalmykia) 163

For me Lithuanians are brothers, we were in Stalin's prisons together for many years. I know what a wonderful, kind-hearted nation the Latvians are. But when we begin deciding who is who autonomous republics come last, even here [Chamber of Nationalities].

Why shouldn't Tataria with around 4 million inhabitants and a budget much larger than many union republics also become a union republic? Why not Bashkiria?

AUTONOMOUS REGIONS, DISPOSSESSED NATIONS AND MINORITY GROUPS

Cultural and administrative autonomy for the ethnic Germans in the USSR would be valuable not only to them but to all of us, too. I have no doubt that the Germans could set us all a model example of such autonomy. [Applause] … Each nation must have a homeland where its historical roots lie. [Applause]
Chingis Aitmatov (Kirgizia) 155

If the rights of autonomous republics are much more limited than those of union republics, then those of autonomous regions and districts are even more vaguely defined.

The dilemma of many nationalities and ethnic groups in the Soviet Union could be defined as the "search for a homeland". Some are still struggling, more than 40 years later, to return the territories from which Stalin ejected them as "traitors" and "collaborators". There is still considerable hostility, for instance, between Chechen who returned from their exile in 1956-8 and the mostly Slavic settlers brought in by Stalin to occupy their villages after deportation in 1945. Other nations then deported by Stalin now face even greater opposition to their return. Neither the local authorities nor the local populations, particularly those who occupied the vacated farms and houses, want them to come back. Even when there is room to spare, as in the inland areas of the Crimea, the local authorities still make trouble for Crimean Tatars who try to buy houses and find jobs there: the Soviet system of obligatory domicile registration with the police makes this harassment very easy.

The Soviet Germans, descendants of those invited to settle in Russia by Catherine the Great, were deported by Stalin to Siberia and Kazakhstan, where they still have to reside. They now demand that their Autonomous republic on the Volga be restored but there seems little chance of that since the local population is firmly opposed (some of them refer to such an eventuality as the "second German invasion", following that of 1941). The government is also reluctant to set up such a republic since it would mean an exodus of the most productive workers from Siberia and Kazakhstan. Even so the exodus started to happen, though on a smaller scale, and not to the Volga but to somewhere on the banks of the Rhine.

One of the most tangible products of perestroika has been a return to the large-scale emigration of the 1970s detente era. Though still a lengthy process, it is now once again possible and, as before, most of the people who want to emigrate, and have the opportunity to do so, are Jews and Soviet Germans. The Germans might benefit from the restoration of some form of autonomy. The position of Jewish people is in no way helped by the existence of Birobijan (the Jewish autonomous region set up in 1934) and their case, though exceptional, exposes some of the problems of the remaining 47 (or 74?) unrepresented nationalities and those who live scattered throughout the country, whether they wish to preserve a cultural identity or simply avoid being labelled as different.

Restricted under the Tsars to living in the Pale of Settlement (roughly present day Belorussia and Ukraine) many Jews moved out of this area after the Revolution and assimilated extensively. After the war official anti-semitism closed Jewish cultural institutions and led to exclusion of Jews from many professions and other forms of persecution. Such rehabilitation as there was, following Stalin's death, did not remove the stigma of this period or restore free cultural activities. The hostility they and the other repressed nations deported by Stalin still feel is not just their imagination. For more than twenty years, the official propaganda against the Crimean Tatars depicted them in books and films as traitors and German lackeys killing Soviet men and women. When the nation was rehabilitated formally no public announcement was made about it. So in the minds of the general public the stigma remains.

Only in the last few months has the Moscow city council given permission for cultural centres for Greeks, Assyrians, Tatars, Jews and Germans (but not yet certain other groups) to be set up. Perhaps this simple fact indicates the obstacles still faced by those without a territorial-administrative base, no matter how unsatisfactory the latter may be.

Pyotr Falk, lieutenant-colonel, Air Force (territorial deputy, Orenburg Region, Russian Federation) 147

I represent a nation of more than 2 million people, the Soviet Germans. The political accusation Stalin made against us in 1941 is now being withdrawn. The question of our nation's political rehabilitation is now being resolved so I want to make only one request to the new President: to make possible the rebirth of a German republic in its national territories in the USSR. (Applause)

Khamzat Fargiev, secondary school teacher, Checheno-Ingush autonomous republic (Territorial deputy, Russian Federation) 150

My voters asked me to request that the autonomy of Ingushetia, illegally abolished in 1934, should be restored. Stalin made his first attempt to abolish Ingush autonomy in 1928.

Voice from hall

Speak to the subject.

Fargiev

I am. My question is not national or territorial in essence. It concerns the creation of a constitutional state. If a nation was illegally repressed it must be given back all its rights. If individuals repressed in 1934 have been rehabilitated then why not rehabilitate the Ingush nation?

At present the views of the Ingush nation on this issue have been expressed in two appeals: one made in October last year, and another in April 1989. The total number of signatures is 60,000, an absolute majority of the Ingush nation.

At the same time I ask the Congress to re-examine the question of fully and legally rehabilitating the Volga Germans, the Crimean Tatars, and the Chechen, Karachaev, Kalmyk and Balkar nations [all the latter are from the North Caucasus, apart from the Kalmyks]. Why? Because no one needs yet another tense situation in this country.

In Checheno-Ingushetia the situation is very complicated because by their actions, the North Ossetian and Checheno-Ingush regional party committees are building up a tense atmosphere.

Evdokia Gaer, research associate, Institute of History, Archaeology and Ethnography, Far-Eastern Branch of the USSR Academy of Sciences, Vladivostok (national deputy, Russian Federation) 161

Perhaps many of the deputies have wondered why this woman was so insistent in getting to this platform [Gaer had earlier occupied the tribune, demanding the right to speak and defending Sakharov after Chervonopisky's remarks]. The reason is that my speech here will bear on the hopes for the success of perestroika of my voters, and among them those of the indigenous nations of the Soviet Far East. Nanai, Ulchi, Orochi, Nivkhi, Udegei — the very names of these nations some of you do not even recognize ...

Nations who, in 70 years of the Soviet state, have never had a chance to talk loudly about their rights, sent me to this Congress to tell of the grievances that have accumulated in all these years...

We are used to talking about our achievements and victories. In my opinion, now is not the time to talk about them... I must talk instead about the problems of our small nations. Public interest in ethnic issues, as it happens, has shifted towards the Transcaucasian region and the Baltic republics. The problems of our small nations who live in the regions traditionally known as the Far East and the North (Northern Siberia) seem negligible in contrast to the massive ethnic conflicts in other areas.

Yes, these small nations cannot hold mass rallies and demonstrations at present. I think they do not need them. But will their faint voice fail to be heard here? The entire country must pay attention to their hard lot, especially as in many instances the question is whether these nation will survive or not. Lists are compiled of endangered animal species or plants but I am talking about endangered nations faced with extinction.

Each nation has an ecological niche of its own, and the life and health of each nation fully depends on the state of the environment. Environmental pollution in the Far East is as bad as in the European part of the USSR. No foreign invasion could have caused so much damage as the invasion of the [Moscow-controlled production-branch] ministries. They determined the export orientation of the Far Eastern economy. As a result, Japan has obtained, what it could only otherwise have obtained by a complete annexation of the Far East: namely, a colony supplying raw materials. The entire Far Eastern population suffers the consequences of this ministerial invasion. But for the indigenous nations the current economic practices lead to terrible tragedies. Take, for instance, the struggle of the Udegei nation to protect the forests in their territory in the Khabarovsk Region. The Forestry Ministry planned wide-ranging logging operations. The Udegei nation has lived in these forests for many centuries. It was only an appeal to the Central Committee that helped to save the forests...

Now the Forestry Ministry has resumed its attacks on the Udegei territories in the Primorsky Region [near the border with China]. I receive letters from Udegei in which they say they will protect their cedar forests and their way of life with firearms if necessary. I hope it will not come to that.

I make an example of the Udegei nation because the Udegei reside at just four sites that are located in four different administrative districts in two separate regions. Meanwhile, their lives depend on various ministries controlling the industries of the Far East. One can imagine how difficult it is for this nation to find the right way to deal with its problems. Other indigenous nations face similar difficulties. The correct historical term for the people who migrated to the Far East since 17th century is "immigrants" but, of course, such problems are significant for them, too.

The entire way of life of the indigenous nations is based on the "taiga" [northern coniferous forest] and the tundra. When the trees are felled and the rivers are polluted, when industrial development leaves no room for trappers, hunters and fishermen, then we cannot call it just economic absurdity. What happens is uncontrolled and brazen destruction of the very foundations of life for these nations. Economic development in the region, over the last decades, completely neglected the lawful rights of the indigenous nations, their specific ethnic and cultural requirements, and their traditional occupations. Their small-scale co-operative enterprises were ordered to amalgamate into large-scale ones or be taken over by the state. These and many other irrational changes were inconsistent with the traditional patterns of life and work for these nations. In the last 20 years numerous small communities were dispersed by the authorities under the pretext of their "inefficiency". About 50 communities of the indigenous nations were destroyed just in the small part of the Amur basin between Khabarovsk and Nikolaevsk.

The indigenous nations were gradually pushed out of the best-paid jobs by the uncontrolled and sometimes subsidised migration of workers in search of easy money from other parts of the USSR. The sphere of traditional occupations is steadily contracting. Though many of the nations in the Far East traditionally made their livelihood by fishing, now only a chosen few of them can get jobs as fishermen. The proportion of trappers and hunters in the indigenous population is decreasing catastrophically. Whaling and sealing are continued only by two or three communities.

At first sight, it seems that the nations of the Far East and North have had a good share of the government's care and attention. Indeed, the USSR and Russian Federation governmental bodies passed dozens of decrees in the last 30 years. All of them started with words about a "further improvement" in social and economic development and promised its acceleration. Most of them, however, were never implemented. Everybody was particularly hopeful about the decree of 1980 which was to be put into practice by more than 40 Moscow ministries. But the Moscow ministries refused to be concerned with the requirements and worries of the far-away ethnic minorities.

The usual promises turned out to be the usual lies for the indigenous nations... Capital investments of 2000 million roubles were made from 1980 onwards, for the development of the territories where these nations live, in the Khabarovsk region, but not a rouble was actually spent for their benefit. The investments were spent for the development of district centres and large-scale industrial project sites where very few people of these nations live. It is no wonder that 57% of the schoolchildren of these nations in the Khabarovsk region attend schools that are unfit for teaching in. Before coming to the Congress I visited many of the Far Eastern communities both with the indigenous and Slav population. I have seen schools where the holes in the wooden walls were plugged with rags... I asked if anything was being done to provide these children with proper schools. The answer was that the next winter they would have to attend the old schools.

The low life expectancy of the indigenous nations has already been noted at the Congress. The figures on the incidence of TB and the infant mortality rate give much food for thought. I am grateful to Klara Hallik, the Estonian deputy, who understands the concerns of the small nations and spoke bitterly about their problems. I belong to one of these nations and I cannot help being even more bitter.

We have, irrevocably, lost much of our national culture. But much can still be saved. First of all, each of the indigenous nations or subgroups of such nations must be allocated certain territories and the exclusive rights to the economic activities there. These will include the hunting grounds, pastures, and inland and coastal waters. Only this will make it possible to stop the assault of the Moscow ministries on what is left of the traditional economies and to preserve at least these remaining elements... In the framework of the suggested reform of the political system it would be reasonable to restore the national administrative units eliminated in the 1930s. Such units as the national territorial district or the national rural Soviet must possess some attributes of national sovereignty and control over all local issues. The elected bodies of such small autonomous units must have wider rights and prerogatives than those of the comparable territorial units. Their decisions concerning various aspects of the national life of the territory of these units, such as languages, culture, economic traditions, must be final and not subject to revision or suspension by the higher administrative bodies. An autonomous unit must be set up in the Amur basin where almost half of the indigenous population of the Southern Far East live. The unit must have the same rights as autonomous regions because the national composition of the population there is varied, the industrial development is considerable, and the environmental problems as well as social and ethnic problems are very acute.

The equality of nations must not be something just written in the Constitution. The equality must be reflected in the rights of the nations. If 10,000 Jews in the Jewish Autonomous Region of Birobijan [located in the Far East region] have their national and political autonomy why can't the 20,000 indigenous citizens of the Khabarovsk region? As an ethnographic researcher, I cannot give a reasonable answer when my fellow countrymen ask that question.

The nations of the Far East and North and the experts who study their problems increasingly agree that a special association of these nations must be set up with support from the government. Such an association would facilitate the political consolidation of these nations, promotion of their rights, and enhancement of their political and social self-awareness.

The Kalmyk deputy David Kugultinov was eminently right when he suggested passing a law on the rights of the Soviet nations. I completely agree with him. When one analyses the ethnic conflicts in various regions of the country one realizes that the main source of ethnic tension is the lack of constitutional provisions for the rights of the nations and the lack of a legal mechanism that would endorse them.

Disputes are raging now in all Soviet republics on the introduction of official languages: Russian or those of the indigenous nations. For us, the small nations of the Far East and North this question does not exist: our languages are dying out. Many nations have practically lost their languages. It goes without saying that when a language disappears a nation disappears. Wherever possible this process must be stopped.

Vladimir Larionov, Director, Institute of Physical and Technical Problems of the North, Yakutian Centre of the Siberian Branch, USSR Academy of Sciences (Communist Party) 153

...The existing national, administrative and territorial structure of the USSR was justified, at a given historical stage, in the construction of the Socialist state. But now, when the priorities are universal human values and the rule of law, questions are raised concerning the status of the national territorial units at various levels. These questions must be clearly answered before the new Constitution is written.

I cannot comprehend why Tataria has a lower level of statehood than Armenia, a country of ancient culture which I deeply respect. Why does Bashkiria with the population of 4 million have a lower status than, say, Estonia. The usual explanation about common borders with foreign countries seems unconvincing. We must lay the foundation for a union of nations possessing equal rights. Our state structure practically ignores such nations as Evens, Nivkhs, Yukagirs, and many others...

The candidates at the first round of elections to this Congress represented only 69, and the elected deputies only 65, of the Soviet Union's nations. This shows how serious the problem is. One may recall that the census of 1926 recorded 194 nations and ethnic groups in the USSR [which then had a smaller territory and population]; later by simple unification they reduced this number to slightly more than 100.

The economic aspects of ethnic relations are of especial importance... The economic rights and duties of the republics must be clearly defined... The development of the North draws special attention. The North faces severe demographic and environmental overloading. Rapid industrial development is accompanied by the irreversible destruction of the environment and damage to protective natural mechanisms.

The mining and logging industries leave dead moon-like landscapes and thousands of square kilometres of flooded, cut-down or burned-out forests. Fish and game are disappearing in Yakutia, reindeer herding is no longer possible. In some instances entire ethnic groups face the threat of extinction. We must work out a humanitarian and theoretically well grounded approach to developing the North which would stop it being regarded as a colony providing raw materials...

Discussion of Nishanov's nomination as the Speaker of the Chamber of Nationalities 159

Unidentified deputy asks Nishanov

How can we distinguish a nation from an ethnic group [according to the standard Soviet classification of nations into four levels]? If the Leninist national policy is successfully carried out can an ethnic group develop to the higher level of a nation within the framework of the Soviet federal structure?

Nishanov

As you know, all these years we have been following Stalin's classification of nations. Now it is being reconsidered by the social scientists and by all of us, too. Our Chamber will also, of course, work on this problem. We must get rid of the old dogmatic approach...

Gaer

[Greets deputies in the Nanai language] What is your attitude to the Geneva Convention on the aboriginal and tribal population signed in 1957? The USSR never signed this convention and hence no policy towards small nations was formulated in our country. When you become the Speaker how will you contribute to the resolution of the problems of the indigenous nations of the Far East and the North? The 1957 Geneva Convention will be reconsidered in June of this year. Will the USSR sign and ratify it?

Nishanov

The concept of this Chamber and its functions stipulated that it would carry out precisely these kinds of activities. The Chamber (if it considers it necessary) will study the 1957 Convention, prepare recommendations and put them before the Supreme Soviet. The Supreme Soviet will analyse them to determine if they are suitable for all nations of the USSR. If necessary this question will be brought to the Congress of People's Deputies.

Secondly, everywhere small nations face problems. In the east, in the west, in the south and in the north. I can't say therefore that I shall concern myself with the matters of the north, otherwise the southerners may say I'm biased. We must do everything for all small nations so that they will be respected and sovereign among the fraternal nations.

Unidentified deputy asks Nishanov

...What do you think about giving powers of veto to the republics, national districts and other national units when problems that concern the vital interests of a given unit are under discussion?

Nishanov

I know from international practice that the veto is used in international organisations comprised of the countries with different social systems, different attitudes to life, different approaches to the resolution of problems. The veto principle was introduced in the UN to prevent the violation of anybody's rights. Until now, we have never failed to reach a mutually agreed decision... So I believe that at present we do not need the right of veto. If somebody has other ideas and is prepared to substantiate them we shall discuss them in this Chamber.

Chapter 5

RUSSIA, MOSCOW AND THE SLAVIC REPUBLICS

> The originality of the historical situation is that the former metropolis, Russia, along with the other republics, itself became a colony of the Centre.
> *Olzhas Suleimeinov (Kazakhstan) 161*

> When we talk of the tragedy of Latvia we must seek for its roots in the tragedy of the Russians, Belorussians and Ukrainians, in the tragedy of the other nations of the Soviet Union. People did not escape from the socially-oppressed territories of Russia and Belorussia, their own sacred homelands, because all was well there ...
> *Janis Peters (Latvia) 155*

The three largest contingents of deputies at the Congress came from the Russian Federation, the Ukraine and Moscow. That the capital had 197 representatives, more even than Uzbekistan and Kazakhstan (not to mention Belorussia), was an immediate source of discontent to many, especially since the Muscovites were far better organised and more vocal than almost anyone else. 'Provincial' Russian deputies were quite as irritated as those from other republics.

The Moscow delegation of 27 elected deputies was vastly boosted by a further 170 deputies from non-governmental organisations, giving it 9% of all the deputies. Its radical spokesmen found allies everywhere, nevertheless, and in the remotest parts of the Russian Federation, an area of such size, population and diversity that regional problems assumed as much importance as that of individual union republics.

In 1988 the Millenium of Russia's official adoption of Christianity was widely celebrated, an unthinkable event until very recently. This was also a commemoration of the East Slavs' (Russians, Ukrainians and Belorussians) common origins and faith. However, the prolonged influence of Western Europe over the western parts of Belorussia and Ukraine, lasting to the late 18th century, means that there are many Roman Catholics in the former and "Greek Catholics" (or Uniates) in the latter republic, forming one focus of national dissent.

The Belorussian and Ukrainian delegations did not form a distinctive bloc at the Congress. In late 1988, however, Belorussia had also experienced the use of troops, gas and police dogs against demonstrators when a large meeting was held at Kuropati, the site of mass executions and burials in the 1930s. This and other events account for the later reference to the Vendée of perestroika, and Ales Adamovich's remarks in the Tbilisi discussion. The most passionately expressed concern of the two delegations was for the environment and nuclear energy, in particular. Yet comments by individual deputies indicated that among stolid and traditionally selected delegations there were highly critical voices, too.

In some cities of the Russian Federation, People's Fronts had also been set up, and the election battle was most intense of all in Leningrad where half of the seats had to be fought a second time.

The clearest expression of national feeling, or resentment, came from the provincially-based 'village prose' Russian writers, Belov from Vologda, and Rasputin from Irkutsk in Siberia. And it was directed against Moscow figures (Medvedev and Evtushenko) as much as other republics. Their attitudes grew from the same sources of complaint and dissatisfaction as the ultra-nationalist Pamyat movement but it would be a mistake to identify their conservative views with the latter's frequent demagogy and anti-semitism. The reasons for such dissatisfaction are clear from other contributions, and both writers have a countrywide respect and reputation that Pamyat (which disrupted rather than participated in the elections) does not have.

The Russian Federation had 902 deputies, Ukraine 262, Moscow 197, and Belorussia 94.

ELECTIONS TO THE CONGRESS

Alla Yaroshinskaya (Zgerskaya), correspondent of *Radyanska Zhitomirshchina* **newspaper, Zhitomir (territorial deputy, Ukraine) 161**

Question to the candidate for USSR Prosecutor General, Alexander Sukharev:

You obviously know of those gross infringements of the electoral law that occurred in Zhitomir. ... After 26 March 48 court proceedings were started against my constituency agents and the activists who helped me campaign. Others were expelled from the Party, and three soldiers, two lieutenant-colonels and a colonel ended up in hospital. ... A commission of four prosecutors came to Zhitomir ... and worked there almost a week. ... a great deal of time has already passed since then, Zhitomir is up in arms, people are indignant about this lawlessness but we have received no clear answer whatsoever from the USSR Public Prosecutor's Office.

Vladimir Kirillov, research worker, polytechnical institute, Voronezh (territorial deputy, Russian Federation) 149

I applauded Yuri Afanasyev but I would like you to note that he did not call for us to divide into factions. It was Gavriil Popov, whom I greatly respect, who made that appeal. The difference is that both Afanasyev and I were elected in proper constituencies and feel the eyes of our voters watching us very attentively. I don't want to offend deputies from public organisations, merely to point out the imperfections of our present electoral system.

THE SUPREME SOVIET: NOMINATIONS OR ELECTIONS?

Moscow

Redzhapbai Allayarov, collective farm chairman (national deputy, Turkmenistan) 147

Certain groups of Moscow and Leningrad deputies and representatives of the fraternal Baltic republics have been given a great many opportunities to speak. Apart from two speakers from the Caucasus, however, neither Central Asia, nor Siberia nor the Far East have yet spoken from this tribune. We've been working for 4 days [including preparatory pre-Congress meetings] and still, one can say, haven't decided anything. ...

... Someone even said that the Moscow delegation is asking for 55 places [in the Chamber of the Union], not 30. Let them choose 30 of these 55 for themselves ...

Gorbachev (in chair) 148/2

[Reads note]
"When will the Moscow group of deputies stop disorganising and confusing the Congress. ... They're holding up the work of the Congress. Perhaps it's quite deliberate?" signed by 4 deputies.

Svyatoslav Fyodorov, director of micro-surgery institute, and chairman of the Soviet Charity and Health Foundation (Communist Party) 148

I have just been listening to a few speeches and it seems to me that we are still in a country broken up into petty principalities, where each "is at war" with another, and therefore wants to elect its own ambassador who would defend the principality interests here in Moscow.

... We must elect the intellect of the nation to the Chamber of the Union ... Therefore the Moscow delegation decided to let the Congress choose the representatives of Moscow from 55 candidates. Choose whom you like. Elect clever people or fools, it's your choice. (Commotion in hall)

Mikhail Gorbachev (in chair)

No comrades. I want to defend the Muscovites. I also belong to the Moscow group.

In the official transcripts Fyodorov's characteristically provocative comments were suitably toned down and the word 'fools' was omitted: "such a transcript inspires little confidence, as far as all the other decisions are concerned," complained Kiselev (151) from Kamchatka. He voiced voters' alarm at such distortion and repeated the demand made earlier by Zolotukhin from Uzbekistan that Fyodorov make a public apology.

Arkady Murashev, research associate, USSR Academy of Sciences (territorial deputy, Moscow) 148

It seems to me that some kind of unhealthy and obviously neurotic atmosphere has developed around the Moscow delegation and its proposals. ...

We make no claims to a single extra seat in the Chamber of the Union. ... Our surplus list is an act of good will ... and confidence in the Congress. Any quota restrictions, after all, and any elections by republic only, are hangovers of distrust towards each other. [1201 voted for, and 948 against, Murashev who was not elected]

Alexei Tkhor, coalmine foreman, Ukraine (trade unions) 148

After looking at the list of candidates for the Supreme Soviet I thought to myself, the whole country is made up of intellectuals, scholars, academicians and professors.

... I know what Moscow means to us. But we shall not give up a single one of our seats! According to the quota, Moscow should possibly not even have 29 seats, but less.

The Moscow delegation had 28 seats in the Chamber of the Union, thus retaining their disproportionately large presence there as well.

Victor Palm, department head, Tartu University (national deputy, Estonia) 149

Whether we like it or not, the group of Moscow deputies have worked carefully and long to come to grips with the actual problems of our society and prepare for the Congress. ... It is perhaps the only real preparation that involved many deputies from different parts of the country. ... Unfortunately there proved to be no other such centre which could have united other deputies.

Belorussia

Vladimir Fomenko, shop manager at textile factory, Mogilev (territorial deputy, Belorussia) 149

The majority of our delegation consider that the quota of seats for Belorussia in the Supreme Soviet means a quota for the proposal of candidatures. I believe these are quite different things and that we can propose more candidates than seats. ... The refusal to let the other deputies stand is, I believe, unjustified and impermissible: the Belorussian delegation is interfering with the prerogatives of the Congress in electing the Supreme Soviet.

Ukraine

Yakov Bezbakh, foreman in steel works, (territiorial deputy, Dnepropetrovsk, Ukraine) 148

I speak for a group of deputies who were elected after 14 May in a third round of elections. We find ourselves at a disadvantage since the selection of candidates for the Supreme Soviet took place without our participation.

Only today did we learn that no choice would be permitted in putting forward candidates from the Ukrainian delegation, which has proposed 52 candidates for 52 seats.

Russian Federation

Alexander Minzhurenko, department head, Omsk teacher training college (territorial deputy, Omsk, Russian Federation) 148

I won't touch on such a delicate issue as the quota for the republics. But quotas for each region in Russia seem unnecessary to me. ... There are 11 in our delegation. It just so happens that out of respect for the regional first secretary [of the party], who is a member of the delegation, 5 or 6 others automatically vote as he does. In this case one individual virtually decides everything. I don't say this as criticism of him but of this kind of system. It turns out, as in former times, that there are no chances of getting into the Supreme Soviet past our first secretary.

In the elections to the Chamber of the Union Moscow offered 55 candidates. As a result, famous but controversial figures like Gavriil Popov, Tatyana Zaslavskaya and others were not elected.

Even more dramatic was the initial exclusion of Boris Yeltsin, the former Moscow party boss, from the Chamber of Nationalities. He came last (1185 for, 964 against) in a list of 12 candidates for the 11 places allotted to the Russian Federation. One of the successful 11 then gave up his seat for Yeltsin. Despite the above protests no names were added to the Ukrainian and Belorussian lists.

Results

Vladimir Zubanov, steel plant party secretary (territorial deputy, Ukraine). 149

The Russian Federation delegation included 4 more candidates [for the Chamber of the Union] than there were seats. We all applauded. But just look what the voting revealed: of the 4 not elected, three were regional party secretaries. That's why we so insistently and stubbornly avoided the principle of choice.

... people now attribute all shortcomings to the work of the Party but .. it's not always so.

Valentin Karasev, department head of Kramatorsk engineering college (territorial deputy, Ukraine) 149

During our election campaign speeches we called for a professional parliament. They must be educated, informed and capable politicians, we said. ... What actually happened? Some examples from the Ukraine.

Of those elected to the Supreme Soviet 35% are manual workers, and 21% high party or state officials. A republic that has an enormous scientific and scholarly potential has provided only 1.5% economists, i.e. deputy Saunin, and not a single legal or political specialist. What kind of professional parliament can we talk about if these proportions are maintained? (Applause)

THE ECONOMY AND POLITICS: OFFICIAL VIEWS

Efrem Sokolov, 1st secretary of Belorussian Party Central Committee (territorial deputy, Belorussia) 151

The suffering of those who live in Belorussia, where 18% of arable land has been contaminated with radioactivity following Chernobyl, has not lessened with time. The USSR government commission was tackling this issue at its first stage but now its efforts are scarcely noticeable. Over 3 years the commission has still not been able to offer a convincing and well planned conception of how people are to live safely, and also assure the health of subsequent generations. ...

The economy will be cured by applying the 3 'D's: democratisation, demonopolisation and decentralisation. ...

In Belorussia we link an improvement in our situation with the rebirth of the Soviets, the transition to territorial self-financing and a tightening of discipline in general, and at work in particular. As territorial self-financing is introduced, of course, regional identities will strengthen and the desire for decentralisation will grow. Therefore when we provide a legal basis for this, using the formula "A strong centre and strong republics" we should precisely define, in my view, ... where the republic has the final word. ...

Relations between republics also need a legal foundation. At the same time, while strengthening the sovereignty and economic independence of the republics we must facilitate in every way a strengthening of the superior sovereignty of the Union. As soon as each republic begins to pull the blanket to its side of the bed the Leninist foundation of the Soviet federation of nations will inevitably begin to break down.

Vitaly Masol, Chairman of Ukrainian Council of Ministers (territorial deputy, Ukraine) 151

We firmly believe that a balanced and efficient development of different territories is only possible within a single economic complex. ... Temporary gains from the introduction of restrictions on inter-regional exchange and cooperation will hardly compensate the purely economic losses, not to speak of the enormous political harm they will do and the growing mutual distrust and uncoupling of our fraternal nations.

... we must make full use of the experience of world economic practice. It's no accident, after all, that the countries of the EEC do not hide themselves away behind their national frontiers. On the contrary, further integration is taking place in the Community and it is moving with increasing confidence towards the introduction of a single currency and the removal of customs barriers.

COMPLAINTS, CONCERNS AND ISSUES

Deputy (unidentified)

I support the comrade who spoke earlier: we must set up a commission on Chernobyl, to study the tragedy that happened there. These secondary issues [Molotov-Ribbentrop pact discussion] can wait. Because this really concerns not only Belorussia, and the Ukraine but Russia as well. 154

Voices of complaint came from both the historic long-settled areas and from Siberia. A graphic description of accumulated problems was given, for example, by a speaker from the Kuzbass, the West Siberian coal-mining and metal-producing region developed only in the Soviet period, from the 1930s onwards.

Vladimir Kazarezov, 1st secretary, Novosibirsk regional party committee (territorial deputy, Novosibirsk, Russian Federation) 153

Our country is in a paradoxical situation. On the one hand, there is excessive centralisation in the management of the economy and, on the other, the centre is helpless when it comes to organising the division of labour and the integration of productive and R & D capacity. ... as far as the degree of coordination and specialisation in industry, especially in engineering, is concerned, we are still at the level of 19th century capitalism using certain indicators.

Knowing that it was futile to expect allocation of much-needed agricultural machinery from the centre ... we decided to organise its production locally in our region. ... "Good lads!" they said in Moscow. "Good"? When the machinery will be several times more expensive and the quality that much lower? ... Yet I know they've done the same in

Sverdlovsk, Voronezh and elsewhere. ...

Like the great majority, I am totally in favour of regional cost-accounting and self-government. I understand what this means at the level of the union republics. But are the regions supposed to insulate themselves in their cocoons also? I think we should think about organising regional units in the administrative system, say, Urals, West Siberia, Far East, the Central regions, etc. And maybe give such regions the same economic rights as union republics. (Applause)

The more rapid development of Siberia's productive forces is an important part of the Party's strategy. But it isn't working chiefly because there is no mechanism for increasing the population of Siberia. Yet if we only remember the late 19th and early 20th centuries, there was a mass, voluntary (not forced) migration to Siberia from Russia, Ukraine, Belorussia and other regions. It was Stolypin, an unjustly neglected Tsarist statesman, who was responsible for the reforms that ensured such migration ...

Siberia does not reach the average republican standards today, so our Siberian specialists consider, in supplies of the most important goods and services: ... the consumer budget must be raised by a minimum of 20-40% in its southern districts and 1-2 times in the north.

Alexander Trudoliubov, collective farm chairman, Smolensk region, Russian Federation (Komsomol) 155

If we don't feed the people there won't be any perestroika. A great many decisions have been taken and the people were promised a long while ago that they would be fed but no decisive changes have taken place.

For us in the central Russian region this is not only an economic but also a political and social issue. The rural community of this region today stands on the edge of the abyss. This isn't a metaphor or an exaggeration and I'm afraid that we may just take that extra step.

Smolensk is only one of 29 regions but its difficulties clearly reflect the problems of the vast area of central Russia (non Black-Earth area) where half the population of the Russian Federation live.

Over the last 14 years three decrees were passed to ensure the more rapid development of our region ... but nothing has changed. This isn't because our peasants are feckless and don't know how to work. Not at all. It's just that, for a long time, other problems were solved at the expense of the central Russian area, among them the industrial development of the cities of Russia with their millions of inhabitants.

Each year 20,000 leave the villages of the Smolensk region alone, and only 10,000 go to towns in the area. The rest go to the Moscow region, Belorussia, the Leningrad region and so on. The educated leave ... and in exchange we get those whom Moscow doesn't need. They're sent here, so to speak, for Chinese [Cultural Revolution] re-education methods, and bring with them their undesirable habits and peculiar ways of life. It's quite dangerous. I now think it's more frightening than environmental pollution. They spoil our peasants, let's put it that way.

The Smolensk region suffered terrible losses during the war but the decision about villages "without a future" [induced or even forcible eviction to new central settlements] brought even more terrible losses. I've always asked who ever thought of suggesting this to the government? (Applause)

Over 20 years more than 2000 villages have disappeared from the face of the earth in the Smolensk region, places with their own history, long inhabited ... And they've gone for good, although, I should add, this is still a historical part of Russia.

... Russians, Tajik, Armenians, Azerbaijanians, Georgians and Ossetians all found their final resting place here during the last war. ... What they didn't surrender to the enemy we are abandoning: the fields are grown over, the villages depopulated, there's no one there.

I also believe that it is essential to stop building factories here for a while. ... I'm not against industry ... but the ministries through Gosplan are still continuing to impose ever new enterprises on us, under various pretexts. There are already 3000 of them in the region and it will take 5 years only to finish building those projects. Yet at current rates of construction, we have calculated, it will take 50 years to build the minimum of necessary roads for our district.

Meanwhile the ministries want to expand all our large factories. 30-40,000 workers will be recruited, again at the expense of the rural community.

Janis Peters (Latvia) 155

Telegram addressed to deputies Janis Peters and Valentin Rasputin:

"Please raise the issue of the Katun hydro-electric power station, the building of which threatens the Altai ethnic group with extinction. ..."

It is terrible to read such a text. Yet even more terrible to realise that aggressive planning is continuing its crusade against various nations.

Iya Egorova, administrator at Altai regional hospital, Barnaul (Women's committees) 160

To this very day, some look on Siberia, Altai included, as a colony or as the private estate of the ministries. Who can tell me why Siberian gas is piped to the European part of the country and to the West but is very little used in Siberia? ... We have been offered gas in the Altai in exchange for supporting the construction of a fertiliser plant in Zarinsk, a town that is already facing difficult ecological conditions because of its chemical industry. I can't help asking why new fertiliser factories should be built when, as we all know, those already in existence are not working at full capacity. We shall not be able to improve social conditions, not only in the Altai but throughout Siberia, when the ministries adopt such attitudes. The time has come to put all resources at the disposal of the local Soviets. Everybody is well aware that today the Soviets do not have sufficient economic capacity to exercise authority in their territory. They are still supplicants of the enterprises located there.

Today enterprises belonging to more than 50 ministries are working in the Altai region and there is a battle with each of them to obtain funding to develop the basic infrastructure of social services there. The centralised disposal of resources has reached such a scale that neither people's deputies nor the public can supervise what's going on. ... A definite percentage of the enterprises' income must be paid into the budget of the local Soviets. Their expenditure thereafter must be made publicly and openly.

Deputies from the Baltic have already mentioned the Katun hydro-electric power station in the Altai region, and so has our respected comrade, Rasputin. However, our dear neighbours from the Gorno-Altai autonomous region have not yet had a chance to speak on this subject, so I am asking the Presidium to give them this opportunity.

Finally, many of my voters ... demanded that the Semipalatinsk nuclear testing ground [in neighbouring Kazakhstan] be closed down. We should not ignore the public opinion and protests of the population in this enormous area. Stop all nuclear explosions in Semipalatinsk! (Applause)

Vladimir Gvozdev, coalmine foreman, South Kuzbass Coal Trust, Mezhdurechensk, Kemerovo region, Russian Federation (Communist Party) 161

Some people have understood democracy in their own way: as freedom to pursue all their own rights and a denial of any, even elementary, obligations. (Applause) I think that certain newspaper articles and television programmes, to a certain extent, have encouraged this.

... frankly speaking, I don't favour the sort of talk that says that we supposedly need other parties, factions and groups or other programmes. ...

We must now take some practical measures. People are already tired of waiting. We must confirm by legislation that the provision of social and health services, housing, recreation etc has priority. ... in practice all this takes second place and working people are justly indignant.

Some examples from the Kuzbass. This is a powerful industrial centre with well-developed coal mines, metallurgy, chemical works and engineering. A fifth of the coal in the country is mined here ...

It occupies 13th place for industrial output in the Russian Federation but comes 43rd as far as housing is concerned, and in 58th place for nurseries and kindergartens.

Environmental problems are critical and water supplies and heating capacity are under severe pressure, especially in the mining settlements and villages. In most of them water is only supplied for a few hours in the day: and it does not reach the upper floors of apartment blocks.

But it's not just the Kuzbass which lives in such conditions — all our rich Siberian and Far Eastern area lives like this. The ministries don't seem to give a damn about the other needs of Siberians. They still give priority allocation of 70% of investment to production. ... We think it's time we stopped coming to Moscow to plead for the necessities of a normal life for the miners and other industrial workers of the Kuzbass and Siberia. We must be given the right, at long last, to resolve these problems locally.

Alexei Yablokov, corresponding member of USSR Academy of Sciences, Moscow (Academy of Sciences' scientific societies and associations) 161

While we support the main theses in Comrade Gorbachev and Ryzhkov's speeches we do not believe that their analysis of ecological problems fully reflected the alarming state of affairs in our country. ... Twenty per cent of the population live in ecological disaster zones while another 35-40% are in ecologically unfavourable conditions. ... Every third man in such areas develops cancer. Infant mortality in certain parts of the country is higher than in many African countries. Average life expectancy is 4-8 years lower than in developed countries. ...

Ecology alongside the economic and inter-ethnic relations has become one of the chief causes for concern in our country. ...

Gennady Bykov, plant foreman (territorial deputy, Leningrad) 160

For many years Leningrad and other major cities have drawn their workforces from the rural areas. People come to us from the small towns of Russia. Part of Leningrad's working class is now made up of immigrants, former *limitchiki* [quota of new, non-resident workers in certain industries] who live in cramped conditions in dormitories and communal flats for years on end. ...

Yet despite the restrictions, the inflow of workers from other cities continues. So I suggest not building any more factories in our big cities, they already have quite enough difficulties. Each city should rely on its own population resources.

UKRAINE AND BELORUSSIA

Boris Oleinik, poet, secretary of Ukrainian republic union of writers, Kiev (Communist Party) 153

As you may have noticed, I am a member of the most unforthcoming and well-behaved republic of all. But I'm not especially shocked by the activity and emotional attitudes of deputies who queue up to speak without being called by the chairman. After all, we're only just learning the ABC of democracy and the elements of parliamentary behaviour. ...

We must take a few specific problems and resolve them before we leave this hall. Otherwise we shall find it difficult to look our voters in the eye.

Above all else, we must find the means to raise the wages and pensions of those who live in poverty or near to it—even if it means halting certain attractive programmes — so that we shall not feel ashamed for our nation. (Applause)

Everything is tied up with the national question. Let us say firmly, ... that many problems can only be untangled by unfaltering support for the idea of federalism by which each republic, and that republic alone, must be the one that corrects the accumulated deformations. The language issue must be solved in such a way that at every level ... the language of the indigenous nation will not be an over-burdened day-labourer but a proud and rightful master in his own home. (Applause)

In a word, I am for the model and idea of the Baltic republics as expressed by the prime minister of Kazakhstan: strong republics, and a strong centre. Naturally in nurturing our national self-awareness (the sacred feeling of love towards the history and customs of our ancestors) we must equally encourage in our ourselves a respect for all nations. For in this interdependent and interconnected world there is nothing more terrible, as [the Ukrainian writer] Oles Gonchar noted, than national isolation.... Of course we have common misfortunes and .. each republic also has its particular problems. In the Ukraine and Belorussia, for instance, parents do not have such a good choice as those in other republics, regarding the language in which their children are taught. Quite simply because in certain towns there's nothing to choose from — there simply are no Ukrainian and Belorussian schools. ... We support making Ukrainian the official language, but have emphasised that the languages of all nationalities living in the republic should be supported.

More recently, however, and not without the help of Central television, the idea of granting Russian the status of official language on equal terms with the national language is being aired. I think that such a step would be an open retreat from the original concept supported by the overwhelming majority of the republic's voters. (Applause) And, did anyone ever ask whether the Russians themselves want that? ...

Is it not a paradox that the Russian people find their national feelings more offended than anyone else. Russia has no Communist Party or Academy of Sciences of its own. Furthermore, it bore the main burdens of the Great Patriotic War [against Nazi Germany, 1941-5], with Ukraine and Belorussia, but is not, unlike the latter two republics, separately represented in the UN. (Applause)

I would ask the government and the Politburo to take notice of those officials on the spot who are furiously opposed to perestroika in inter-ethnic relations, and to set an example by punishing them. To speak plainly they have been persecuting the Shevchenko Ukrainian Language Society [Taras Shevchenko, 19th century national poet of Ukraine].

Environmental problems bear directly on the strengthening of republican sovereignty: the republic must be protected from the onslaughts of the union ministries which irresponsibly and with impunity build nuclear power stations, chemical monsters, and canals wherever they please. Since they lay these "cuckoo's eggs", as a rule, in long-established historical and cultural centres such as Kiev, Chigirin, Kanev, Zaporozhe, Rovno and Khmelnitsky, and plant these mines under the whole republic, not just its national treasures, the struggle against these new industrial invaders is now of the first importance. Mark my words, another one or two Chernobyls and there will be no one to quarrel over language and culture at all. (Applause)

In this often unequal struggle the first victories have already been won. The government decision to stop building the Chigirin nuclear power station was the cause for national rejoicing in the Ukraine. But what about the Crimean station? There is not a single nuclear power station in the world where there is such a terrifying combination of geo-physical dangers (earthquakes up to 10 on the Richter scale, tidal waves, ...) as the site where the Crimean station is being erected.

After the Chernobyl tragedy in Belorussia alone, not to mention the Ukraine, more than 520,000 people have been exposed to radiation. The Chernobyl station still remains an unpredictable source of radioactive contamination. ... we should today take the only reasonable decision and once and for all shut it down. (Applause)

There are now rumours that a plant will be built within the 30-kilometre exclusion zone ... for the burial of toxic by-products. I demand that these rumours be either confirmed or disavowed.

In a word, all government departments and ministries, including the atomic energy commission, should at long last understand that before they install the next reactor they must ask the permission of the nation and government of the relevant sovereign socialist republic.

It was probably Boris Oleinik who first spoke at an official televised Party event of millions of victims of Stalin's policies. He was referring, at the 19th Party Conference in June 1988, to the 1932-3 famine in the Ukraine. (In November 1987 Gorbachev had only referred to "tens of thousands" of victims.)

Zoya Tkacheva, hospital administrator, Slavgorod, Mogilev region (territorial deputy, Belorussia) 155

The official report of the Ministry of Health published in Pravda on 29 May 1989 does not display sufficient concern for the health of those living in areas affected by the Chernobyl disaster, nor for the fate of future generations. It is the first time such an accident has happened and so there is no available experience in health monitoring ...

I think the health experts have not coped with the task they were entrusted with. Wouldn't it be better to turn to our foreign colleagues for help since they have more reliable equipment and greater experience? It's not just the fate of one region that is being decided today, after all: this affects the entire Belorussian nation.

The assessment medical practitioners give of the population's health in the affected districts diverges more and more from that offered by the medical specialists and the country's leading health officials. ... The latter attribute the observable changes in health to other factors — nitrates, poor nutrition, lack of breast-feeding — but not to radiation. These factors, we could tell them, can only intensify the effect of radiation but not account for it.

All of this creates a tense situation in these areas. We believe that people should be resettled, stage by stage, from the affected districts. ... we have offered the people sausage produced elsewhere, personal radioactivity meters and tractors with air-conditioned cabins. They have no use for such offers. They simply ask to be re-settled as soon as possible so they can resume a normal life, and begin working on the land again.

Yaroshinskaya (Ukraine) 155

Our region lies in the zone of high-level radioactive contamination [following Chernobyl]. The Narodich district has now become a zone of high-level silence. For 1 years I have been unable to publish anything anywhere about what is happening there. At first 18 villages were affected; now, three years later, there are 90 villages in the zone of high-level radioactive contamination. ... Four more districts are now affected.

Yet the Ukrainian minister of health Romanenko tells us that we are living in some kind of Swiss health resort. It's simply disgraceful. If you look at the documentary made by Moscow film-makers then you will see what's actually going on there. This affects us all. We know about Tbilisi and other events. But what is happening in the Zhitomir region is very important. ...

In the Supreme Soviet the nominee as chairman of the Soviet atomic energy commission later gave the first ever public acknowledgement and details of the Chelyabinsk nuclear waste disaster which occurred 30 years earlier.

RUSSIAN REACTIONS

Vasily Belov, writer, secretary of Russian Federation union of writers (Communist Party) 153

I would like to begin by saying that I do not understand or appreciate the two or three highly offensive attacks that were made yesterday against the recently elected president [reference to Afanasyev, Vlasov etc]. (Applause) Even the Americans, and they're a very clamorous people, don't demand impeachment on the second day after election

[Adamovich]. They respect their president. (Applause)

And are we really the people's deputies I ask myself? I understand the nobility of Kazannik [who surrendered his seat in the Chamber of Nationalities in favour of Yeltsin]. I also remember the emotional gesture of the two Leningrad deputies who offered to withdraw their candidature in favour of another republic [Nagorno-Karabakh]. If I was a Leningrad voter, however, I wouldn't vote for deputies who abandoned their rights so easily. (Applause) We must follow the will of our voters … and be aware of a hierarchy of values.

Thousands of letters and telegrams precisely and clearly express their instructions, and these dictate my hierarchy of values as a deputy. … First, to improve the electoral system; second, to confirm a widening of local Soviets rights by decentralising authority; third, and most important in my view, … that the right to private ownership of land, with the right of inheritance, be specially set down in our constitution alongside the collective and state farm property. I'm convinced that this can and must be decided at the present Congress.

… a new law about land-use would considerably ease a great many of our economic and ethnic problems. It would facilitate ecological improvements and the linguistic and cultural renaissance of all the nations in our multinational state.

The people, as represented by of their local Soviets, must decide what to do with land and water — not the central ministries. Over the last 20 years the Ministry of Water Resources has spent 150,000 million roubles of the people's money, ruined millions of hectares of the best land, and brought agriculture to the brink of disaster. Together with the dam-builders and chemists, the Ministry has ruined the Volga, a great river on the banks of which dozens of different nations have lived for centuries.

The policy of ruining the economy through ministerial intervention is continuing. Recently Murakhovsky [now retired deputy prime minister] sent a note to the Politburo suggesting that the area of irrigated land be increased by the year 2005 to 40 million hectares. The ministry of Water Resources is demanding another 230,000 million roubles from us for these destructive aims. Don't give it to them! (Applause) This money could be used to build 500,000 kilometres of roads, 10 million well-designed rural homes, hundreds of thousands of schools, hospitals and shops. … The Ministry received thousands of excavators and bulldozers in 1988 while the few hundred allocated to the roads programme in central Russia were never in the end supplied.

… It wouldn't do any harm to talk of the political, economic and financial inequality of the republics. Experts believe that the unequal position of the Russian Federation is a source of Russophobia. Since the Federation lacks such important bodies as its own Party Central Committee and Academy of Sciences it is presumed that their functions are filled by all-union bodies. Isn't that why the latter are perceived as Russian bodies? Their mistakes and miscalculations are perceived as the mistakes of Russians. ... Many years of inequality can be attributed to the demographic situation ... which is unfavourable not only in the Russian Federation, Ukraine and Belorussia but also in Estonia, Latvia and Lithuania. However, economic inequality is particularly characteristic of Siberia and Central Russian regions. The majority of deputies simply do not know the depressing statistics about this. ... I shall simply say that before the Revolution, Russians and Ukrainians had a very high population growth rate. Now both are faced by the threat of depopulation. The villagers continues to vote with their feet. And I do not envy the governments of the Baltic republics where the growth in population is due to immigration and not to an increasing birth rate of the indigenous population. I'm sure deputies from all the union republics and the autonomous republics of the Russian Federation will correctly understand this part of my speech. I am not at all sure, however, that the "democratic minority", or rather the press, will not pin another label on me. *Moscow News* has already once called me a misanthrope in six different languages. If certain members of the Politburo, and Mikhail Gorbachev himself, have already learnt to put up with slander then it is hardly for us, plain mortals, to complain. Yet I am nontheless very concerned that the mass media, especially television, are all in the same hands and often do not reflect the interests of all the people but only of particular groups, moreover of those located in the capital. (Applause) There is no hint of pluralism here yet. To judge by their speeches the Moscow group place great reliance on expert knowledge. Indeed, no country in the world has so many Academicians ... but why, in my village, does the peasant still cut hay in the same way as in the 12th century? (Applause) And what is the result of the latest economic theories? ... In four years of perestroika the economists in Moscow and elsewhere have been able to come up with nothing new apart from urban cooperatives, which should been have started in the villages not the towns. (Applause) And how can we respect the kind of science that gave us Chernobyl? I'm not at all against science and experts but they musn't think just of their own academic interests. ...

Here, there has been talk of the danger of hooliganism and extremism for our young democracy. But who, pray, is to blame? Aren't we ourselves to blame, and the television, variety shows and cinema which promote the cult of cruelty and violence? (Applause)

Centralising cultural policy, and entrusting it to the same permissive people will lead to no good. Let me read an excerpt from a telegram: "… stop the debasing of our culture. Commercial films, variety shows, pornography, the avantgarde, alcohol and drugs are destroying all hopes of a renaissance." Incidentally, people were disappointed by the Politburo's failure to implement the 1985 law [restricting production and sales of alcoholic beverages]. It was not a bad law. But it came and it went. … It's time to understand a simple truth: a sober economy is impossible with a drunken budget. We must ask those who complain today about the severe budget deficit why it came into being? Is it not because there are 18 million people employed in administration? What about the war in Afghanistan? And Cuba, Nicaragua and Ethiopia? And the space programme? How much do our lavish festivals, olympiads and international forums cost? … It's not surprising there's a budget deficit when we have such ministers as Vasiliev and Murakhovsky who have spent billions for no visible result … (Applause)

I must read out another letter sent to Valentin Rasputin and myself. "Please table a law enabling the Supreme Soviet to annul all deals and leasing of Soviet territory to foreign firms and joint ventures … As if it's not enough that the country should be turned into a dumping ground for nuclear waste they are now selling off the land of their own country". (Applause)

… I would add the demand that the terms of all international agreements be published and discussed … because they are agreed and signed by a a very small number of people. I also suggest that the Congress and its presidium vote to hold a referendum, without delay, on nuclear energy. (Applause)

Proud, at times even jubilant, words about political power have several times sounded from this tribune. Henceforth and forever, political power belongs to the people's deputies. Don't hurry so hastily, as they used to say in Odessa. Power still belongs to other people, to those whom we often simply do not know. It is in the hands of those who control the TV cameras and the newspapers. It belongs to those who sit nearer the tribune and have already learned how to make use of photocopiers. Even here at the Congress, power belongs to such people. And there are people who long for any kind of anarchy and chaos. Please don't forget that…(Applause)

Yuri Chernichenko, TV commentator on agricultural affairs, (territorial deputy, Moscow) 153

I was born in the Kuban region, where in the 1960s old grandmothers still threatened disobedient children, "Look out, the Muscovite is coming after you". They meant no harm by it. Yet when the euphoria of the elections had passed — I fought against 11 other very deserving candidates! — and preparations for the Congress began, we came under pressure and lists were imposed on us and secret agendas were followed. ... It was then that the scarecrow or bogeyman "Muscovite" appeared. ... For 5 weeks people famous throughout the country met at the deputies' club in Moscow. Late into the night they hammered out quite impermissible things — the conception and programme of this Congress.

These proposals, which represent such a danger to us and to you, were copied and circulated at the meeting of the Russian Federation delegation, though not without considerable opposition: who ever gave you permission, so to speak?

The attitude to the Moscow delegation reveals a fear of taking real political initiatives. [The Soviet saying is] Initiative must be punished. So, subtly responding to the half-spoken command, one deputy suggested to a professor (pure Mao Tse Tung!) that he should be re-educated in the factory; another demanded to have an answer why there were shortages; and a third, pointed accusingly, "That's where these filthy cooperatives and leasehold farming come from!"

It was only a short while ago that such obedient indignation denounced Pasternak and yelled "Crucify him!" at Sakharov. ... Now, as a result, none of our economists (Abalkin, Bogomolov, Shmelev, Tikhonov, Petrakov and Popov), nor naturally the sociologist Tatyana Zaslavskaya nor the historian Yuri Afanasyev are members of the Supreme Soviet. There are hardly any legal experts there. ... What is this, "cultural revolution"? Just don't talk to me about rotation. We all know that this was not at all accidental: as the old collective-farm refrain goes, "The tractor-driver drives the tractor, it doesn't drive itself." (Applause)

... Soon I will have been a party member for 40 years. ... The elections were nothing if not communist: the people neatly separated the party from its officials. But in private, during the pre-Congress preparations, the party bureaucracy took its revenge. It even began to decide at the Central Committee plenum who would head the parliamentary commissions, thereby provoking the most loyal to disobedience ...

If the millions who became politically aware, rejected the district commissions [during the elections in March] as bureaucratic inter-ference, they will never approve such tactics here.

... I must confess that at 168 pre-election meetings I said that comrade Murakhovsky is not to blame for anything. "Don't shoot the pianist, he's playing the best he can." Because up to 8 government ministers and their deputies have to sit in the reception, waiting to see the deputy head of the Central Committee's agricultural department.

I greatly enjoy watching Yegor Ligachev on television. He travels about the country and learns a great deal, evidently because he hasn't dealt with agriculture before. ... I only want to ask why someone who knows nothing about the subject and who made a mess of ideology [when he headed the Central Committee department], was put in charge of such a politically important branch of the economy. How could it have happened?! (Applause)

No one, alas, has mentioned our shameful exports here. We sell 200 million tonnes of oil each year, and mainly crude oil! ... Then we import produce that we can grow here ourselves. ...

Last year we bought 21 million tonnes of wheat. Who in their right mind can tell me why we bought them when we produce two times more wheat here than we need ourselves? ... Last year I marked the 25th anniversary of this anti-national import. ...

And about the Moscow group. Drop the word "Moscow": there are already so many deputies from Orenburg, Chelyabinsk, Kamchatka, Chukotka, Kursk and who knows where else, who come to talk to us ...

Valentin Rasputin, writer, secretary of USSR union of writers, Irkutsk (USSR union of writers) 159

An involuntary contradiction has been revealed between those of us who were elected in competitive elections and those approved by non-governmental organisations. Several times we have heard that some are the choice of the people, and the others have been imposed so as to slow down the pace of perestroika. I also agree that the electoral law is imperfect. Can it really be right when one individual votes three, and sometimes four, times: first in his constituency, then somewhere like the Cultural Foundation, the Union of Writers, and yet again in the Acade-my of Sciences? (Applause) The further discussion goes, however, the more convinced I am that representation from non-governmental or-ganisations was essential in the initial states of democratic elections. I say this for the sake of pluralism, which we repeatedly insist is an essential condition of democracy. For perestroika has now climbed to that summit inhabited by birds of prey which try to remain in sole possession. Any who do not agree with them are declared enemies of perestroika.

... We hear that if perestroika is a revolution then there must be a counter-revolution. As you yourselves understand, we must deal with counter-revolution in a special way, without any pluralism. ...

It's not a question of the differences of opinion that inevitably arise ... but of something much more important: the fate of perestroika and democracy. I like the idea stated here by Olzhas Suleimeinov: if you pull on the left oar all the time, you will immediately swing to the right. So be careful about declaring others to be "forces opposed to perestroika". Logically you yourselves are the first in that category.

The words aren't mine, but I would like to repeat them here with a slight alteration: "You need great catastrophes, gentlemen, we need a great country" [Stolypin]. (Applause)

Our young men died senselessly in Afghanistan, and now they are just as senselessly crippled in the undeclared war on morality ... Never since the war has the stability of the state been put through such tests and upheavals. We Russians look on the national feelings and problems of all the nations and ethnic groups of our country without exception, with respect and understanding. But we want to be understood as well. That Russians are chauvinist and blindly arrogant is a fabrication of those who play on your national feeling, respected brothers. But they are playing, I must admit, with considerable skill. Russophobia has spread in the Baltic and Georgia and is also penetrating other republics ... Anti-Soviet slogans are combined with anti-Russian slogans. Emissaries from Lithuania and Estonia form a common front and take these slogans to Georgia. Thence local agitators set out for Armenia and Azerbaijan. ... The great activity of the Baltic deputies is very noticeable at the Congress: using parliamentary methods they secure the amendments to the constitution that would allow them to say farewell to this country. It's not my job to give advice in such cases. ... But the Russian custom of helping others leads me to wonder: perhaps, Russia itself should leave the Union (Applause) if you hold her to blame for all your ills, and if her underdevelopment and unwieldiness hampers your progressive aspirations? It would help us, incidentally, to resolve a number of existing and future problems. ...

Believe me, we're fed up with being a scapegoat and putting up with insults and abuse. We are told, this is your cross. (Applause) However, this cross is becoming ever more difficult to bear. We're very grateful to Boris Oleinik, Ion Drutse and others who said kind words here about the Russian language and Russia. They're allowed to, but we're not forgiven if we do so.

... it is not Russia that is to blame for all your ills, but the common thrall of the administrative-industrial machine that has ... so degraded and robbed Russia that she is barely alive ... Whether we are to live together or not, do not be arrogant towards us, and do not blame a person for something that is not his fault. It would be best of all if we set things right together. ...

It is also true that the same industrial machine which is destroying nature is to blame for inter-ethnic complications. I agree ... that we should not unnecessarily alarm our deputies and, by implication, the whole country, which has been constantly watching us on television ... Yet, whatever we might say and however much we might exaggerate, our words would still not be strong enough to describe the ecological crisis ...

All large-scale projects must be discussed in the commissions of the Supreme Soviet and passed for a final decision to the Congress. Otherwise government decrees, taken without the people's knowledge, will appear time and again: for example, the decree on the construction of 5 oil and gas-processing complexes in Tyumen [West Siberia] that will be disastrous for the country, extremely destructive for the environment but, probably, profitable for foreign firms. ...

In conclusion I would like to say that if we introduce countrywide referenda then it would be good to hold the first one on nuclear power stations. Thank you. (Applause)

Nikolai Shmelev, senior research associate, Academy of Sciences Institute of USA and Canada, Moscow (Academy of Sciences) 160

Let me begin by saying that, as an economist, I am not very worried by our long-term prospects. I think that as a nation or country we are not intending to commit suicide and, having tried out in our history every conceivable and inconceivable means of organising the economy, we cannot help returning to the path that Lenin identified in the last two years of his life. In 70 years we have had only 7-8 years of a really efficient economy [the New Economic Policy of 1921-8]. We simply cannot help returning to this path since there is no alternative. On average a bankrupt firm in the West needs 8-10 years to get more or less back on its feet. A much greater period will be needed, of course, for our vast economy.

I am very disturbed, however, by our short-term prospects. The next 2-3 years are what worry me. Let me not mince words: if we do not halt the accelerating inflation, the recession in the consumer market and the horrendous budget deficit (a world record, if related to GNP) then we may in 2-3 years face economic failure.

... Then everything will be rationed, the rouble will drastically decline in value, the black market and the "second" economy will flourish and we shall be forced to return, for a certain period, to the strict discipline of the command economy.

After Nikolai Ryzhkov's speech I was again convinced that the government understand that we face such a danger ... but I have grave doubts that they appreciate the immediacy of this threat. ...

A commonly-heard explanation is that the rapid rise in wages is to blame. This is unjust. ... The degree of exploitation of labour in our country is the highest of all industrial countries: approximately 37-8% of our GNP goes on wages compared to 70% in the West. Our working class has the moral right to raise its share of GNP. ... A second widely-held explanation is that cooperatives are to blame ... This is a ludicrous explanation. The population's annual income is roughly 430,000 million roubles. All of the incomes received by cooperatives amount to 2000 million roubles, ...

... Nikolai Ryzhkov justly referred to our terrible legacy ... Yet in the three Five Year Plan periods he referred to the average budget deficit was 20,000 million roubles while now it is more than 100,000 million roubles. In the last 3-4 years major mistakes were made in managing the economy. First, there was the totally incompetent action taken to restrict the sale of alcohol... Fine intentions here did colossal damage to the balance of the market and of the budget. The second mistake was the short-lived but very fateful campaign in 1986 against "unearned or illicitly earned incomes" which had a dreadful effect on agriculture. The third mistake, which we could also have avoided, was a consequence of the fall in oil prices and the enforced cutbacks in our imports. Instead of cutting imports of grain or machinery we slashed ... the import of consumer goods, which give the budget 8-10 roubles for every hard-currency rouble spent abroad. Finally, a mistake for which I can find no rational justification: last year the deficit stood at 50-60,000 million roubles but this year it soared to over 100,000 million roubles and, at the same time, our capital investment also raced ahead. Where did the money come from? Evidently the government from the start decided to cover these expenditures by printing more money. ... a quite conscious step towards inflation.

... Let me warn you straightaway that the programme I'm proposing will perhaps not please many and is hardly likely to gain the support of the government.

... First, we must return to a normal selling of hard liquor. ... I want to say the following to the writer Vasily Belov. If I were to call him the ideologue of the mafia, the black market and the herald of speculation he would probably be terribly offended. ... yet even if we refer to official data, one half of the hard liquor in the country is distilled by moonshiners. And that only refers to alcohol distilled from sugar [now rationed in Moscow, as well as elsewhere], not to tomato paste, cockroach sprays and so on. People aren't drinking any less ... and drinking has little relation to price. People drink because of the lies, idleness and depressed state of our society. We must find ways of treating this problem without destroying one of the mainstays of the country's budget. (Applause)

Second, there are roughly 150,000 million roubles waiting for goods to appear on the market. We need roughly 15,000 million dollars' worth of imported consumer goods to mop up this sum. Then, while the economy is still in an unbalanced state, we must import about 5-6000 million dollars worth over the next 2-3 years. ... Yesterday Nikolai Ryzhkov gravely told us that there was no such money available. With a will, I beg to differ, these sums can be found.

Has the government ever seriously considered offering our collective-farm chairmen hard currency for any grain and meat they produce above the usual level, with the right to spend it as they like? (Applause) ... Each year unused imported machinery costs us 10,000 million dollars. Perhaps we could halt the import of machinery for 5 to 10 years ...? (Applause).

Third, and here I am forced to use foreign estimates since the Soviet government does not publish such figures, has anyone ever thought how much our involvement, say, in Latin America costs us? American specialists put the figure at 6-8000 million dollars annually. ... A large part is in hard currency and much of that, for no reason anyone can understand, goes in paying 400% of the world price for Cuban sugar, for example. This source alone would be enough to support the consumer market in equilibrium for those few essential years until we have turned the economy around and set out on the path of reforms.

Finally, loans. I can understand when Nikolai Ryzhkov says he does not want to leave his grandchildren with any debts to pay, but there's still something provincial in this attitude ... All we have to do for the time being is pay the interest on these loans, and any of the three above-mentioned sources would be sufficient ..

I believe that the state budget is such an important and serious matter that when we meet again in October or November the approval of the budget must already be the prerogative of the Congress. (Applause)

ELECTIONS IN CHAMBER OF NATIONALITIES 163

The Speaker Nishanov proposed the Ukrainian textile-worker Wanda Venglov-skaya as one of his deputies. In the subsequent discussion objections were politely but firmly raised to this candidacy. The delicate observation of quotas — for women, for nationalities and for social classes — was critically re-examined. The tacit understanding that representatives of the Slavic republics would hold leading positions was also broken.

Boris Yeltsin led the demand for a choice of candidates, and Klara Hallik objected to the coefficient "of lower competence" applied to the token women candidates. As a result no less than 4 names were canvassed, including Yeltsin, David Kugultinov, Tufan Minullin and Klara Hallik. The latter all stood down in favour of Evdokia Gaer.

From benches

Does the level of education of the proposed candidate play any role in her aspiration to the post of deputy speaker? Is she studying at night school perhaps?

Nishanov

We do not set any specific level of education or any other restrictions on election to this post. We are all members of the Supreme Soviet and have equal rights.

Wanda Venglovskaya, textile worker, Zhitomir (national deputy, Ukraine)

I only went to secondary school, and then worked for 23 years at the textile factory. ...

From benches

Are you ready to carry out such an important function?

Venglovskaya

... We all have the same rights here and without your help, of course, I cannot get by.

Genrikh Igityan (Armenia)

Perhaps she is a splendid person, and an excellent textile-worker, and I have nothing against her. But this isn't the 1920s when an able-bodied seaman was given the keys and told, "You'll be in charge of the bank."

Neither Venglovskaya or Gaer gained sufficient votes. As the female quota was abandoned, the Ukrainian poet, Boris Oleinik was later easily accepted for this post.

Then a Belorussian, Tarasevich, was suggested as chairman of the Chamber's commission on national policy and inter-ethnic relations. (He had already headed the Soviet government's fact-finding mission to Tbilisi in early May.) This time the objections were not to lack of competence but to the political credentials and independence of the candidate.

From benches 163

I have very grave doubts about the proposed candidate. They are linked to what we know about the attitude of at least a sizable part of the leadership of Belorussia to the democratic changes taking place there. ... I know it would be an exaggeration to say that Belorussia is the Vendée of perestroika ... But there is something to it. ... So I want to propose Klara Hallik for this serious post.

Tarasevich

I understand that the comrade deputy has some specific objections to my candidacy, and not to the republic or the Belorussian people as a whole. Am I right? If so, I would ask him to say exactly what they are.

From benches

There was no question. I was proposing another candidate.

Khudonazarov (Tajikistan)

I welcome Boris Yeltsin's proposal that we choose between different candidates and support the candidacy of Klara Hallik.

Nishanov

We decided not to return to this question. Your job is to support or reject our proposal.

Khudonazarov

I ask that you include Klara Hallik as an alternative candidate.

Nishanov

Very well ...

Baltic deputy

Do you speak Belorussian? Is it true that there are very few schools in Belorussia where children are taught in that language, or even not at all? What does the Belorussian people think about this?

Georgi Tarasevich, Chairman of Presidium of Belorussian Supreme Soviet, Minsk (national deputy, Belorussia)

I went to a Belorussian-language school and naturally know the language. As far as schools are concerned, the problem of language is perhaps most acute in our republic. In the rural areas the majority of schools do teach in Belorussian. Unfortunately, ... in the towns, the majority of schools — well, one couldn't say there aren't any Belorussian-language schools — but the majority teach in Russian. This alarms all Belorussians and me in particular and we have been especially active more recently in looking for a solution.

From benches

Did you have an opponent during the elections?

Tarasevich

Yes, but unfortunately he withdrew just before the elections. ... It wasn't because anyone made him do so. I even made a special trip to visit him and ask why he'd withdrawn.

Tarasevich was approved by 152 votes to Hallik's 75 votes.

Chapter 6

CENTRAL ASIA AND KAZAKHSTAN, NEO-COLONIAL REALITIES

The Central Asian delegations at the Congress were criticised several times by more radical Russian and Moscow deputies for their passivity, conservatism and unanimity. In turn they reacted to stereotyped and condescending views, as they saw it, of their backwardness. During the second week of the Congress the events in the Ferghana valley in Uzbekistan focused attention on the ethnic complexity and tensions of the region.

Central Asia was, with the North Caucasus, the last area to be incorporated into the Russian empire, in the later 19th century, and much of it then continued to be indirectly ruled through the local feudal potentates. Kazakhstan, a nomad-inhabited steppe, was steadily encroached on from the late 18th century onwards, and before and after the Revolution many Russians and Ukrainians went to settle there.

The religion of Central Asia has been Islam (of the Sunnite confession) since the 11th century but the area had long been a centre of ancient cultures lying on a major East-West trade route. All the main nations there are Turkic-speaking (apart from the Tajik). When Soviet rule was established in the region in 1921-22 the feudal lords organized a fairly successful guerrilla campaign that was crushed by the Red Army only in the early 1930s. The population was then overwhelmingly rural and largely illiterate.

In the 1920s and 1930s there was an attempt to untangle the complex ethnic web of the area to form 4 modern and more homogeneous territorial and national republics. Rapid industrial development achieved 100% literacy rates, considerable urban growth and the accompanying social problems that are in many ways similar to those of the Third World countries. Central Asia, as opposed to Kazakhstan, remains still largely rural today. The infant mortality rate per 1000 newborn babies is 46 in Uzbekistan and 56 in Turkmenia, which is close to that for the poorest countries in the world. For Latvia the same indicator is only 11 and the difference illustrates the striking contrasts between the regions of the USSR. The per capita income in Estonia is greater than that in Uzbekistan by a factor of 2.3. The labour productivity in the Baltic republics increased by about 83% in 1971-1986 while in Turkmenia the corresponding increase was just 2%.

Some observers think that the Central Asian republics have a considerably greater potential for a rapid readjustment of their economies if the suggested radical economic reforms are implemented. These nations have old and vital traditions in various kinds of artisanship and handicrafts which might help to mop up some of the high rate of unemployment (an unofficial estimate is about 6 million). There are still many vacant jobs, nevertheless, in the chemical and textile industries built in the regions in recent decades and manpower had to be imported at a great expense from other regions of the USSR. The attempts to draw Uzbek workers to other regions, such as Central Russia and Far East, are also a failure, though no expense was spared to implement such programmes.

The Central Asian region had 266 deputies at the Congress (108 from Uzbekistan). The Kazakh delegation was 99 strong.

PARTY LEADERS ARE UNANIMOUS BUT ARE THEIR NATIONS?

Vladimir Zolotukhin, correspondent of Turkestan military district newspaper (territorial deputy, Uzbekistan) 148

I'm very concerned that, as candidates to the Supreme Soviet, the Uzbek delegation is putting forward 8 of the leading Party and Soviet officials from the republic. How will they be able to sit in our parliament if they retain those posts as well? (Applause)

I was rather hurt by the statement [Fyodorov's remarks] that the country's intellect is concentrated in Moscow. Are there only stupid people in Uzbekistan then? ... At the same time we must avoid an undemocratic procedure for choosing our candidates to the Supreme Soviet: so far our republic's proposed list was not drawn up collectively. We didn't even formally vote for these candidates.

Absamat Masaliev, 1st Secretary of the Central Committee of the Kirgiz Communist Party (territorial deputy, Kirgizia) 153

Our constituencies expect from us reasonable approaches to the acute problems. Emotions, rallies, or vicious speeches are no good for that...

It is too much to hold two Congresses and two sessions of the Supreme

Soviet every year. What is important are the concrete actions, the practical sense. What we see here is mostly emotions rather than reasonable ideas...

We know too little about the difficult problem of ethnic relations. The Central Committee is searching for constructive approaches to this problem... We Kirgizian deputies fully support this work and hope that it will produce new relevant legislation. Firstly, purely economic relations must be established between the republics and Moscow and between individual republics. There are many distortions in this field. For instance, the Kirgizian economic development has been one-sided; the emphasis was made on mining industries and, generally, on production of raw materials. This produces adverse financial and social results...

We believe that the further development of nations and ethnic groups must not be isolationist but should combine organically the independent interests of the republics with the interests of the union as a whole. The union will be really strong if it has strong republics and a strong centre and is based on the sincere trust and mutual respect between our nations. When we, the people's deputies, try to resolve our regional problems we must remember our great responsibility for preserving the unity of the multinational Union of the Soviet Socialist Republics. Any other attitude will lead ultimately to serious losses for a given region or nation... At this difficult stage we must concentrate our attention not on changing the established forms of national statehood, and not on redistributing territories between various republics but on tackling the multitude of economic problems we are facing ... Each republic also has many rights and opportunities for resolving ethnic conflicts, eliminating distortions in the spheres of languages, culture and education.

...The current democratic process is undoubtedly a significant achievement of perestroika. We must not, however, forget about the need for strengthening discipline. Unfortunately, our efforts in this field have slackened. It is no accident that democracy has brought with itself extremist groups that whip up the nationalist sentiments and purposefully undermine the authority of the Soviet State and the Communist Party, the Party's policies and ideology. We know even of sacrilegious attempts to question our eternal values... Even Lenin has been slandered...

Some economists regularly appear on TV and write in papers and magazines about our economic failures and financial troubles. They address the Congress here too. But they suggest no reasonable ways out of this situation. Do they live outside society? (Applause)

Voice from the hall.

They make suggestions.

Masaliev.

You make them all right, but we, the sovereign Kirgiz republic, have not seen a single research economist in all these years. We have not received a single suggestion from you. (Applause)...

The complicated situation in some regions seriously affects the social and political life in the entire country. Various groupings and organizations that spring to life there often produce social conflicts, instigate confrontation with the party and government authorities, and push the ethnic relations in a dangerous direction... Our people for the first time have known real democracy but some circles already attempt to transform it into anarchy...

Some speakers accused the deputies from Central Asia of being too obedient in voting unanimously for anything. This is not serious, to say the least. Let us dispense with imposing unsuitable opinions on others. We would like Moscow, the capital of the USSR, and Leningrad, the birthplace of the October Revolution, to be in the forefront of the fight for perestroika: we would like communists, workers and intellectuals of these cities to demonstrate to us model order and discipline.

Kakhar Makhkamov, 1st Secretary of Tajik Communist Party Central Committee (territorial district, Dushanbe, Tajikistan) 153

I represent the capital of Tajikistan and I support the concept of the strong centre and strong republics. Many press reports suggest that the so-called "raw-materials" republics are quietly withdrawing from the concept of territorial economic independence. This is entirely untrue. We support the concept of self-financing and self-administration on the whole but believe that it can be realized only under the following three conditions.

First, there must be a reform of the system of wholesale prices and prices for raw materials.

Second, the concept must be realized simultaneously throughout the country.

Third, a legal foundation must be set up in the form of a law on the economic relations between territorial units in a federal state.

We shall not achieve our goals without satisfying these conditions...
In the nearest future 150,000 new jobs must be made in Tajikistan to give

work to the ever increasing population. Since the amount of arable irrigated land area in the republic per capita is only 0.11 hectare, the new jobs can be generated only in new industries...

We clearly see the many problems and difficulties in ethnic relations. This heavy legacy of the past is the product of our reluctance to face the truth and we must overcome it together, by common efforts, under the conditions of goodwill and dialogue. In Tajikistan we still encounter the results of the incompetent demarcation of the boundaries between the republics of Central Asia. The errors made long ago are still felt now. Some of these problems we can resolve ourselves but some we cannot. The tiniest of these problems is the following. Many Tajiks and some Uzbeks who reside in Tajikistan and Uzbekistan want to change the nationality shown in their passports since these entries were incorrectly made in the past. In November 1988 the governments of Uzbekistan and Tajikistan asked the USSR Council of Ministers for permission to do this, but it still has not been granted... Together with the Uzbek leaders we do everything we can for strengthening the friendship between our nations and resolving the current problems. We have started a joint programme for developing the economic and cultural relations between our republics....

A Georgian deputy questioned the tradition of [sending from Moscow] 2nd Secretaries of the Central Committees of the republican communist parties. Let Georgian comrades deal with their own problems if they have them. This question must not be put on behalf of other republics. Undeserved reproaches aimed at the party have been heard at the Congress. Yes, the party has made some mistakes. But it was the party that made the October revolution. It was the party that led the Soviet people to victory in World War II. Now the party has started the revolutionary perestroika of the society. Let us all together help it to achieve a new victory that will decide the destiny of the country and of the Socialism as a whole.

Saparmurad Niyazov, 1st Secretary of Turkmenian Communist Party Central Committee (territorial deputy, Ashkhabad, Turkmenia) 153

...Lenin used to say that Marxism is based on facts, not on potentialities. If we see that conflicts between nations and various social groups are a fact of our life, we choose the policy of unity and consolidation... We respect the quest of the Baltic nations for independent development... We, though, would like a more systematic and differentiated approach... Even in Central Asia not everything is uniform. Each republic has its own way of implementing social, political and economic programmes in accordance with the historical, territorial and psychological characteristics of its nation.

The tendency towards national isolationism is not typical of our nation; it has no historical roots. The Turkmenian nation was consolidated after the October Revolution and it had assistance from practically all the nations of the country and particularly from the Russian nation. We have achieved a stable state of bilingualism. I do not agree with Comrade Drutse in his evaluation of bilingualism in various regions. For us it is the most suitable approach since we have in our population 12% Russians, 7% Uzbeks, 3% Kazakhs and 1-2% Armenians, Azerbaijanians, Ukrainians, etc. At present it would be unreasonable to divide the people by giving any single language the official status. We have consulted the people about that.

We share the special concern about social troubles voiced by some deputies. The bane of our republic is the high infant mortality rate, social backwardness of rural areas and demographic distortions [very high birth rate]. And the life of our women is, probably, harder than anywhere else...

The economic structure of the republic is considerably distorted. The per capita production of consumer goods is 3 times lower than the USSR average. Though Turkmenia has the largest per capita production of cotton it is difficult to find cotton fabrics in our shops. Not more than 5% of the cotton grown in the republic is processed there.

Turkmenia meets all plans in supplying cotton, natural gas, oil products, chemical and other commodities to the fraternal republics but we often face difficulties in getting deliveries from them. For instance, the Ukraine failed to deliver the planned amount of cotton yarn though it is made of our own cotton... We think such a situation is abnormal; some of our leaders suggest selling our products to foreign countries and buying what we need from them...

The deficient economic structure adversely affects the employment indicators, and the numbers and skills of industrial workers. The number of industrial workers in the republic is only 69 per 1000 compared with the average of 130 for the country as a whole... The Supreme Soviet, in particular the Chamber of Nationalities, must supervise the provision of basic incomes and employment throughout the country. The long-range social development programme for various regions must be financed by the USSR budget... This will prevent the possible ethnic conflicts...

We have started eliminating the anomalies we inherited from our recent and distant past. But can we put everything right in a single blow? We would be poor politicians and strategists if we forgot about the tactical opportunities for our own social, economic and ethnic policies. Democratisation poses the question of greater independence of the republics and their greater responsibility for the destiny of the Union. Unfortunately, we often forget about the dialectical priority of unity. This is our political principle. Its old dogmatic interpretation is hopelessly dated now. We need new approaches, new tactics, this is what perestroika is about...

We are profoundly satisfied with the activities of the Central Committee, the USSR government and Mikhail Gorbachev, particularly those aimed at improving foreign relations. Turkmenia, which shares borders with Afghanistan and Iran, is especially interested in good neighbourly relations.

Mukhtar Umarkhodzhaev, Rector, Andizhan Languages Teachers Training College, Andizhan (national deputy, Uzbekistan) 155

More than 70 deputies submitted a memorandum which has not been read out. All cotton-producing republics ask that the cotton wholesale price be increased by 50%. If it is not done, our standard of living will not improve.

The birth rate in Uzbekistan and Central Asia in general is very high. It is very difficult for school-leavers to find jobs. Now there are 760,000 people who cannot find jobs in Uzbekistan and soon the number will be in millions.

Lukyanov (in the chair).

Let us hear five more deputies, three minutes for each [in the general discussion].

Unidentified voice from the hall.

No!

Lukyanov.

Let us allow one more person to speak since he has already slipped onto the platform. [The young man pushed his way to the platform through the deputies crowding near it.]

Pulatdzan Akhunov, Assistant School Headmaster, Andizhan Region, Uzbekistan (Young Communist League) 155

I must table a protest. Only those deputies from Uzbekistan are admitted to the platform whose opinions are unanimous [and agree with those of the leaders]. I demand an opportunity to speak for the minority who have their own views on conditions in Uzbekistan. Why are we not allowed to tell about the catastrophic situation there? Uzbeks hoped that perestroika would allow them to get rid of the monoculture of cotton. Unfortunately, nothing is being done about that. The area under cotton must be cut by 50%. I have much to say, allow me to speak at the next session.

THE NATIONS OF CENTRAL ASIA AND KAZAKHSTAN
9th sitting, Friday 2 June

Chingis Aitmatov, writer and chairman of Kirgiz SSR writers' union, editor-in-chief of the influential Moscow-based Russian-language literary journal *Inostrannaya Literatura* (Communist Party) 155/4

... after the economy the next most acute problems concern the relations between nations. The commission on the Tbilisi events at any rate will contribute to legal guarantees for protecting nations from violence in this country. On the whole, I agree with the concept of complete Socialist sovereignty of the union republics: without it their federal status becomes a fiction. But the development of sovereignty must proceed methodically, reasonably and consistently, by introducing new legal instruments rather than emotions, and without attempting to kill all birds with one stone. What we possess is too valuable, and what we aim to achieve is too important.

The problems of language are of especial significance for me [Aitmatov writes and is published in both Russian and Kirgiz] ... I have in mind the concept of official languages in the union republics and the legal justifications for introducing the relevant laws. The correct attitude is to work out a general model for such processes. In my opinion, the federal state must provide for the federative principle of national languages in the sense that the languages of the indigenous nations of the union republics must be given the status of the official state languages. The same requirements of applying reasonable consistency and a logical and commonly-agreed framework apply to the introduction of such status.

The languages of the indigenous nations of the union republics were for a long time neglected by the republican authorities. Now they must be given preferential status simply to ensure their revival and their rights. This is a very complicated issue, particularly in Central Asia. Many of our fellow citizens have never had the experience of using the local languages in an official environment and regard this attitude as a challenge to the authority of the Russian language. Let us consider this issue.

The genius of the Russian language has served us all. I cannot imagine our future without the spiritual heritage of the Russian language which belongs to us all. Russian is universal and irremovable in this respect. It faces no threat within the Soviet Union as a whole. But it must not squeeze out the languages of other nations that live side by side with it, although there have been good historical reasons why it spread everywhere. In this connection, one must appreciate that each nation remains a nation only when it possesses a language of its own, and that is where its cultural sovereignty lies. As soon as it loses the opportunities to use and develop its language, no matter why this occurs, a nation ceases to be what it was and what it must continue to be.

Hence our goal should be to harmonize the language situation primarily through the concept of bilingualism, with preferential treatment for the national language of the nations possessing statehood [the second language for all Soviet nations must be Russian]. Not everyone is yet prepared to accept this fact. Compromises, dialogue and mutual attempts to narrow the gaps between positions are the only ways to reach mutually beneficial and honourable solutions here.

Unfortunately, the mass media, particularly those based in Moscow, do not always promote such understanding. It is now almost a vogue among them to charge any citizens concerned about their natural ethnic requirements with nationalism or an obsession with local issues. At the same time, the media promote a national nihilism, depreciating ethnicity and berating any of its normal manifestations. Such press reports (intentionally or not) help to spread undesirable bad feeling between different ethnic groups in regions where they traditionally used to live peacefully, side by side, sharing common problems and needs and understanding each other's individual needs... *Komsomolskaya Pravda* [The Young Communist League countrywide daily newspaper (circulation 5 million)] claimed as established fact, for instance, that the events in Alma-Ata [violent youth riots in 1986 caused by the removal of the Kazakh party leader and his replacement by a Russian, Kolbin] were largely a result of the continuing provision of Kazakh-language school education for many young people there...

Kazakhstan must have all the sovereign rights of a socialist republic. It cannot be made an exception: the Kazakh nation, one of the most ancient in the region, is not to blame because the USSR needed a sharp increase in wheat production. To open the Kazakh virgin lands (the steppes) for cultivation, millions of settlers were brought from the European part of the USSR [in the mid-1950s], thus sharply reducing the proportion of Kazakhs in the overall population of the republic. Yet some people never miss an opportunity to remind Kazakhs of their present minority status and thus put them in their place.

The law and the Constitution must protect the cultural self-sufficiency of each nation. This is especially important since many indigenous nations, for instance, Kazakhs and others in Central Asia, have no ethnic groups residing outside their homelands that would provide at least a theoretical possibility of preserving the culture and language of the nation, if this cannot be done within their republics.

Each nation's destiny is unique. The Soviet mass media, in my opinion, are also unfair towards the Uzbek nation when they repeatedly gloat over the "Uzbek" affair to delight their less sophisticated readers and viewers [a wide variety of crimes by highly-placed party and government officials in Uzbekistan in the 1970s and early 1980s. Falsified reports on the cotton crops were claimed to have then generated illegal gains of several thousand million roubles]. Why the Uzbeks? Why such slander? Because this uniquely hard-working nation had to build their lives around such a thankless occupation as cotton growing? Because for decades cotton used to be a major source of hard-currency earnings for the USSR government, apart from having other [military] uses? If organized crime exists here or there, let the law-enforcement agencies deal with it without smearing the honour of the entire nation. I should like to say the same about the Crimean Tatars. When will we finally stop delaying a solution to the tragedy of this nation? Our mass media still present their case (in particular, the official TASS news agency) as if this nation were itself largely responsible for the inhuman, genocidal treatment it received [an estimated half of the nation perished in 1944 when it was deported as a whole to Central Asia by Stalin]. This is an absurd attitude. Is there a law that punishes entire nations? Who has the right to make decisions? Our Lord Himself cannot claim such a right [the speaker's background is Muslim]. Even if some Crimean Tatars did become defectors and traitors during the Second World War, were other nations free of those evils? War is war. It involves fighting, heroic deeds, and suffering. It produces prisoners and deserters. It means both victories and defeats. And this can happen to any nation, we must be dialecticians and realize it all, we must protect the honour of the entire nation. (Applause)

Neither can I remain silent about the injustice done to the ethnic Germans in this country ... During the war they were deported from their homes and subjected to numerous humiliations and suffering; and political discrimination against them continues to the present day. Cultural and administrative autonomy for the ethnic Germans in the USSR would be valuable not only to them but to all of us, too. I have no doubt that Germans could set us all a model example of such autonomy. (Applause)

Let us learn from the terrible lessons of our past to prevent any repetition of the same experiences. Constitutional guarantees must be worked out that protect absolutely the ethnic integrity of nations, that prevent absolutely deportations of any ethnic groups on any political, administrative or racial grounds, and provide equal justice for everybody. Each nation must have a homeland where its historical roots lie. (Applause)

KAZAKHSTAN

Olzhas Suleimenov, 1st Secretary, Kazakhstan Writers Union (territorial deputy, Semipalatinsk district, Kazakhstan) 161

The principal aspect of perestroika for me is the continuation of the decolonization process which was suspended in the twenties. It is now exhibiting all the features characteristic of decolonization ...

My constituency is in the Semipalatinsk region — the oldest existing site of nuclear tests in the USSR. It is also the most active testing site, accounting for 18 nuclear explosions a year. It is located almost at the very geographical centre of the country but for 15 years open nuclear weapon tests were conducted there on the land surface and in the air. According to minimal estimates, the total power of the weapons exploded there is about 2,500 times that of the Hiroshima bomb. Could such tests fail to affect the health in the surrounding communities? Though the official experts give a negative answer, we still do not believe them. Experts of the voluntary anti-nuclear movement Nevada-Semipalatinsk have terrible data at their disposal. The USSR Ministry of Health keeps secret the relevant research information... In contrast to Japan, our government has shown less care and respect for its citizens. During 40 years of nuclear testing, the military have not spent any money on building any kind of health care institutions in the communities around the testing site. The fallout from the open nuclear tests will affect health levels throughout the country for many years to come...

That underground tests are also unsafe is shown by the discharge of radioactive gases into the atmosphere that occurred on 12 February 1989. Such discharges have happened more than once, for instance, during the last summer. On the same day thousands of children in the area became sick with nosebleeds, dizziness and other symptoms which are hardly typical for flu, the official diagnosis ... We strongly hope that a complete test ban treaty will be signed ...

Our further development will increasingly depend on how open the dialogue between the people and the government will be. The troubles in this country began in the late 1920s precisely with persecution of dissent. To maintain democratisation and glasnost special legislation must be introduced to provide for the right of dissent, regarding it as a productive, rather than seditious factor. (Applause) We must pass special resolutions condemning the crimes of Stalin's clique against Socialism, such as the physical elimination of its opposition. We must condemn as criminal the Leftist theory and practice of the "forced development"... 350,000 Kazakhs lost their lives in World War Two while more than 4 million dead were the result of such periods of "forced development" [Kazakhs now account for an estimated 30% of the republic's population. During collectivisation in the early 1930s, an estimated 2 million Kazakhs starved to death. Then and later there were also mass deportations to Kazakhstan]. Each Soviet nation has similar periods of suffering. History senselessly repeats itself if its lessons are not learned. We must publish at last the statistics of Stalin's crimes against all Soviet nations.

We do not want to deny our entire history indiscriminately. It has given rise to common cultural values, and it has, apart from the sad pages, some positive aspects that must be preserved and continued. This is precisely why we must separate the bloody pages from the pure ones. We remember the millions that perished without a murmur; now we are able to condemn arbitrary violence. It is the evidence of the speed with which our ethics and sense of legality are developing. The students and workers of Alma-Ata were the first in the country to stage rallies without official permission in December 1986. If these events had been widely and democratically discussed, perhaps there would have been no Tbilisi tragedy in April. I believe the tragic events in Alma-Ata must be examined by a special commission of the Supreme Soviet within the framework of the new humanitarian approach. I call on my fellow countrymen, those who live in Kazakhstan — Kazakhs, Russians, Germans, Koreans, Ukrainians, Uighurs and Turks — to have faith in justice which is possible if we retain self-discipline and preserve our common interests and values.

The country is overflowing with sorrow... Each nation has its own, still open, wounds... Many of the deputies received appeals from the Meskhetian Turks, Crimean Tatars, Abkhazians, and other dispossessed nations. The Supreme Soviet Commission of Ethnic Relations will have much to do before the next Congress... A full and comprehensive understanding of history is mandatory. The reason for many ethnic quarrels and misplaced ambitions is the circumscribed knowledge ... Special volumes of documents must be published on these acute issues. Genuine culture implies taking steps to meet each other half-way. Such a volume [on Karabakh] must include objective historical data, the terrible truth about Sumgait, and also the report about the crash of the military transport plane in which 50 Azerbaijanian soldiers died when they were en route to Armenia to help in the rescue work after the earthquake. These lads contributed their lives to the restoration of friendship between nations...

Mukhtar Shakhanov, secretary, Kazakh Writers Union (territorial deputy, Alma-Ata, Kazakhstan). 159

Nineteen deputies from Kazakhstan make the following statement in the hope of preventing new ethnic conflicts from arising in the current tense conditions in the republic.

Our voters in Kazakhstan send us numerous letters and telegrams asking us to re-open the subject of the December events in 1986 in Alma-Ata. It was the first time that sappers' spades and police dogs were used to disperse a peaceful demonstration. Special troops kicked girls and hit them with clubs. The number of casualties among the demonstrators is still kept secret. According to incomplete sources, about 2000 people were arrested and many of them sentenced to long terms in labour camps. A thousand students were expelled from their schools and many lost their jobs.

The first attack on the era of stagnation produced a monstrous response and hundreds of politically inexperienced young men and women fell victim to it, their lives irrevocably shattered.

It is true that the Kazakh party headed by the prominent internationalist figure of Comrade Kolbin did much to improve the situation. However, information on the Alma-Ata events and the illegal actions of the special police force is still classified. This causes the spread of unhealthy rumours in Kazakhstan which cast a slur on the friendship of nations and produce ethnic resentment. The statement of the Central Committee of the CPSU issued after the events referred to them as a manifestation of Kazakh nationalism. One can lay blame on 5,000 people or on 100,000 people, but it is impossible to charge the entire nation with nationalism. We ask for justice, for removal of these harsh and un-deserved charges...

The Kazakh nation repeatedly proved its faithfulness to the friendship of nations, in its history, by shedding its blood. The ethnic problems will soon be discussed at the special plenary session of the Central Commit-tee. Since many of the deputies are not members of the Central Commit-tee and thus will not be able to take part in these discussions a group of Kazakh deputies make the following suggestion to the Congress. Before the scheduled Central Committee session is held, the Congress must approve a decree providing for the official status of the languages of the indigenous nations in the union and autonomous republics, autono-mous and national regions and the territorial units populated by ethnic minorities...

COTTON, POVERTY AND CORRUPTION

Adyl Yakubov, 1st Secretary, Uzbek Writers Union, Tashkent (USSR Writers Union) 162

...Among the many values we have lost in the last 70 years and are still losing there is one that is the most difficult to repair. It is one of the noblest human properties — charity and compassion. It has been re-placed with cruel indifference and unwillingness to sympathise. Yester-day I heard two very pretty women in the lobby in front of this Hall saying "Why do these Uzbeks keep on babbling about their cotton? It's just too boring, they have no culture at all." I thought bitterly, whose fault is it that our proud villagers find themselves in such tragic condi-tions?

Where could they get culture from when they were robbed of every-thing by the "father of all nations", by Stalin, who ordered the USSR to become self-sufficient in cotton. Hundreds of thousands of hectares of orchards, pasture and shady almond and walnut-tree groves were mer-cilessly cut down to plant cotton. The country got its self-sufficiency in cotton and immense riches with it. But what did our villager, his wife and children get? Just twelve hours of hard work under the sultry Southern sun daily, without holidays or vacations.

The numerous reports in the press on corruption in our republic give you a chance to calculate precisely how much each of the corrupt officials has stolen from the people. These officials must be punished... But what have our villagers got for their back-breaking toil...?

Our women work under scorching sun in fields sprayed with poisonous chemicals. This results in an increasing incidence of cancer, hepatitis, intestinal infections, and gynaecological disorders leading to higher death rates for women and children.

When they return from the fields at dusk they have to cook gruel for their children with no other fuel but dried dung just like hundreds years ago. One can't help weeping when one looks at these dark faces, as if they had been singed with some fire; women in whom nothing feminine is left — just eyes full of hopeless sadness...

I know that all farmers, particularly Russian farmers, lead hard lives in this country... But cotton-farming is a special matter ... Remember how the cruel American planters had brought hundreds of thousands of African slaves to work in their cotton fields since they thought this work was not fit for the white men. Remember also how these evil planters gave their slaves enough to eat ... And today the descendants of these slaves excel in American sports and arts, too ... What about our village children? Do they have a chance for sports or for arts? Poor nutrition (20 kilograms of meat per year on average) and work too heavy for children thwart their physical development to such an extent that they are judged unfit to be drafted into the army even as auxiliary troops... I'd like to ask Comrade Ryzhkov if it is true that our country needs cotton so much...? If so, then why are our cotton prices the lowest in the world? (Applause)

Before the October Revolution Russian merchants (who introduced this bothersome crop to our region) exchanged one pood of cotton for 18 poods of wheat. Now the price of a kilogram of cotton is 50 kopecks, or in other words the price of half a kilo of cucumbers at a private market in Tashkent...

Central Asia was famed from ancient times for its unique climate which makes it possible to grow the sweetest fruit and vegetables on Earth, priceless water melons and cantaloupes of an exquisite flavour.

After 70 years of our history, the cruel and irrational wasting of natural resources has brought our region to the brink of environmental catastrophe... We must set up a special commission of top experts on economics, ecology, health and agriculture to analyse the situation in

Uzbekistan and to present a true picture to the government. I am convinced Uzbekistan can feed half of this country and not in the distant future but in a few years. But we must lift the burden of monoculture from it and to allow the hard-working nation to spread its wings...

Tulepbergen Kaipbergenov, writer and chairman of the Karakalpak ASSR writers union (national deputy, Karakalpak autonomous republic) 152

In his speech Mikhail Gorbachev mentioned the ecological crisis, but only in passing. The catastrophe that has befallen the Aral sea, and which is still unfolding, is comparable to the most recent world catastrophes in its scale and long-term consequences. Experts estimate that each year 440 kgs of sand and salt swept away from the former sea of Aral fall on each hectare of land in Karakalpakia and in parts of Turkmenia.

It is now dangerous to grow fruit and vegetables on our land ... Science has as yet found no way to cleanse the land of the herbicides, pesticides and defoliants that in the past were tipped onto each hectare by the ton. ... The vast concentrations of poisonous chemicals near Aral is affecting our genetic systems and the incidence of congenital deformities has risen sharply.

We now live like this not through our own will, but thanks to the central [Moscow] planning agencies.

The death of the Aral sea threatens not only the whole of Central Asia but will lead to unforetold, and most probably catastrophic, climatic changes over a very wide area. Agriculture in Central Asia, as we all know, exists thanks to two rivers that flow into the Aral sea. Now that natural cycle is disrupted. ... We must quickly and drastically cut back on cotton production. And in no circumstances, sell it abroad: this is literally to trade in the health of our fellow-citizens.

The "Uzbek affair" or the "Gdlyan affair"?

A fascinating side issue during the Congress was the so-called "Uzbek affair". After the death of the long-time Uzbek party chieftain Sharaf Rashidov, a personal friend of Brezhnev's, it became at last possible for the Moscow law-enforcement agencies to do something about the massive corruption in Uzbekistan and other Central Asian republics. The investigations in Kazakhstan came much later since the Kazakh party leader Dinmukhamed Kunaev, another close friend of Brezhnev's, is still very much alive and Gorbachev managed to engineer his dismissal only by the end of 1986.

In about 1984 (the exact date is kept secret) the USSR Prosecutor-General's office, supported by the KGB, started investigation of a universally known fact: that Uzbekistan never produced the amount of cotton planned and paid for each year. The reports on cotton crops were falsified at the collective farm level, huge bribes were paid to the local officials to cover the falsification and thus the chain of corruption went further up and reached into the Kremlin.

The team of investigators sent to Uzbekistan from Moscow was headed by an ambitious special investigator, Telman Gdlyan, an Armenian, and his no less ambitious Russian deputy Nikolai Ivanov. 200 investigators worked for more than 4 years and secured long prison sentences for thousands of former high officials in Uzbekistan. There was at least one death sentence for corruption. But when the investigators started to trace the links of the Uzbek mafia to the top men in Moscow, the attitude of the authorities to their activities started changing. In May 1988 in an unprecedented appeal to the public in the popular Ogonyok weekly the investigators complained that they were prevented by the party from carrying out their duty and arresting important officials. Faced by a wave of enraged public opinion the party had to give way and a few top Uzbek officials were arrested (to do this a decision by the Central Committee is needed).

Later that year in Moscow the USSR Supreme Court tried for corruption the son-in-law of Brezhnev, Yuri Churbanov, the former first Deputy Minister for Internal Affairs, and a number of top Uzbek police officials. The only defendant who cooperated with the investigators was given a very heavy sentence while the others, Churbanov included, were acquitted. The public was infuriated while Gdlyan and Ivanov complained to the press about the biased court. In response, the Prosecutor-General suspended them from their jobs and ordered an investigation into their cases under the pretext of numerous complaints from those arrested by Gdlyan's group.

In the elections to the Congress of People's Deputies in a Moscow constituency, Gdlyan won with the second-best majority in Moscow after the charismatic populist leader Boris Yeltsin. Ivanov won a heavily contested seat in Leningrad. In a televised election debate in early May, Ivanov indirectly accused a conservative Politburo member of protecting the corrupt party and government officials and of an involvement in the organized crime. This charge, the first of this kind against a party leader since early 1920s, had far-reaching consequences. Of course, the accusation was denied, and an investigation was demanded. On 12 September the Prosecutor-General's office issued a statement according to which evidence against the Politburo member was given by a former Uzbek Prime-Minister who had been arrested by the Gdlyan team and charged with corruption. Later this piece of evidence was withdrawn.

While the fact of corruption was undeniable, doubts began to surface about the methods the investigators had used, keeping suspects and even their families *in detention for several years at a time. Both sides made dark allusions to the lawless methods and terror of the 1930s. The Uzbek deputies at the Congress bitterly complained about the term "Uzbek affair" saying that it was slander against the hard-working Uzbek nation. Gdlyan hurried to explain that fundamentally what they were trying to investigate was the "Kremlin affair" since it concerned the corruption in the holy of holies — the Central Committee and the USSR government. In the end it became the "Gdlyan affair" since the Congress set up a commission to investigate the charges brought up by Gdlyan and Ivanov and the charges against them made by various government and party bodies and officials.*

Nikolai Ivanov (during the discussion of the composition of the "Gdlyan" commission) 154

It is typical that all serious questions to be decided are suggested for discussion at the end of the day when we are all tired... While we discuss setting up commissions, the investigation of corruption is being halted ... The Prosecutor-General removed 64 of the most experienced investigators from the group ... Three chief suspects have been released... The fight against organized crime is being curtailed. Only the Uzbek bribe-takers have been punished, the Russian ones have been released, the ones from Moscow are shielded from prosecution...

Voice from hall [question to candidate Chairman of Supreme Court] 160

Over the last 3½ years more than 450 verdicts have been overturned by appellate judges in Uzbekistan. Has anyone from the law enforcement agencies, and the prosecutor's office in particular, been punished for permitting such infringements of justice?

At a plenary session of the Central Committee held in Moscow on 19-20 September the USSR Prosecutor-General declared that the most careful investigation carried out by his office demonstrated that all charges against Ligachev had no foundation whatsoever. The Central Committee issued an official statement to that effect.

In late August the deputy head of the "Gdlyan" commission set up by the Congress complained bitterly to the press that his commission had no chance of working since the Prosecutor-General's office refused the people's deputies access to all the relevant documents. Gdlyan and Ivanov are still on the staff of this office as special investigators, though they have been suspended from duty pending the inquiry. All documents about their cases are technically the property of the office. Moreover, they are classified as top secret material and any persons handling them must have special clearance.

FERGHANA: A VALLEY OF BLOOD AND TEARS

As the Congress entered its second week the country experienced probably the worst ethnic conflict after the long-drawn out Azerbaijanian-Armenian confrontation. The Ferghana valley in Uzbekistan, the most productive agricultural area in Central Asia, became in early June the scene of violence of unprecedented brutality and viciousness.

Sixty thousand of the Meskhetian Turks deported by Stalin were brought to Uzbekistan and had since lived there alongside the Uzbeks and other deported nations (Crimean Tatars, Chechens, Koreans and others) under fairly good and friendly conditions. However, the lopsided economic development in Central Asia, and particularly in the Ferghana valley with its heavily polluted environment and accompanying social problems gave rise to ethnic tension. In recent years the replacement of thousands of corrupt Uzbek party and government officials produced, ironically, a surge of national self-awareness in Uzbekistan with a resulting hostility towards all non-Uzbeks in the region. It was a quirk of chance, probably, that the first violent outpouring of this hostility happened to be directed against fellow Muslims, the Turks, rather than Koreans or Russians. (Leaflets distributed in Tashkent and other towns and signed by an underground fundamentalist Islamic Uzbek movement stated later explicitly that they wanted all infidels and new-comers out).

After several days of indiscriminate rioting and attacks on the local police stations to get firearms and on the local party offices, 12,000 special troops were brought in. Because of poor coordination and reluctance to use fire-arms, it took them several days to crush the stubborn resistance of the rioters. It was said that the events had been carefully prepared by the Uzbek organized crimes groups which include many former and still active party and local officials, some of them even from the law-enforcement agencies.

For a few days the reports about the events were rather confusing and thus a variety of horrifying rumours spread throughout the region (there is some evidence of people being skinned alive). Thousands of Turks' homes were burned down. Tens of thousands of refugees were guarded by the army in makeshift camps in temperatures of 30°C with poor water supplies and practically no sanitation. An airlift was set up to take refugees away, but in the largest country in the world it proved hard to find a place for them. Georgia was reluctant to take them back in large numbers. Thousands of Turks were finally brought to villages in Central Russia where new housing had to be provided for them, for which the local population had been waiting for many years. Thus the seeds of future conflict were sown here as well.

Sober-minded observers suggest that the basic reasons for that particular ethnic conflict were social and economic. To put it plainly, there are too many people in Uzbekistan and especially in the Ferghana valley. The standard of living has been actually decreasing in the past years, while the unemployment grows alarmingly. The birth rate is so high that each third family in the rural areas where most Uzbeks live has five or more children below the age of 18. These families are often so poor that their basic diet is just bread and tea. Turks as a group (as well as Koreans, Crimean Tatars, Jews and Russians) are more active and prominent socially and economically, producing envy and hatred on the part of indigenous Uzbeks.

Rafik Nishanov, 1st Secretary, Uzbek Communist Party Central Committee (national deputy, Tashkent, Uzbekistan) 159

[Question period in the Nationalities Chamber. Nishanov is a candidate to be elected as the Speaker of the Chamber.]
... The Ferghana events started with small everyday quarrels. Forty five years ago Uzbeks accepted the deported Turks as brothers and sisters and provided them with all the conditions for work, education and a good life... There are 60,000 Turks in Uzbekistan, 12,000 in the Ferghana valley. All of them have jobs, they are members of local councils and party bodies.

In recent years, however, there have been repeated demands by Turks for the return of their homeland. In connection with the Congress these demands have become somewhat more urgent, but the conflicts originally started over a tiny everyday quarrel. A Turk at a local market rudely addressed a woman who was selling strawberries she had grown herself. The Turk claimed that the strawberries were too expensive and overturned a plate of them. The people around saw it as an insult and a skirmish occurred. This fight was stopped but soon a small group of Turks attacked local youngsters and one Turk was killed. Measures were taken and everything was quiet after that for almost a week. Then, quite unexpectedly for the local authorities, large groups of young Turks and Uzbek men aged from 15 to 22, some under the influence or alcohol or drugs, armed themselves with iron bars, clubs, bicycle chains and hatchets and started attacking homes of Turks, burning them down, and beating everybody in sight. Only Uzbeks and Turks were involved in these fights. Troops were sent there, curfew was introduced and the situation came under control. Some Turkish families had to be evacuated to an Army base for the sake of their safety.

I have visited the area and talked to the Turks. In the name of the Uzbek party and all workers of Uzbekistan I deplored the vandalism of the Uzbek youngsters and brought our deepest apologies to our Turkish brothers and sisters... The working people of Uzbekistan, no matter what their nationality, are generally hospitable, hard-working, humble people. These acts of barbarity are deplored by all and we must learn lessons from them to prevent anything of the kind happening in the future...

Anonymous [Baltic] deputy

I am not satisfied with Comrade Nishanov's answers. He did not give a specific answer to any of the questions.... When you were asked about Ferghana you told us about the strawberry incident that had happened almost a week before. Then a few days later some drunken and drugged people started a rampage. And as a result people of another nation were murdered. You said you went there to investigate. So I want you to give a direct answer: what were the causes—strawberries, alcohol and drugs, or was it nevertheless an ethnic conflict? If an ethnic conflict was to blame then tell us precisely what were the reasons for it.

Nishanov

I believe I gave you quite an objective and reasonable answer. Whether you were satisfied with it or not it is another matter. The deeper reasons for these events are being studied by the Uzbek government and party commission. A careful and principled analysis and political assessment are needed in such circumstances. I said I deplore this vandalism. What in my answer did not satisfy you?

Chapter 7

RESPONSES AND SOLUTIONS

Chairman of Congress sitting reads out an appeal:

The time has come to find real solutions to our present problems, and not simply state those shortcomings we all know perfectly well.

I think that deputies should also stop trying to frighten the Congress by ending their speeches with the words: 'I cannot guarantee the consequences if ...' 154

Conservative deputies often objected during the Congress to the "alarmism" of the radicals and spokesmen for national minorities. They were seeking a cheap popularity, the former suggested. It seems more likely that they were uncomfortably aware, as one put it, of "the voters breathing down our necks". The opportunity to explain their demands to other regions and republics, and to the whole country may have moderated the views of some deputies, and of the millions of viewers and listeners. One Central Asian deputy who had insisted that time must not be wasted in "endless" discussions over procedure and that decisions must be taken, was some days later complimenting the Moscow group for their "concern" and the Baltic delegations for "teaching us parliamentary procedure and etiquette".

However, the momentum already generated, partly by the elections, and the events that followed the Congress, suggest that these warnings were instead the voices of restraint.

THE ACHIEVEMENTS OF THE FIRST CONGRESS AND FIRST SESSION OF THE SUPREME SOVIET

On the second day there was a crucial vote on the notorious Decree on meetings, demonstrations and rallies. Referring to disturbing reports about the police breaking up a meeting in Moscow, the sociologist Tatyana Zaslavskaya demanded a statement from the Minister of Internal Affairs on the application of this decree. The Minister replied immediately, an unprecedented novelty, and insisted that no one anywhere had been arrested the previous day, and no meetings had been dispersed although many of them did not have official approval.

Reactions to this exchange were strong. Those who supported and attended such meetings were accused of demagogy and Gorbachev read out an indignant note demanding that "deputy Zaslavskaya apologise to the Moscow police for her improper remarks": 'I don't think things have reached that point yet,' he himself commented. Zaslavskaya, already a well-known and controversial figure, subsequently came last among the 55 Moscow candidates for the Chamber of the Union, with 591 votes for and 1558 against (the president of the new USSR cooperative union, Professor Tikhonov, was almost as unpopular).

A vote to suspend the operation of the decrees, at least during the session of the Congress, was taken — at the insistence of the Lithuanian delegation — and 831 were in favour. This was the high-tide mark at the Congress in the alliance of "democrats" and republican national movements. (As a compromise gesture a large area near Moscow's biggest sports stadium was thereafter made available for informal meetings which attracted many thousands.) Towards the end of the session this alliance took more permanent form. It was announced that an inter-regional and inter-republican group of deputies was being set up: and it was at this point that TV cameras were hastily turned off. Subsequently Boris Yeltsin became its figurehead and to date its membership numbers around 400.

In the dramatic closing days of the Congress, many more questions were raised. An unsuccessful attempt was made to bring the media under the Congress's control, by submitting the nominees as editor of *Izvestiya* and head of state broadcasting to the approval of the deputies. Demands were made, echoing Major Chervonopisky's concerns, for proper public hearings on the Afghan war with its thousands of Soviet dead, and million dead Afghans. An investigation was needed, Sobchak from Leningrad insisted, into the Novocherkassk events of 1962, when tanks were used against demonstrators in that southern Russian city protesting against rises in food prices. And in the wake of the Tienanmen massacre of 6 June, Andrei Sakharov called for the Soviet ambassador to be recalled from China in protest.

Sakharov's final major speech (he spoke 7 or 8 times in all), listed all that had not been resolved by the Congress. Interrupted repeatedly from the hall, and, finally, from the Presidium as well, he called for a radical dismantling and re-assembling of the Federation.

"As economic disaster looms ahead and relations between nations become tragically intensified," he warned, "certain dangerous developments are taking place. One symptom is the universal crisis of public confidence in the country's leadership. If we just drift along, comforting ourselves with the hope of gradual changes for the better in the distant future then the growing tension may erupt with the most tragic consequences for society. ... If the Congress cannot take power in its hands, then there is not the slightest hope that the Soviets at a lower level will be able to do so." (162)

When it came to the state of the Union, Sakharov saw the only solution to the oppression suffered under the inherited Stalinist model by all nations, including the Russians, as "the transition to a horizontal federal system" that would provide "all existing political structures for different Soviet nations, irrespective of their size and present status, with equal rights (while preserving present borders)". At this point the microphone was turned off, and though Sakharov's remarks continued to be audible they were not included in the official transcript ... (The full text was immediately published in Lithuania, and some time later in a Moscow monthly.)

The Congress thus raised numerous important issues without solving very many of them. Universal support, and wider application, of a government proposal to increase the appallingly low allowances received by the poorest pensioners was almost the only gesture to an impatient public, though an important and well-appreciated one.

In the subsequent sessions of the Supreme Soviet, the members grilled Ryzhkov's nominees as ministers throughout most of July and rejected no less than 5 of them. Indeed, if the rules of election had not been changed soon after the first such upset from 50% of all members to 50% of those present, the Minister of Defence would have also been among those not approved. Gradually more and more deputies revealed in discussion the qualities for which they had been elected and, if appointees, were perceptive enough of the popular mood to change their tone. After debate they permitted the Estonians and Latvians to proceed as of 1990 with *their* own plans for cost-accounting, not those of the central government. They also participated dramatically in the resolution of the miners' strike.

If then the Congress orators were not deliberately provoking the ethnic clashes and industrial strikes that succeeded one another through the summer into the early autumn, the Congress was in one sense certainly responsible. For what it did achieve, if nothing else, was a demystification of power in Soviet society as ministers and even Gorbachev himself were publicly called to order.

The pace of events quickened in every part of the country, as a glance at our Recent History appendix shows. Policy-making was subjected to criticism and supervision but had still hardly changed — indeed how could it? The Central Committee of the Party continued to follow traditional Soviet methods of resolving issues, and many of these traditions offered little guidance in the field of inter-ethnic conflict.

THE TRANSPLANT OPERATION

Why were the optimistic Western reactions to the Congress so rarely shared by the Soviet public, a Western journalist asked. Soviet observers were indeed moved and often passionately interested, even fascinated by the Congress and the Supreme Soviet but, at the same time, very wary in their judgements and expectations. There was a weary scepticism fully justified by a steady worsening of daily living conditions. Many others felt, in the spirit of Zalygin's quotation about such assemblies in the past, that the Congress must decide everything at once or would achieve nothing.

Perhaps the appearance of a democratic if still very disorganised assembly involuntarily led outsiders to draw false parallels with Western parliaments. In the Soviet case, however, the underpinning democratic institutions, in the economy, the administration and so on, are simply not yet there. Although the system's natural resistance had been progressively weakened by ever increasing doses of glasnost everyone feared there would be a terrible reaction, sooner or later. Two particular weaknesses might be noted in this respect. Most important of all, as was frequently and publicly admitted, the Party itself which provides the country's Cabinet or Politburo and also possesses the most powerful administrative and decision-making body in the Soviet Union, the Central Committee, is not yet under internal democratic control.

Secondly, the lower levels of Soviets or representative councils are still largely rubber-stamping assemblies of the old kind. So the Congress, and even the new-style Supreme Soviet, were for the time being dangling precariously in mid-air. Alexei Emelyanov, a Moscow deputy and Moscow University professor of economics, uncompromisingly asserted that "The people take precedence over the Party, and our Congress over a Party Congress. The Supreme Soviet is superior to the Central Committee. The constitution is superior to the Party regulations." (161) Yet deputies were still over-worked dealing with leaking roofs, and other tasks that should have been resolved at the local level by those who already realised they would not themselves be re-elected, and they were therefore reported to be achieving nothing.

It was probably no bad thing at all that half the deputies would not be in Moscow, sitting in the Supreme Soviet and on its commissions and committees, but spread out, however thinly, across this vast and diverse country, breathing quite a different political atmosphere to that in the hot-house environment of the Kremlin in late May to early August 1989.

Most pressing of all, the republican supreme soviets had to be re-elected. Here there were immediate positive gains, following the Congress discussions. The draft for the Russian Federation electoral law excluded the indirect election or nomination of deputies from non-governmental organisations and, except where there were 10 and more candidates in one constituency, did not permit the dubious district electoral commissions to intervene and filter out "undesirable" candidates. Soon there would even be suggestions that these republican supreme soviets should also be bicameral bodies with their own Chamber of nationalities (or at least, as far as the Russian Federation was concerned). On the other hand, the unpublished draft of the Ukrainian electoral law was denounced by the more democratic Ukrainian deputies as even more retrogressive than that applied in the countrywide March elections. And when it came to the Baltic republics, Estonia erupted into widespread strikes when a citizenship and length of residence qualification was introduced for voters.

PARTY AND GOVERNMENT START TO ACT

By the end of 1986 the party leadership finally admitted the need for new ethnic and national policies. It was announced that the Central Committee was preparing a special plenary session at which the fundamental ethnic and national issues would be decided. Thereafter, however, nothing more was heard for months on end. The session was finally scheduled for July 1989 — but even in early September there was still no word of it. Then in the week before the Supreme Soviet was due to resume sitting, the long-delayed plenum was held on 19-20 September.

Gorbachev spoke in unusually harsh terms about the terrible costs of the ethnic strife in Karabakh and elsewhere in terms of human tragedies and economic losses. In his new capacity as Head of State he warned Soviet citizens that the continuation of such strife was madness. Future generations, he said, would damn those extremists who strove to generate hate between the Soviet nations, and those who had failed to prevent them. He spoke of criminals who were exploiting valid national grievances in their own sinister interests and threatened them with prosecution under

G

the relevant laws. At the same time, he admitted that decades of Communist rule had left a legacy of social, economic and cultural problems so closely interconnected with ethnic issues that any measures designed to tackle them would fail if the ethnic dimension was not taken into account.

THE LAST PEACEFUL SUMMER?

One sign that the plenum was finally on its way was the publication in mid-August of the Party's draft proposals on ethnic and national issues.

The Soviet practice for releasing major party or government documents is to publish them simultaneously, in full, in all the newspapers (national, regional and local) that exist in the country, i.e. in hundreds of millions of copies so that they reach each reader more than once. Editors have long complained about this mandatory practice but, in this case, most of them were only too willing to publish the "National Policy of the Party under Current Conditions (the CPSU Platform. A Draft)" even without explicit orders to do so.

In the weeks that followed the press published a wide variety of (mostly favourable) opinions about the Platform from all sections of the public: from farmers to academics, and even Western comment, which would have been unthinkable just three years ago. Yet the reports of strikes, rallies and sporadic but persistent violence from all over the country that continued to appear alongside this discussion were deeply disturbing, especially to the traditional outlook of the average Soviet person. It was not just the way things were going but the fact that the authorities seemed to be unable to do much about stopping them.

A Moscow observer wryly commented that Soviet people would soon look back on 1989 as the last peaceful summer for several years.

THE CAUCASUS: THE TURMOIL CONTINUES

In July violent riots swept through Abkhazia. They were sparked off by an unprecedented cause of ethnic conflict in the Soviet Union — the opening ceremony for the Abkhazian branch of the Tbilisi State University in Sukhumi, the capital of Abkhazia. Tension there was so high that this genuinely cultural event was regarded as a challenge by Abkhazians, and a further deliberate violation of their cultural autonomy by the Georgian nationalists. There may be some truth in this. The Georgian authorities could hardly fail to realize that an institution where teaching would be conducted in Georgian would not be welcome to the Abkhazians, especially under the present tense conditions.

Dozens of people were killed in the riots, hundreds were injured, and crowds attacked and ransacked police stations seizing hand guns, automatic rifles and ammunition stored there. In the resulting mayhem large numbers of the prisoners held in the police station cells escaped into the wooded mountains a few miles away. Abkhazia has a long tradition of bandits, hiding out in the mountains, being aided and abetted by the local population. Special peace-keeping troops were speedily brought in and house-to-house searches for weapons were conducted. Thousands of rifles, pistols, and even heavy machine guns were confiscated from private citizens. Large caches of explosives, mines and hand grenades were also found. For a few days the major railway that connects Georgia and Armenia with the rest of the USSR was put out of operation by engineer's strikes, and by explosions and attacks on the trains. The economic costs were staggering and thousands of holiday-makers had to be evacuated by chartered aircraft and boats. By August the troops had the situation under control in the coastal regions but helicopter patrols have still to be sent to the mountain areas to search for hundreds of bandits still hiding there. In September massive strikes were started by Abkhazians in all major towns. Ironically, their demands are just the opposite of those of Armenians in Karabakh. They appealed to the USSR Supreme Soviet to institute direct rule in Abkhazia thus effectively taking it out of the jurisdiction of the Georgian republic. Some Abkhazian activists even insist that if independence as a separate republic is impossible for Abkhazia they would then prefer to join the Russian Federation with which they have a common border just so long as they can escape Georgian rule.

The Georgian authorities have many more concerns, in addition to the conflict with Abkhazia. The Commission on Tbilisi set up in May by the Congress has not delivered its verdict. For an outside observer, life in Georgia seems calm but Georgians claim that an explosion could occur at any moment; at the slightest provocation. Apart from some halfhearted attempts to pacify the nation, the Moscow authorities did not do much to meet the demands of the national movements in Georgia. And even what they did do seemd more like a show of strength by Moscow. For instance, General Rodionov kept his position as commander of the regional military district, a post that ranks third from the top in the USSR military hierarchy, until early September when he was quietly removed to another position.

The Karabakh affair continues to be a prime source of conflict in the region. In mid-August most of the strikes that had been going on there since 3 May were halted but the decision was accompanied by other controversial actions. Armenians in Karabakh for a long time protested against direct rule, arguing that it was unconstitutional. Since the Azerbaijanian and Moscow authorities did nothing about Armenian demands to restore the suspended powers of the local Soviets and party committees (which are controlled by Armenians) and to retain the Direct Rule Committee merely as a body representing the Moscow authorities, Armenians convened a Congress of Representatives from Karabakh communities. The Congress elected a National Council and charged it with the administration of Karabakh "in the name of the people". The Congress announced that it would exercise the constitutional right to self-determination by passing a resolution to secede from Azerbaijan and join Armenia. The National Council also promised to work for a stabilization of the situation in Karabakh and to prevent ethnic conflicts there but did not offer any concrete details.

In response protest rallies and demonstrations were held in Baku and other Azerbaijanian cities involving hundreds of thousands (mostly men, as Islamic traditions there are growing in influence). The protesters also demanded official registration of the People's Front of Azerbaijan set up to support perestroika and to protect the national rights of Azerbaijanians in Karabakh and elsewhere. Meanwhile, the Karabakh Azerbaijanians seemed quite capable of looking after themselves. In late August a 100-strong crowd of them captured, and held hostage for 5 hours, three Army generals including the three-star general commanding all special troops stationed for peace-keeping in the region. The hostages were released only after the authorities met demands to transfer several Azerbaijanian prisoners from an Armenian prison to an Azerbaijanian one. Numerous incidents were reported in September when Azerbaijanians attacked and sometimes killed the Russian peace-keeping troops and police.

Azerbaijanians cut off virtually all road and railway links to Karabakh and Armenia thus establishing an economic blockade, since all but 15% of freight goes to Armenia via Azerbaijan. Addressing the Central Committee plenary session on 20 September, Arkady Volsky, the Head of the Special Rule Committee for Karabakh, said that Armenia and Azerbaijan were on the brink of an "ethnic war" over Karabakh. No solution was offered at the session.

The conservative Azerbaijanian leadership for a long time refused to recognize the People's Front which eventually called for a general strike.

The activists of the Front claim that all major industries in the republic went on strike from 4 September. The official news agency admits reluctantly that some strikes are going on. Indeed, the authorities seem to be so confused about what is happening that they resorted to an old and well-tried approach, a clampdown on news. What served them well in the 1930s and even early 1980s now has the effect of further angering and confusing people, since they get abundant (though sometimes distorted) news coverage from other sources: foreign radio stations, which are no longer jammed, numerous unofficial publications and, of course, the traditional and most popular news source in the USSR , rumour. By mid-September the Azerbaijanian authorities had to give way. The People's Front was officially registered and the strikes were stopped.

Another hot bed of ethnic tension involving Azerbaijanians lies in Georgia in a fertile valley not far from Tbilisi. A small settlement of Azerbaijanians has existed there since the last century. In recent decades it has been steadily expanding due to migration of Azerbaijanians from their republic where the standard of living is considerably lower, and the exceptional corruption of local officials makes life hard for enterprising individuals. The migrants compete with indigenous Georgians for available housing and for customers in the local markets since they are highly accomplished market gardeners and the prices for produce in the private markets in Georgian cities and towns are notoriously high. The old resentment of local Georgians against the Azerbaijanian migrants erupted in July in violence in the villages and towns where they live and special troops had to be brought in to stop the ethnic fighting. Owing to the speedy response of the authorities and the small scale of the problem the casualties were few but the tension persists in this region.

We should also note here the large expatriate community of Chechen engineers and workers in the oil fields on the Mangyshlak Peninsula in Kazakhstan. Recently they were involved in violent clashes with the local Kazakhs and thousands of them had to flee with their families from Kazakhstan and to return to their homeland. There the housing shortage and other social and economic problems reinforce the ethnic hatred between the indigenous Chechens, who returned from their exile in 1956, and the mostly Slavic settlers brought there by Stalin to occupy the Chechen villages after their deportation in 1945.

"BALTIC CHAIN"

The events in the Baltic republic proceed in a much more orderly manner but their speed is no less breath-taking. Immediately after the Supreme Soviet of Estonia had approved the election law in mid-August, massive strikes by the Russian-speaking workers began in major industries. For the first time in the history of the USSR, strikers were making purely political demands. At first, the republican leadership was not prepared to make concessions to the strikers and some even saw the "hand of Moscow" in them. But when the transport workers joined the strike, the economy of many regions in the country was hit, since the Estonian capital Tallin is an important Baltic sea port. In general, the transport-ation system in the USSR is in a state of permanent crisis and even a small additional disruption can be disastrous. On 16 August the Presidium of the USSR Supreme Soviet declared that the new Estonian election law was unconstitutional. Behind-the-scenes pressure was applied both to the strikers and to the Estonian leadership: there was an unprecedented TV screening of parts of the discussion in the Presidium of the Supreme Soviet. The Estonian Supreme Soviet promised to reconsider the matter at a special session in early October. Strikes were stopped and the talks are now going on between the strikers and the Estonian government.

In late August the Baltic nations marked 50 years since the signing of the Molotov-Ribbentrop pact. A commission was set up by the Congress to re-evaluate this pact but by the time of the anniversary it still had not published its report. A similar commission of the Lithuanian Supreme Soviet concluded that the pact was illegal and invalid from the moment it was signed and hence the unification of Lithuania with the USSR in 1940 was also illegal.

On the anniversary, 23 August, the People's Fronts of the three Baltic republics organized numerous rallies, parades and demonstration. In an extraordinary show of solidarity more than a million people holding lit candles, praying and singing national songs formed a human chain — the Baltic chain — along hundreds of miles of roads between the capitals of the three republics. At a signal the word "freedom" was passed from one person to another along the chain.

This spectacular display of national intransigence enraged the conser-vatives in Moscow and on 29 August the front pages of all papers in the country carried the "Declaration of the Central Committee on the situ-ation in the Soviet Baltic republics". It came as a shock to the Baltic nations. The Declaration stated plainly that the goal of the People's Fronts was secession from the USSR and that this concerned the fundamental interests of all Soviet nations. The Central Committee charged the party and government leaders of the Baltic republics with an inability or unwillingness to control and regulate the perestroika process which had got out of hand. The declaration warned of civil conflicts, mass rioting and hinted of the possible heavy price to pay. In no uncertain terms it said that the consequences would be catastrophic and the very existence of the nations would be uncertain if the "bourgeois nationalist extremists" were not curbed. It ended with the call to communists and nations to "preserve the unity of the family of Soviet nations and the integrity of the Communist Party of the USSR". This last appeal was prompted by the growing trend towards an independent status for the Communist parties of the Baltic republics. This has been particularly pronounced in Lithuania where the next party congress will make a decision on the issue.

This attempt to threaten the national movements in the Baltic republics produced a mixed reaction throughout the country. Its intention was clearly understood as a warning to the People's Fronts and movements in all republics that they cannot go too far. In the Baltic republics the response was almost uniformly indignant. The party and government leaders had consultations and issued statements that they had the situation well under control, that no secession plans were intended and that the extremists were really a harmless, though perhaps unsavoury, product of democratisation. The Moscow threats were mostly taken as a bluff and the central mass media were accused of misrepresenting the Baltic case and even of falsifying some reports about the anti-Soviet activities in the republics.

More sober leaders warned, however, that nobody could confidently estimate how much bluff there was in the Declaration, not even its anonymous authors.

One interesting but unexpected consequence of the Baltic striving for sovereignty took place on 7 September in Lithuania. The Soviet of the Shalchininkai district where 81% of the 40,000 population are ethnic Poles, declared its new status as a self-governing Polish national district, despite the promises of the Lithuanian authorities to grant them some form of autonomy in future. The Moscow press relished the fact of Lithuanians getting some of their own medicine.

The strikers in the Baltic republics inspired the Russian-speaking workers in Moldavia, who staged strikes with similar demands in late August and early September, protesting against the law that made Moldavian the official language in the republic. The Moldavian legislators also learned their lesson and their new law allowed for Russian to be used as the second official language. As a result, neither the Moldavian People's Front nor the Russian-speaking workers were entirely satisfied and ethnic tension has not relaxed.

STIRRINGS IN THE SLAVIC REPUBLICS

In late June the Belorussian People's Front, having failed to get permission to hold its inaugural meeting in Minsk, was finally established at a meeting in Vilnius, the capital of neighbouring Lithuania. In early September a People's Front (the Rukh) was officially set up in the Ukraine, perhaps heralding the passing of the Ukrainian party leader Shcherbitsky, the last of Brezhnev's generation, and certainly indicating a major shift in this large and crucial republic. (The retirement of Shcherbitsky was, indeed, announced at the session of the Central Committee on 20 September).

Russia itself continues to present a highly contradictory picture. The national identity of Russians is quite diffuse. The territory the nation occupies cannot be readily identified with the Russian Federation, the historical culture has been severely undermined, and the morale of the people is very low. In many respects, the standard of living in Russia proper is considerably lower than the average for the USSR. But what worries Russian intellectuals (as can be seen from the speeches at the Congress) is that while other nations began to exhibit an enhanced self-awareness and a stronger sense of national identity this cannot be confidently said about Russians.

Many place their sole hope on reviving the national spirit of Russia in the Russian Orthodox Church. Even the communist party with its tradition of virulent anti-religious policies, now admits that religion has a contribution to make in improving the cultural and moral environment. To mark the recent 1000-year anniversary of the official adoption of Christianity by Russia, the government allowed the Church to open several, formerly closed, monasteries. Religious literature can now be brought from abroad and it is permissible and even fashionable for young couples to be married in church, for babies to be baptised and so on.

Unfortunately, the slow revival of Russian national culture is accompanied by less wholesome developments. The unofficial cultural groups are often influenced by the notorious Pamyat movement whose anti-Semitic and generally chauvinistic concepts find tacit support among some high-ranking party and government officials in the Russian Federation. The neo-Slavophiles in turn support the neo-Stalinists, hoping to preserve the existing strict rule and administrative structure of the Communist Party but use it for the purpose of restoring the Great Russian spirit and culture. These Russian patriots, as they tend to call themselves, also blame Communists for all the troubles that Russia has experienced since the October Revolution. They resolve this apparent contradiction by noting that the Communist Party leadership at the time of the 1917 Revolution and many years after consisted mostly of non-Russians, particularly Jews. The more chauvinistic of the "Russian patriots" even claim that the Communist Revolution was nothing but a plot by Jews and Masons to destroy the Russian nation.

The Russian national movement, if and when it emerges, thus remains the big unknown factor. The isolationist trend in conservative Russian thinking is becoming more pronounced. Solzhenitsyn, as early as 1976, warned in his letter to the Soviet government that time was running out for Russia, that its cultural and human resources were almost exhausted, and that the last chance for Russia to rise again was to retreat to the great expanses of the North-East and to seek its future there.

In the summer of 1989 the Russian nationalists who are mainly intellectuals, made special efforts to recruit industrial workers to their groups. A Russian Workers Front was set up in Leningrad in mid-June with the behind-the-scenes support of the local party officials, evidently to oppose the strong People's Front there. The former's programme is quite vague but the intentions are unmistakable: they are for a return to the Stalinist methods and for suppression of all liberal, democratic and ethnic movements, and one method was to insist that candidates as people's deputies only be put forward by mass meetings at factories and in the workplace. Similar groups were set up in other Russian cities and in early September they held a foundation conference for the National Russian Workers Movement in Sverdlovsk. There they announced their opposition to the political and economic reforms advocated by Gorbachev. This movement apparently enjoys support of the top party conservatives but they are rather poorly organized and popular support for them in Russia seems to be weak. On the other hand, if social and economic conditions continue to deteriorate, if there are fewer goods in shops at higher prices, and if the crime rate soars any higher their influence may be decisively enhanced. A recent sinister move by the party authorities in some regions, started in the city of Gorky, is to set up volunteer workers militia. The volunteers (preferably veterans of the Afghan war) will receive basic police training, they will be armed and work with the police performing "special duties" for three months a year while their wages will be paid by their employers (an enforced deduction imposed by the party authorities). The pretext is provided by the extraordinary measures against crime announced by the Supreme Soviet in July but some observers see it as a political move.

In response to comments at the Congress and to these subsequent developments, the Prime Minister of the Russian Federation, Alexander Vlasov, promised Russians much greater autonomy in the near future, especially in cultural matters (interview in *Izvestiya*, 1 September). Emphasising that he fully supported Gorbachev's political and economic reforms, he announced that the Russian Federation would gain its own party, trade unions, Komsomol organisations, and Academy of Sciences. Large Russian regions would also be given some economic independence (regional cost-accounting).

THE NEW PARTY DOCUMENT

The draft document of 16 August (see page 164) was introduced as the programme to be discussed at the plenary session of the Central Committee. (It is implied that this document will be approved and used as guidelines in national and ethnic policy in the future.) The anonymous authors of the Platform are apparently high-ranking Central Committee officials who lead teams of specially selected academics each preparing a section of the document. They claim to have analysed the views expressed by the party and government bodies, academics, the public at large, reports in the mass media, and statements by the deputies in their speeches at the Congress. Since the draft document was published, numerous comments and suggestions have been printed by the party press though no formal invitation for its discussion was made.

The document briefly but fairly described the history and the current state of ethnic relations and problems in the USSR. It claimed that Lenin's concept of the federation of Soviet republics did much to help the development of all nations and, at the same time, the integration of economy and society that the Soviet nations started merging into a historically new community — a Soviet supernation. But then Stalin's deviations from the genuine Socialist principles and the misguided policies of his heirs gradually gave rise to a variety of ethnic conflicts and problems that are everyday news in the mass media. Society is undergoing radical changes at present, the Platform continues, which must preserve everything valuable from the past and give new impetus to the economic, political and cultural development of each nation.

Up to this point it is all more or less standard party propaganda. What is new in the Platform are the suggested radical changes in the federal structure of the USSR.

Apparently, the party is prepared to give the republics much more political sovereignty and economic independence than they have now. Major changes in the USSR Constitution are envisaged. However, various limitations on independence are carefully inserted into the Platform. For instance, the republics will own the land, waters, mineral and other resources but the principles of using them will be decided by Moscow authorities "in the interests of country's security and inter-republican and all-union concerns". This is less independence than the Baltic republics are demanding and, probably, more than the Central Asian republics can immediately cope with.

Another important reform is the promised "restoration of full rights of the nations of the autonomous republics, regions and districts". Autonomous republics will have self-government and economic independence on the same principles as the union republics. This approach, properly implemented, will eliminate a large number of existing and latent inter-ethnic conflicts. The upgrading of the rights of smaller autonomous formations (regions and districts) will also contribute to a weakening of ethnic friction. Even the ethnic minorities that possess no autonomous territorial units are promised a much better deal in future, particularly in languages and culture. The dispossessed nations, such as Crimean Tatars, Meskhetian Turks, and Volga Germans, are given only vague assurances that their problems will be resolved "taking into account the interests of all nations concerned and current realities". It is a vivid indication of changing times that the Platform ends by explaining that it only contains proposals to be analysed and approved by the Congress of People's Deputies and the Supreme Soviet. This is the first major party document that includes such a stipulation, demonstrating that the party has started thinking in real terms about sharing power and responsibilities with elected people's representatives.

CONCLUSION

These are fine intentions. Finding the way and will to implement them is another matter. Meanwhile ugly rumours and distorted reporting do not help to ease the tension. Deteriorating economic conditions add to the general sense of desperation. Some analysts suggest that the morale of the people in the country is at its lowest since the days of heavy losses in World War 2. No segment of the society feels confident that it is being listened to by the authorities. The conservatives demand discipline and firm actions, liberals ask for sweeping economic reforms leading to a market economy and further democratisation. The authorities have lost much of their authority, and waver dangerously between the two. The Congress and Supreme Soviet do not yet have the experience or power to share the responsibility or take their place.

When the Congress was debating Gorbachev's candidacy as President, the Ukrainian writer Yavorivsky warned that if the people's deputies did not set an example of greatness and principle at the "top of the pyramid" then the people would turn their backs on them and "retreat again into silence and vodka, and anecdotes — about you, Mikhail Gorbachev, and about us deputies". This timely reminder of the recent past, however, is probably already out of date, even for the hitherto more passive Slavic republics. Under the cumulative pressure of economic, ecological and above all national problems the former unproductive but manageable apathy is rapidly being replaced by active involvement of both hopeful and disturbing kinds.

APPENDICES

APPENDIX I
Recent History

1989

25 March	Elections for 1500 deputies to USSR Congress of People's Deputies
2-9 April	Second round in 275 constituencies
9 April	Troops used to disperse demonstration in Tbilisi, 20 dead as result
14 May	Third round in 76 constituencies
15 May	Gorbachev in China
25 May	**Congress opens in Moscow**
	Gorbachev elected Chairman or President
26 May	Elections to Supreme Soviet
May	Turkmenian urban riots
3 June	First session of Chamber of Union
	Rail catastrophe, near Ufa, Bashkiria
	Tienanmen square massacre in China
	Pogrom in Ferghana valley, Uzbekistan, begins; more than 100 dead, thousands of refugees
6 June	First session of Chamber of Nationalities
	First free elections in Poland
7 June	Ryzhkov elected Prime Minister
9 June	**Congress closes**
June	Riots in Novy Uzen, Kazakhstan, more refugees
10 June	Second sessions of Chambers, break for a week
12 June	Gorbachev to West Germany
20 June	Supreme Soviet resumes sitting

late June	Belorussian People's Front set up in Vilnius
1 July	Gorbachev TV appeal for ethnic calm
4-6 July	Gorbachev in France
July	Kirgiz-Tajik border clashes
15 July	Selection of new government ministers completed
Early July	Coal-miners strike throughout the country
July	General railway strike narrowly avoided; partly provoked by failure to approve minister
July	Scheduled Central Committee plenum not held
Mid-July	Ethnic riots in Abkhazia
July-August	Political strikes in Moldavia and Abkhazia
16 August	Communist Party Draft Platform on National Policy published for discussion
16 August	USSR Supreme Soviet Presidium Declares Estonian Election law unconstitutional
20 August	Supreme Soviet goes into recess
Mid-late August	Strikes in Estonia against new language and election laws
23 August	"Baltic chain" demonstrations, 50th anniversary of Molotov-Ribbentrop pact
29 August	Central Committee issues threatening declaration about Baltic republics
Late August	Karabakh people's congress declares intention to secede from Azerbaijan
Early September	Massive industrial strikes in Azerbaijan, demands for registration of People's Front
Early September	First non-Communist government in Soviet bloc takes office in Poland
7-10 September	Founding congress of Ukrainian Ruch (People's Front), Adam Michnik of Solidarity among official guests
10 September	Ingushi People's Front set up in Grozny (Northern Caucasus)

9 September	Gorbachev's TV address to the country
13 September	Gorbachev meets Baltic party and government leaders
Mid-September	Economic blockade of Karabakh
17 September	Extraordinary sessions of Armenian and Azerbaijanian Supreme Soviets on Karabakh
19-20 September	Central Committee plenum approves Platform on National and Ethnic policy
25 September	Supreme Soviet renews sitting
October	Autumn session of Congress
October	Estonian Supreme Soviet meets to reconsider election laws

1990

1 Jan 1990	Baltic republics, Belorussia, Tataria, and various regions of Russian Federation begin cost-accounting
Feb 1990	Provisional date for elections to new-style Supreme Soviet of the Russian Federation
	Elections to republican Supreme Soviets and local Soviets

APPENDIX II

The National Composition of the USSR population 1979 (figures and % in brackets are for 1959)

	000s		%	
Total	262 436	*(208 826)*	*100.0*	*(100.0)*
Main nationalities of the union republics				
Russians	137 397	(114 114)	52.4	(55.0)
Ukrainians	37 252	(42 347)	14.2	(18.0)
Belorussians	9 463	(7 913)	3.6	(4.0)
Uzbeks	12 456	(6 015)	4.8	(3.0)
Kazakhs	6 556	(3 621)	2.5	(2.0)
Azerbaijani	5 477	(2 939)	2.1	(1.4)
Armenians	4 151	(2 786)	1.6	(1.3)
Georgians	3 571	(2 692)	1.4	(1.3)
Lithuanians	2 851	(2 326)	1.1	(1.1)
Moldavians	2 968	(2 214)	1.1	(1.1)
Latvians	1 439	(1 399)	0.5	(0.7)
Tajik	2 898	(1 396)	1.1	(0.7)
Turkmenians	2 020	(1 001)	0.8	(0.5)
Estonians	1 020	(987)	0.4	(0.5)
Kirgizians	1 906	(968)	0.7	(0.6)
Main Nationalities of the autonomous republics				
Tatars	6 317	(4 967)	2.4	(2.4)
Chuvash	1 751	(1 469)	0.7	(0.7)
Mordovinians	1 192	(1 285)	0.5	(0.6)
Bashkiri	1 371	(989)	0.5	(0.5)
Main nationalities of the autonomous regions and districts				
Jews	1 811	(2 267)	0.7	(1.1)
Ethnic groups of the North	158	(127)	—	—
Remaining nationalities and ethnic groups				
Germans	1 936	(1 619)	0.7	(0.8)
Poles	1 151	(1 380)	0.4	(0.6)

Note: these figures are based on census findings in 1959 and 1979, i.e. what people said their nationality and that of their children was. Data about nationality are preserved in two important types of Soviet document.

In 1932 internal passports (identity and domicile registration documents etc.) were reintroduced. They are formally acquired at the age of 16 and since the war have imposed a strict choice between the nationality of one or other parent (there are an estimated 40 million children of inter-ethnic marriages in the USSR today).

In addition, the famous 5th item on standard application forms for jobs, places in higher education etc., also requires applicants to state their nationality. This has permitted controversial quotas of various kinds to be applied ('positive discrimination' for students from Central Asia and other less developed regions, anti-semitism in many professions).

APPENDIX III

The populations of the republics

No less than 55 million live outside their nominal homeland or republic. There are over 24 million Russians, and more than 1 million Armenians living outside the Russian Federation and Armenia respectively. And, of course, only 10,000 Jewish people live in Birobijan (the Jewish Autonomous Region) on the Soviet-Chinese border.

The following tables give certain basic information on four regions and the larger autonomous republics:

1 Baltic republics and Moldavia

2 Caucasian republics

3 Slavic republics

4 The largest autonomous republics in the Russian Federation

5 Central Asia and Kazakhstan

In each case the total republican population is compared to that of the indigenous (or eponymous national) population, in 1979 and for the first post-war census in 1959. The degree of urbanisation, in 1989 and 1959, is also provided as a rough measure of economic development.

So far, only crude figures for the total population of each republic, and their relative numbers of urban and rural inhabitants, have been provided for the latest regular decennial census held in January 1989 (Pravda and Izvestiya, 29 April 1989). These are included here in brackets.

1 Baltic Republics and Moldavia

Total 000s (1)	"indigenous"			urban % (5)
	000s (2)	% (3)	(1959 %) (4)	
Lithuania: Russians (303), Poles (247) and Belorussians (57)				
3391 (3690)	2712	78	79	(68) 39
Latvia: Russians (321), Belorussians (111), Ukrainians (67) and Poles(63). In the 1935 census Latvians were 75% of total pop.				
2503 (2681)	1344	54	62	(71) 56
Estonia: Russians (409), Ukrainians (36) and Belorussians (23).				
1464 (1573)	948	65	75	(72) 56
Moldavia: Until 1940 an autonomous republic and part of Ukraine. Ukrainians (561), Russians (506), Gagauz (138).				
3950 (4341)	2526	64	65	(47) 22

2 Caucasian Republics

Until 1936 combined in Transcaucasian Federation.

Total 000s (1)	"indigenous"			urban % (5)
	000s (2)	% (3)	(1959 %) (4)	
Georgia: Contains Abkhazian and Adzharian ASSRs and South Ossetian autonomous region. Ossetians (160), Abkhazians (85), Armenians (448), Russians (371) and Azerbaidzhanis (256)				
4993 (5449)	3433	69	(64)	(56) 42
a) Abkhazian autonomous republic: Demoted to autonomous republic status within Georgia in 1931. Georgians (213), Russian (80), Armenians (73).				
486 (535)	83	17	—	(48)
b) South Ossetian autonomous region: 65,000 Ossetians and 28,000 Georgians				
Armenia: Azerbaidzhanis (161), Russians (70) and Kurds (51).				
3037 (3283)	2725	90	88	(68) 50
Azerbaijan: Includes the Nakhichevan ASSR (bordering Turkey) and the Nagorno-Karabakh autonomous region. Armenians (475) and Russians (475).				
6027 (7029)	4709	78	68	(54) 48
a) Nogorno-Karabakh autonomous region: Azerbaijani (37) and Russian (1000).				
162 (188)	123*	76	—	52
b) In Nakhichevan 230 of 240 thousand population are Azerbaijani.				

*Armenian Population

3 Slavic Republics

Total 000s (1)	"indigenous"			urban % (5)
	000s (2)	% (3)	(1959 %) (4)	
Russian Federated republic: Over 100 different nationalities and ethnic groups. Includes 16 autonomous republics, 5 autonomous regions and 10 autonomous districts. Ethnic Russians still form overwhelming majority.				
137,410 (147,386)	113,522	83	83	(74) 53
Ukraine: After Ukrainians the next most numerous nationalities are Russians (10,472), Jews (634), Belorussians (406) and Moldavians (294).				
49,609 (51,704)	36,489	74	77	(67) 46
Belorussia: Apart from Belorussians, Russians (113), Poles (403), Ukrainians (231) and Jews (135).				
9533 (10,200)	7568	79	81	(65) 32

4 The Largest Autonomous Republics in Russian Federation

Total 000s (1)	"indigenous"		Russians 000s (4)	urban % (5)
	000s (2)	% (3)		
A UPPER VOLGA/URALS AREA				
Tataria				
3445	1642	48	1516	73
Bashkiria				
3844	936	24	1548	64
Chuvashia				
1299	888	68	338	58
Udmurtia				
1492	480	32	870	70
Mordovia				
990	339	34	591	57
B NORTH CAUCASUS				
Chechen-Ingushetia				
1156	611	53*	336	41
C SIBERIA				
Buryatia				
899	207	23	647	62
Yakutia				
852	314	37	430	67

*Chechen population: Ingush 135,000

5 Central Asia and Kazakhstan

Turkestan as it was called before the Revolution was divided in the 1920s
and 1930s into 4 republics. Kazakhstan became a union republic in 1936.

Total 000s (1)	"indigenous"			urban % (5)
	000s (2)	% (3)	(1959 %) (4)	
Uzbekistan: Contains Karakalpak ASSR. non-Uzbek population includes Karakalpaki (282), Russians, Tatars, Kazakh, Tadzhik and Koreans.				
15,389 (19,906)	10,569	69	62	(41) 34
Tajikistan: Union republic in 1929; includes Nagorno-Badakhshan autonomous region (115 of 128 thousand are Tajiks). Uzbeks (837), Russians (395), Tatars (80) etc.				
3806 (5112)	2237	59	53	(33) 33
Turkmenia: Union republic in 1924. Russians (349), Uzbeks (333), Kazakhs (80) and Tatars (40).				
2765 (3534)	1892	68	61	(45) 46
Kirgizia: Union republic in 1936. Russians (912), Uzbeks (426), Ukrainians (109), Germans (101), Tatars, Kazakhs and Tadzhik.				
3523 (4291)	1667	47	41	(38) 34
Kazhakstan: Union republic in 1936. Russians (5991), Ukrainians (897), Germans (900), Tatars (313) and Uzbeks (263).				
14,684 (16,538)	5289	36	30	(57) 44

Notes: Figures in text for each republic are from the 1979 census.
Columns:

1   1979 total (1989 census preliminary report)

2 & 3   1979 census

4   1959 census figures

5   1959 census (1989 figures)

MAP

Overleaf is a map of the Western and Central part of the USSR, showing the principal republics.

RUSSIAN SOVIET FEDER

FINLAND

•Moscow

ESTONIAN
SSR

LATVIAN SSR

LITHUANIAN
SSR

BELORUSSIAN
SSR

•Kiev

UKRAINIAN SSR

POLAND

MOLDAVIAN SS

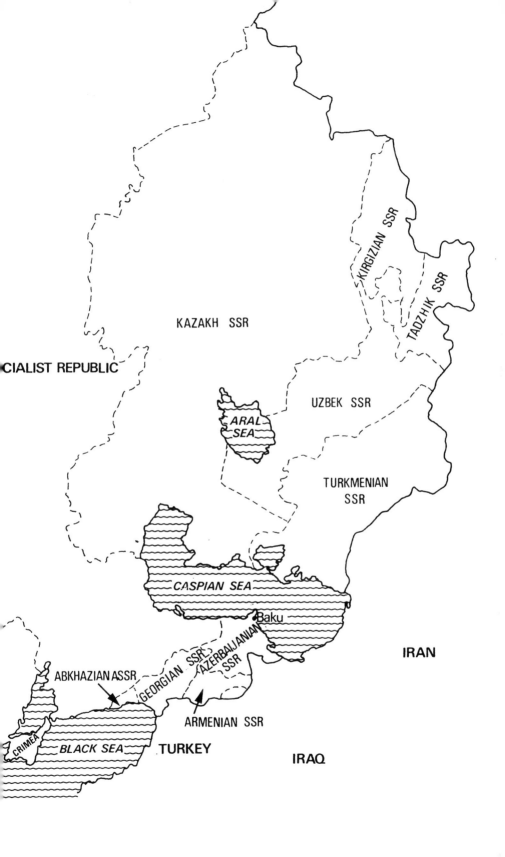

INDEX OF SPEAKERS
(and others mentioned in the text)

Note: Deputies whose names are in bold type were elected on the 2nd day of Congress to the Supreme Soviet (Chambers of Union and Nationalities). Mikhail Gorbachev's interventions have not been indexed.